**BIBLE STUDY
COMMENTARY**

ROMANS

BOOKS IN THE BIBLE STUDY COMMENTARY SERIES

ROMANS

BIBLE STUDY COMMENTARY

CURTIS VAUGHAN
BRUCE CORLEY

ZONDERVAN
PUBLISHING HOUSE OF THE ZONDERVAN CORPORATION
GRAND RAPIDS, MICHIGAN 49506

ROMANS: BIBLE STUDY COMMENTARY
© 1976 by The Zondervan Corporation
Grand Rapids, Michigan

Library of Congress Cataloging in Publication Data
Vaughan, Curtis.

Romans: a study guide.

(Study guide series)
Bibliography: p.
1. Bible.   N.T.   Romans—Study—Text-books.
I. Title.
BS2665.5.V38   227'.1'06   76-26485
ISBN 0-310-33573-6

Printed in the United States of America

Unless otherwise indicated, the Scripture references used in this book are from the American Standard Version of the Bible.

83   84   85   86   87   88 — 10   9   8   7

Contents

Preface

This small volume is sent forth with the hope that it may offer guidance to pastors and laymen who desire to gain a better understanding of the message of Romans. Two suggestions may be given to the person who uses it: First, *read* the Epistle to the Romans many times — if possible, in several different translations. To master any book of the Bible one must read that book continuously, repeatedly, and prayerfully. No commentary or study guide can take the place of this. Second, *study* the Epistle to the Romans. Bible reading is a part of but cannot be equated with Bible study. The latter requires disciplined thinking and just plain hard work. It is hoped that the present volume will aid in such a study. Since it is a study *guide* it is designed to be a companion to the epistle. Those who use it with an open Bible will derive the most help from it. Technical matters usually discussed in more scholarly works have, with few exceptions, been omitted.

Our debt to others who have written commentaries on Romans will be apparent throughout the book. We have tried, particularly in handling some of the more difficult and/or controversial sections of the epistle, to give the reader an indication of the positions taken by those whose works we consider especially valuable. A complete listing of commentaries quoted or referred to is given in the Bibliography in the back of the book. We are indebted to the Zondervan Publishing House for requesting the manuscript and are deeply grateful for the patience, courtesy, and kindness with which the editors have treated us in the course of completing the work. Miss Paula Buford and Mrs. Bruce Corley both rendered invaluable assistance in preparing the typescript.

**BIBLE STUDY
COMMENTARY**

ROMANS

Chapter 1

Background for the Study of Romans

"O St. Paul," wrote Frederic Godet, "had thy one work been to compose an Epistle to the Romans, that alone should have rendered thee dear to every sound reason" (p. x) — and no believer would be disposed to disagree.

The influence of the book upon the course of Christianity — indeed, the history of the world — is beyond measure, and testimonies to its value and power, extending from the patristic period to the modern era, could be multiplied. Chrysostom, whose homilies on the epistle are still available, had it read to him twice each week. It was, as is well known, the instrument used of God to bring spiritual life to Augustine, and its message concerning the righteousness of God was that which to Martin Luther "became the gateway to heaven." To the great reformer Romans was "the true masterpiece of the New Testament, the purest gospel. It deserves," he said, "not only to be known word for word by every Christian but to be the subject of his meditation day by day, the daily bread of his soul; for it can never be too much or too well studied and the more time one spends on it the more precious it becomes." These words are taken from the Preface of Luther's commentary on Romans. Most of our readers will recall that while that Preface was being read publicly in a Moravian meeting in Aldersgate Street in London, John Wesley felt his heart "strangely warmed." Matthew Henry thought of the Psalms of David and the Epistles of Paul as "stars of the first magnitude"; but Romans, he said, "is superlatively excellent, the largest and fullest of all." Farrar spoke of it as "one of the greatest and deepest and most memorably influential of all compositions ever written by human pen." And Deissmann, writing in *The Expository Times*, affirms that "fire, holy fire, glows between its lines. This holy divine flame is what warms and interpenetrates us. The deep understanding of human misery, the terrible shuddering before the power of sin, but at the same time the jubilant rejoicing of the redeemed child of God — this is what for all time assures to the Roman Epistle a victorious sway over the hearts of men who are sinful and who thirst for redemption" (XI, 10).

A. The Church at Rome

It will be helpful, in approaching the study of this book, to consider briefly a few pertinent facts about the church at Rome. Actually, we know little about it, but there are indications that it was quite large and important at a relatively early date. Clement, writing around the close of the first century, refers to the Christians in Rome at the time of the Neronian persecutions (mid-sixties) as "a large body" (1 Clement 6:1), and Tacitus (*Annals* 15:44) speaks of them as "an immense multitude."

There are two principal questions relative to the church at Rome. First, how did it come to be established? It is impossible to give a dogmatic answer to this, but there are several matters of which we may be reasonably sure. (1) The church was not established by Paul, for he had not yet visited Rome at the time of the writing of the Roman letter (cf. 1:8-15). (2) It was not founded by Peter. That apostle was in Jerusalem at the time of the Jerusalem Conference (A.D. 49) and appears, prior to that time, to have engaged only in missionary activities which did not take him far from Jerusalem (cf. Acts 9:32 - 11:18). Yet there is good reason to believe that there were Christians in Rome before A.D. 49, the approximate date of Claudius' edict banishing Jews from Rome, for (as is generally felt, on the basis of a statement by Seutonius) the reason for the Jews' expulsion involved controversies among them concerning Christ. Aquila and Priscilla were in Corinth a few months after Claudius' decree (Acts 18:2), and the New Testament at least implies that they were believers before leaving Rome. In the New Testament the only possible reference to Peter's being in Rome is in 1 Peter 5:13, and this passage can be so interpreted only if "Babylon" is understood as a cryptic name for Rome. (3) It is unlikely that any other apostle founded the Roman church, for in the Roman letter Paul affirms that it was not his policy to build on another person's foundation (15:20). Yet he appears to consider the Roman church as within the sphere of his commission.

Positively, two possibilities emerge: (1) The church may have been established through the witnessing of early converts[1] who, following their conversion, visited Rome or settled there. Godet, who subscribes to this view, likens the founding of the Roman church to the founding of that at Antioch (cf. Acts 11:19ff.). (2) Another possibility, not radically different from the foregoing, is that the Roman church was organized as a result of the witnessing of Roman Jews or proselytes who were in Jerusalem on the day of Pentecost (or some subsequent festival) and

---

[1]Some would say these were *Gentile* converts, arguing that Acts 28 represents the Jews of Rome as declaring an amazing ignorance of Christianity (cf. Godet, p. 65).

were converted through their contact with believers in Jerusalem. (That there were Romans present on the day of Pentecost we know from Acts 2:10.) This latter view is advocated by F. J. A. Hort (*Prolegomena*, pp. 8,9). Perhaps the truth of the establishment of the Roman church combines both these factors.

The second question, which perhaps is more important than the former for one's interpretation of Romans, concerns the composition of the church at Rome. The epistle clearly implies that it was both Jewish[2] and Gentile, but was it *predominantly Jewish or predominantly Gentile?*

A relatively small number of scholars hold that the church at Rome was preponderantly Jewish. Theodor Zahn, for example, argued that "in Rome the Gentile Christians constituted a comparatively small minority" (*Introduction to the New Testament*, II, 422).

The traditional view is that the church was essentially a Gentile church. Paul addresses the Roman Christians as Gentiles (e.g., 1:5,6, 13-15; 11:13); in the progress of his argument he speaks of the Jews in the third person (cf. chs. 9-11); and the majority of the names cited in chapter 16 are Gentile names. Among others, Godet, Hort, Gifford, Sanday and Headlam, Denney, Dodd, and Murray subscribe to this view. Cranfield thinks no decisive answer can be given and suggests that we "leave the question open" (p. 21).

B. The Epistle to the Romans

Several definite historical allusions within the epistle help us to *date* it with a measure of certainty and confidence. For instance, from the introductory portion of chapter 1 we gather that Paul had not yet visited Rome at the time he wrote this letter (1:8-15; cf. 15:23,24). Again, from 15:24-31 we learn that the apostle, at the time of writing Romans, was about to leave for Jerusalem with an offering contributed by Christians of Macedonia and Achaia for the needy saints in Jerusalem (cf. Acts 19:21; 20:1-3). This set of facts places the writing of Romans near the close of the third missionary journey. Moreover, in 16:1,2 Paul commends Phoebe to the church at Rome and identifies her as a member of the church at Cenchrea (the eastern seaport of Corinth). She probably was the bearer of the Roman letter to its destination, and if this assumption is correct Paul must have been in Corinth when he wrote the letter. Another passage of interest is 16:23, where Paul sends greetings to the Romans from "Erastus, the city treasurer." Erastus is associated with Corinth in 2 Timothy 4:20, and an inscription was found in Corinth

---

[2]Hort thinks chapters 2 and 4 suggest that some of the original readers must have been Jews. He also thinks that the scruples of Judaism are in the background of chapters 14 and 15, and on the evidence of 15:7-13 he concludes that there must have been some Jewish members in the Roman church. With this view, there is general agreement.

some years ago which mentions an Erastus as an official of the city. Finally, in 16:23 we learn that one Gaius was Paul's host at the time Romans was written. This was a rather common name of the day, but we know that there was a Gaius at Corinth who was baptized by Paul (1 Cor. 1:14).

The cumulative evidence of these passages suggests that Romans was written some time between A.D. 55 and 58, near the close of his third missionary journey while the apostle was in Corinth. Dodd dates Romans in February of A.D. 59; Barrett, in the spring of A.D. 55. Franzmann (*The Word of the Lord Grows*) prefers A.D. 55/56 as the date; Cranfield, A.D. 55/56 or 56/57; Bruce, "the early days of A.D. 57." A.D. 57/58 is widely held (e.g., Lightfoot, Sanday and Headlam, and Murray).

There are three leading views relative to the *occasion* of Romans. One says it was a crisis in the life of the church, namely, the threatening danger of the Judaizing heresy (cf. Galatians), which called forth this epistle. On this view, then, Romans was written to combat a tendency on the part of at least some of the Romans to embrace this heretical teaching. A second theory understands the occasion for the letter to be, not a crisis in the life of the church, but a development in Paul's own plans. The apostle, it is explained, wished to visit Spain and felt he needed to win the support of the Roman church for that mission. The Epistle to the Romans accomplishes this end by displaying the merits of, and by removing the objections to, Paul's gospel (cf. 15:14-33). (See Dodd, Cranfield, et al.) The third view takes the occasion to be Paul's conflict with unbelieving Jews. It seems, so the argument goes, that at the time of writing Romans the apostle's most dangerous enemies were not the Judaizing teachers, but Jews who professed no relation to Jesus Christ (cf. 2 Cor. 11; Acts 20:23; 21:11,27). Gifford champions this theory and presents a convincing case for it.

There is more to be said for the second and third views, but there is some truth in each of them. Therefore, the true occasion of Romans may be learned by combining elements of all three.

The *purpose* of the book is necessarily bound up with its occasion. So one's understanding of this matter will, to a large measure, be determined by what he thinks of the occasion of the book. The traditional position is that Romans is a theological treatise written with a general didactic aim. On this view, it was occasioned by no special set of circumstances either in the life of the church, the plans of the apostle, or the nature of his opposition at the time. Advocates of this theory think that Paul wrote Romans to put his ideas into systematic form and give a full statement of Christian doctrine simply for the satisfaction of his own mind. Some who take this position feel that Paul might have written this book as his "testament" to Christendom. Romans probably comes closer to being a general and systematic statement of Christian doctrine than any other of Paul's epistles, but it is questionable that this was Paul's primary purpose in writing the book.

A more recent view is that the apostle wrote Romans to win the support of the Roman church for his intended visit to Spain (see paragraph on occasion, above). He did this, it is explained, by setting out a reasoned and orderly statement of the gospel as he preached it.

Gifford believes that "As the main purpose of the whole Epistle we can acknowledge nothing less comprehensive than the desire of the Apostle, at a momentous crisis in his own life's work and in the history of the whole Church of Christ, to set forth a full and systematic statement of those fundamental principles of the Gospel, which render it the one true religion for all the nations of the earth, and meet especially those deepest wants of human nature, which Judaism could not satisfy, righteousness in the sight of God, and deliverance from the power of sin and death" (p. 20).

For Further Study

1. Read Romans at one sitting. If you cannot do this, read chapters 1-11, then at another sitting chapters 12-16. Or, read chapters 1-8, then chapters 9-16. If possible, do your reading in a translation which you have not used before — or at least in a translation which employs modern English. An accurate, readable rendering is *The New International Version*, published by Zondervan.

2. In your first reading of Romans be alert to historical references and allusions which shed light on the circumstances under which Paul wrote the book.

3. As you read Romans, watch for recurring words and phrases.

4. Read Acts 20:1ff. for Luke's account of Paul's ministry in the period during which Romans was written. Use a map to check the location of Rome in reference to Corinth.

5. If you have a Bible dictionary, read articles on Paul, Romans, Aquila, and Phoebe. *The Zondervan Pictorial Bible Dictionary* and *The New Bible Dictionary* (Eerdmans) are good one-volume works. More detailed discussions may be found in *The Zondervan Pictorial Encyclopedia of the Bible*.

Chapter 2

Introduction

(Romans 1:1-17)

The opening words of the Pauline letters are in every instance appropriate to the occasion. Usually, they indicate the relation of the apostle to the people addressed; in addition, they often give at least a suggestion of the matters to be stressed in the body of the book. The introductory portion of Romans, written with sensitivity, dignity, and graciousness, is one of the clearest examples of this. It contains an address (vv. 1-7), an explanation (vv. 8-15), and a statement of the theme of the letter (vv. 16,17).

A. The Address (1:1-7)

Greek letters of ancient times customarily opened with the formula, "A to B, greetings." Paul follows this formula in his epistles, but gives it a decidedly Christian flavor and varies it somewhat according to the circumstances of the readers. In the Epistle to the Romans the address has a special fullness, perhaps because the apostle was writing to a church to which he was not personally known. Indeed, the address of this letter, containing slightly more than thirteen lines in the Nestle Greek text, is longer than that of any of the other Pauline writings. It is especially significant for its doctrinal emphasis, making mention of such themes as the prophetic witness of the Old Testament; the humanity, deity, resurrection, and lordship of Christ; the calling of believers; and the fatherhood of God.

1. *Paul presents his credentials (1:1)*

In the opening verse the apostle introduces himself to the Romans and explains the capacity in which he writes to them. It was especially appropriate to begin in this manner, for the Roman church was not founded by Paul, and most of the people there had had no contact with him. Three things are said: First, Paul calls himself "a servant of Jesus Christ." The Greek word (*doulos*), which literally means "slave," suggests Paul's consciousness that he belonged to Christ and that he was therefore obligated to serve Him. Some think Paul was alluding to the fact that in the Old Testament "servant of the Lord," or an equivalent, was a title accorded such men as Moses and Isaiah, and that Paul therefore was claiming to be in the line of the prophets (spokesmen for God). Perhaps it is better to understand the words simply as a claim on Paul's part to be a Christian. "Servant of Jesus Christ" is, to be sure, an especially appropriate designation for an apostle, but it also is a true description of any Christian.

Second, Paul says he was "called to be an apostle." That is to say, he is an apostle not because he presumptuously chose the office for himself, but because God called him to it. The Greek word for "apostle" suggests an authorized representative, an official delegate, a commissioned messenger. It is generally used in the New Testament of those who were in a special way Christ's representatives. As used by Paul, it reflects his consciousness of divine commission and divine authority. Cranfield calls it "a very humble word" but points out that it is "at the same time expressive of the most august authority" (p. 52).

Third, Paul describes himself as "separated unto the gospel of God." This means that he was set apart, consecrated by God, for the *preaching* of the gospel.

2. Paul describes his gospel (1:1b-5)

The Greek word for gospel, *euangelion*, is used four times as frequently in the epistles of Paul as in all the other New Testament writings combined, and is a term most characteristic of Paul.[1] Tyndale describes it as a word that "signyfyeth good, mery, glad and ioyfull tydings, that maketh a mannes hert glad, and maketh him synge, daunce, and leepe for ioye." "Good news" is perhaps the best English equivalent.

Paul's description of the gospel is threefold. First, it is "of God" (v. 1b). This phrase may mean either that the gospel is good news *from* God (i.e., having its origin in God) or that it is good news *about* God (i.e., having God as its subject matter); or both of these ideas may be present. Perhaps the statement of verses 3-5 (discussed below) should lead us to interpret the phrase as basically denoting the idea of origin. Second, it is a gospel promised in Scripture (v. 2). This suggests that Paul's gospel is not a novel thing; it is rather a fulfillment of and is continuous with the prophetic message of the Old Testament. This is a concept brought in elsewhere in the epistle (cf. 3:21ff.; 4:1ff.). Third, it is a gospel "concern-

---

[1] "Gospel" appears sixty times in Paul's epistles, ten times in the Gospels, twice in Acts, once in 1 Peter, and once in Revelation. It does not appear at all in the Gospel of John nor in his epistles.

ing his [God's] Son" (vv. 3-5). The meaning is that Christ is the sum and substance of the gospel; He is its central theme. The apostle expands the reference to Christ considerably, and in so doing, leaves us with a passage of great christological importance. Christ, he says, was "[born] of the seed of David according to the flesh" and "declared to be the Son of God with power, according to the spirit of holiness, by the resurrection from the dead." This shows that Christ, though one person, belonged to two realms — the human and the divine.[2] "[Born] of the seed of David" means that He was, on the human side, descended from Israel's great king. His resurrection from the dead, however, was a powerful demonstration of his divine sonship. He was, by that great event, "miraculously designated Son of God" (TCNT).

The two phrases ". . . flesh" and ". . . Spirit"[3] mark respectively Christ's incarnate and exalted states.[4] In the days of His flesh He fulfilled the office of Messiah ("seed of David"), and in His risen, exalted state He is shown to be the Son of God. It is not that He *became* Son of God by His resurrection; it is rather that His divine sonship was proved and made apparent by His resurrection. Godet, however, aptly points out that the resurrection of Jesus not only proved and showed what Christ was; "it wrought a real transformation in His mode of being" (p. 79).

Christ, Paul further declares, is the One "through whom" he received "grace and apostleship." "Grace" may be employed here in its usual sense of unmerited favor. Moffatt connects the word closely with "apostleship" and renders it "the favour of my commission" (cf. *Modern Language Bible*, "the undeserved gift of apostleship"). Others, however, think that here "grace" is a synonym for power or ability from God (cf. Rom. 12:3,6; 15:15; 2 Cor. 12:9). The meaning then would be that Paul through Christ had received the ability to perform the work of apostleship.

The purpose of Paul's commission as an apostle was to promote "obedience of faith among all nations [Gentiles]." This could mean either the obedience which *consists in* faith (i.e., saving trust) in Jesus or the obedience which faith in Jesus *produces*. Perhaps it would be better to understand the Greek word for faith as a simple attributive genitive

---

[2]Compare Barrett's translation: ". . . the sphere of the flesh . . . the sphere of the Holy Spirit" (p. 15).

[3]Moffatt, RSV, NEB, NASB, NIV, and others capitalize "Spirit." KJV, ASV, Goodspeed, TCNT, and others use lower case. Knox has "the sanctified spirit that was his." Williams translates "on the holy spiritual side." Bruce points out that "spirit of holiness" is simply a Hebraism for Holy Spirit.

[4]See Bruce, p. 73, who quotes T. W. Manson: "The antithetic terms 'flesh,' 'spirit,' do not divide His substance, but unfold the economy of His manifestation." Others, e.g. Meyer, see a contrast between the outward ("flesh") and the inner ("spirit") person of Jesus.

and render the phrase by the expression "believing obedience."

3. Paul greets his readers (1:6, 7)

In greeting the Roman Christians, Paul describes them as Gentiles, as divinely "called," as "beloved of God," and as "saints" (i.e., the people of God). The greeting (v. 7b), which is in the nature of a prayer, is the familiar "grace and peace." Luther's definition of these terms is apropos: "Grace releaseth sin, and peace maketh the conscience quiet."

B. An Explanation of Paul's Interest in the Roman Church (1:8-15)

The apostle's purpose in these verses is to establish rapport with the believers of Rome. He had never visited their city and had no official connection with their church. This paragraph, therefore, was necessary to prepare the readers for a sympathetic reception of his message.

1. Paul begins with an expression of appreciation for the Roman church (1:8)

In this verse he uses language which reveals that the church at this early date had made its presence widely felt. Paul sincerely thanks God for them, acknowledging (as the grounds for his gratitude) that their faith in Christ is spoken of throughout the empire (cf. 1 Thess. 1:8).

2. The apostle reveals that he had for a long time had a deep desire to visit Rome (1:9-13)

Paul had, in fact, made it a matter of constant prayer (vv. 9,10), even though (as he explains in 15:20) it was not his custom to build on foundations laid by others. The sincerity of his statements is indicated by his calling on God as witness to his continual mention of them in his prayers.

Paul's reasons for wanting to visit Rome are stated in verses 11-13.[5] First, he felt that such a visit would bring spiritual enrichment both to their lives and to his own life (vv. 11,12). He could, through his presence, be the instrument of God in imparting "some spiritual gift" (v. 11). We cannot know what special gift Paul had in mind. Gifts (*charismata*) of the Spirit, which are endowments emanating from and bestowed by the Spirit, are treated at length in 12:6ff. and also in 1 Corinthians 12-14. Weymouth understands the meaning here to be simply "some spiritual help." The result of this divine bestowal, whatever the gift might have been, would be the strengthening of the Roman believers (v. 11b). The form of the verb (second person passive) implies that in Paul's thought God was the One who would do the strengthening. But to be doubly certain that his words would not be misunderstood as an arrogant boast, he delicately and tactfully explains in verse 12 that the spiritual advantage resulting from his stay in Rome would not be a one-sided thing.

---

[5]Compare 15:24, where another reason is mentioned.

There would be, he points out, mutual benefit — they and he being encouraged[6] by their mutual faith.

Second, Paul desired to visit Rome in order that he might obtain fruit among them as well as among other Gentiles (v. 13). The imagery is that of gathering a harvest, and in this context the reference must be to the winning of new converts and the building up of the church.

Verse 13a affirms that Paul often had intended to visit the Romans, but that he had been prevented from doing so. Here he merely states the fact; no further insight into the matter is offered.[7] The hindrance may have been an awareness of urgent responsibilities that required him to remain in the East (cf. Rom. 15:18f., 22f.).

3. *Paul affirms* a sense of spiritual obligation *toward the believers of Rome (1:14,15; cf. 1 Cor. 9:16-19)*

Indeed, he felt it his duty to preach the gospel to the whole Gentile world[8]—cultured ("Greeks") and uncultured ("barbarians"),[9] educated ("wise"), and uneducated ("foolish") (v. 14). "So" (i.e., in accordance with his sense of debtorship to all ranks and classes of people) he was "ready to preach the gospel" to the Romans (v. 15). "As much as in me is" (v. 15a), an awkward construction in Greek, may allude to the hindrances mentioned earlier (v. 13). The thought then is: "If there is a hindrance now, it is not on my part. I for my part am ready, etc." But it may simply mean "to the extent of my ability." The word rendered "I am ready" expresses eager desire.

C. Statement of the Theme of the Book (1:16,17)

Practically all commentators agree that verses 16 and 17 give the "text" or theme of the entire epistle. For example, Sanday and Headlam (p. 22) speak of the verses as expressing the "thesis" of the epistle; Davidson and Martin (p. 1016) use the expression "seed-plot." Barrett thinks they might be thought of as "a summary of Paul's theology as a whole" (p. 27). The heart of the passage is summed up in the word "gospel," which has already appeared in verses 1 and 9.

Verses 16 and 17 are closely related to the statement of verses 14 and 15. There is, in fact, "a progressive unfolding of reasons" in the passage, indicated by the threefold repetition of "for" in verses 16 and

---

[6]The Greek word conveys the ideas of comfort, strengthening, and encouragement. Encouragement, however, seems to be the dominant meaning here.

[7]One should compare 1 Thessalonians 2:18, where a hindrance in his plans is ascribed to Satan.

[8]Each pair of terms refers, from different points of view, to the whole Gentile world.
[9]By the Greeks anyone who did not speak Greek was considered a barbarian. NIV, therefore, translates it "Greeks and non-Greeks."

17. The apostle is ready to preach the gospel to those in Rome *for* he is not ashamed of the gospel. He is not ashamed of the gospel *for* it is the power of God unto salvation. The gospel is the power of God unto salvation *for* in it is revealed a righteousness of God. Three things then are here affirmed in reference to the gospel:

1. *Paul is not ashamed of it (1:16a)*

The use of the negative concept ("not ashamed") probably was dictated by Paul's awareness that in the proud capital of the Roman Empire the message of a crucified Redeemer was a stumbling block, a thing of scorn and ridicule. The statement is an example of the figure of speech called litotes. Positively stated, the apostle's meaning is that he gloried in the gospel, counted it a high honor to be a preacher of it, and had unbounded confidence in it.

2. *The gospel is the power of God unto salvation (1:16b)*

This is why Paul was not ashamed of it. "Power" is the translation of the Greek word *dunamis*, from the root of which we get such words as dynamo and dynamic. It is here understood by Sanday and Headlam in the sense of a "force" (p. 23). Cranfield defines it as "effective power" (pp. 87, 89). Murray feels that "power of God" can be best conveyed in our language by the expression "omnipotence of God." To say, then, that the gospel is the power of God unto salvation is to affirm that "the gospel is the omnipotence of God operative unto salvation" (I, 27). Cranfield sums it up in the phrase, "God's almighty saving power" (p. 87).

"Salvation," a word used elsewhere in this epistle in 10:1, 10; 11:11; and 13:11, denotes deliverance, rescue, or preservation from danger. The term is probably used here with its widest meaning, "including the whole process of mercy from the time of belief onwards; deliverance from doom, sin, and death" (Moule, p. 56).[10] Paul's use of the verb form in 5:9 shows that salvation may be thought of in the narrower sense of deliverance from the wrath of God. The reference in 13:11 shows that our complete and final salvation is yet future. Barrett therefore thinks of the term as belonging to the framework of eschatology and defines it as "man's eventual safe passage through human trials and divine judgment to eternal bliss" (p. 27).

"To everyone that believeth" reveals that the salvation available through the gospel is not unconditionally and universally experienced. It is effective only for those who believe, that is, for those who put their trust in and dependence on Jesus Christ. A hint as to the meaning of

---

[10]Unless otherwise indicated, all references to Moule are to his commentary on Romans in *The Cambridge Bible for Schools and Colleges.*

belief or faith was given in 1:5 (see discussion at that point). Its fullest meaning gradually becomes clearer as the epistle unfolds. The words "every one" point up that such things as race and culture are not obstacles to the effectiveness of the gospel — so long as there is true faith.

3. In the gospel there "is revealed"[11] a righteousness of God" (1:17)

It is this which gives the gospel its power to save. The "righteousness of God" is one of the most important concepts in Romans. It is indeed the dominating theme of the epistle. Therefore, it is imperative that one understand Paul's use of the term. Found at least eight times in Romans, the Greek expression may literally be translated "a God-kind of righteousness," or simply "a God-righteousness" (cf. TCNT, "Divine Righteousness").[12] But in what way is it a "God-righteousness"? A few interpreters have explained that it is a God-righteousness because righteousness is thought of as *an attribute of God* (i.e., His personal righteousness).[13] Many more interpreters take the position that it is a God-righteousness because righteousness is thought of as *an activity of God* available for men.[14] Old Testament usage, it is contended, shows that the righteousness of God and the salvation of God are practically synonymous (cf. Isa. 42:21; 51:5; Ps. 24:5; 31:1; 98:2; 143:11). Righteousness, then, in this view, is the saving activity of God (cf. TEV, which interprets the phrase in terms of God's putting men right with Himself). Knox translates it, "God's way of justifying us." Others understand the reference to be to *a status of man* resulting from the saving activity of God.[15] This is the view which we prefer. Compare Weymouth's rendering: "a righteousness which comes from God." C. B. Williams renders it, "God's way of man's right standing with Him."

Perhaps the best commentary on the phrase is found in Paul's own words, recorded in Philippians 3:9: " . . . and be found in him, not having a righteousness of mine own, even that which is of the law, but that which is through faith in Christ, the righteousness which is from God by faith." Similar words are found in 2 Corinthians 5:21: "Him who knew no sin he made to be sin on our behalf; that we might become the righteousness of God in him."

---

[11]The tense is present, "is being revealed" (cf. 3:21, where a perfect tense is used for "manifested"). The thought seems to be that the righteousness of God is continuously being disclosed wherever and whenever the gospel message is preached. However, the context implies that though human lips may be employed in the proclamation, the revelation in that proclamation is God's doing.

[12]Interpreted in this manner, "of God" is a simple attributive (descriptive) genitive.

[13]In this view, "of God" is a possessive genitive.

[14]In this view, "of God" is a subjective genitive.

[15]In this view "of God" is an ablative of source.

This divine righteousness is said to be "from faith unto faith," an expression which perhaps is simply a rhetorical device to emphasize the importance of faith; righteousness begins in faith, it ends in faith (cf. NEB). Hodge therefore understood it to be a formula equivalent to "by faith alone" (p. 32). Barrett translates it "on the basis of nothing but faith." Knox's rendering is similar: "faith first and last." Phillips has, "a process begun and continued by their faith."Others (e.g., Calvin) interpret the phrase as referring to the advance from one degree of faith to another. Compare TCNT: "resulting from faith and leading on to faith." The thought in Williams' rendering is similar, "The way of faith that leads to greater faith."

Paul confirms his teaching by citing a passage found in Habakkuk 2:4: "But the righteous shall live by faith." Perhaps a better rendering is "He who is righteous-by-faith shall live." Bruce observes that for Paul and many other Jews "life" and "salvation" were practically synonymous. To "live" then is the equivalent of "be saved."

For Further Study

1. In a Bible dictionary, read articles on Apostle, Rome, Saint, Righteousness, Gospel, etc.

2. Use a map to trace out the course of Paul's third missionary journey. Read Luke's account of this journey in Acts 18:23 - 21:16.

3. Why do you think Paul was hindered from going to Rome when he had on previous occasions wanted to do so? In your opinion, *how* was he hindered? Compare Romans 1:13 and 1 Thessalonians 2:18.

4. Using a concordance, check the references to "Rome" in this epistle and in the Book of Acts.

5. Use a concordance to check every reference in Romans to Faith or Believe.

Chapter 3

The Wrath of God:
The Doctrine of Condemnation[1]

(Romans 1:18-3:20)

Before giving his exposition of the righteousness of God (i.e., God's way of putting men right with Himself), Paul shows why it is so urgently necessary for men to receive that righteousness. This he does in 1:18-3:20. In short, the passage teaches that all men need the divine righteousness because they have no righteousness which will enable them to stand before God. They are all morally and spiritually bankrupt, and they therefore stand under the wrath of God.

To some, divine wrath is incompatible with the love of God, or even the righteousness of God. And in this connection, it has been pointed out that Paul uses the phrase "wrath of God" in only two other passages (Eph. 5:6; Col. 3:6) and that he never uses the verb "to be wrathful" with God as subject. From this it is concluded (wrongly, we think) that the apostle thought of divine wrath as a kind of impersonal principle built into the structure of the universe — a kind of automatic force which resists evil. This position is summed up by Barclay as follows: "There is a moral order in this world, and the man who transgresses the moral order, soon or late, is bound to suffer." "Moral order," he says, "is the wrath of God at work" (p. 18).

There is truth in this view, but it is not the full truth. There is a sense in which wrath *is* a sort of impersonal force at work in the world. But Scripture requires that we see the wrath of God as something more than this. "Wrath," write Sanday and Headlam, is "the reaction of the Divine righteousness when it comes into collision with sin" (p. 35). Barrett concludes that "Wrath is God's personal (though never malicious or, in a bad sense, emotional) reaction against sin" (p. 33). And

---

[1]Most interpreters see 1:18-3:20 as a unit, and all agree essentially on the place of this unit within the argument of the epistle. Murray sees it as setting forth "The Universality of Sin and Condemnation." Bruce calls it "Sin and Retribution: The universal need diagnosed"; Shedd, "The necessity of gratuitous justification"; Dodd, "The Universal Sway of Sin and Retribution"; Gifford, "The Unrighteousness of Man"; Nygren, "Under the Wrath of God."

Moule reminds us that the wrath of God "is the wrath of a Judge. In its inmost secret it is the very opposite of an *arbitrary outburst*, being the eternal repulsion of evil by good" (p. 58). The divine wrath, then, is not like human anger; but it is personal. It is the expression of God's holy hatred of sin. Murray states it well: "Wrath is the holy revulsion of God's being against that which is the contradiction of his holiness" (I, 35).

Paul's statement about the divine wrath — that is, the argument that all men are under the wrath of God and therefore in need of the gospel — is presented in three movements: (1) The wrath of God is upon the Gentiles (the pagan world) (1:18-32); (2) upon the Jews (2:1-3:8); and (3) upon the whole world (3:9-20).

A. The Wrath of God Upon the Pagan World (1:18-32)

These verses give a terrible but accurate portrayal of the sinful condition of the pagan world. In so doing, the passage depicts with appalling vividness the Gentile world's deep need of the righteousness offered in the gospel. Gifford explains that Paul here is not giving a history, "but a Christian philosophy of history; he is not narrating the growth of idolatry and vice in this or that nation; but showing in a broad generalized view the condition of the heathen world and the causes of its corruption" (p. 62).

The burden of the passage is that the visible degradation of heathen life is proof that the wrath of God is being poured out upon those who have rebelled against His sovereignty. It speaks of (1) the revelation of the wrath of God (v. 18), (2) the grounds for or justification of that wrath (vv. 19-23), and (3) the execution of it (vv. 24-32).

1. *The revelation of God's wrath (1:18)*

Melanchthon called verse 18 "an exordium terrible as lightning." Gifford calls attention to the striking contrast between it and the preceding verses. In the one (v. 17), reference is made to a revelation of the righteousness of God which makes the gospel the power of God for salvation; in the other (v. 18), reference is made to the revelation of "the destroying power of God's wrath" (p. 62).

In affirming that the wrath of God is "revealed," Paul means that there is a positive, dynamic, active expression of the divine displeasure. The tense of the verb is present, suggesting that this expression of the wrath of God is a fact in the ongoing life of the world. As Moule puts it, it is a *standing* revelation, "for all places and all times, and ever repeated to individual consciences" (p. 59). Perhaps we are to look to verses 24-32 for a statement of the *manner* in which the divine wrath is revealed, namely, "in the debasing vices and conscious misery to which the sinner is given over" (Gifford, p. 62).

This divine displeasure is revealed "against all [i.e., every kind of] ungodliness and unrighteousness of men." "Ungodliness" denotes irreverence, impiety — perversity that is religious in character. Murray thinks the primary reference is to idolatry. "Unrighteousness" is perhaps a wider word, essentially denoting the lack of a right attitude inwardly and right conduct outwardly. Moule understands it to include "the idea of injustice to God as well as to man; spiritual rebellion" (p. 59). The NEB translates the two terms as a hendiadys, "all the godless wickedness of men."

The divine wrath is revealed against the wickedness of those "who hold the truth in unrighteousness" (KJV).[2] This is more accurately rendered "who *hold down* the truth, etc." The thought is that those against whom God's wrath is revealed do, by their wicked lives, resist, hinder, stifle, repress, and thwart the truth. What is meant by "truth" is brought out in the following verses, namely, that which is known about God from His handiwork in creation. In verse 25 it is specifically identified as "the truth of God."

2. The grounds for God's wrath (1:19-23)

The intent of these verses is to show that God's wrath upon the Gentile world is justified.[3] That is, it is fitting and proper in spite of the fact that that segment of the world had, in Paul's day, never heard the gospel. The justness of the divine wrath springs from two facts: (1) that God has revealed Himself to all mankind (vv. 19, 20) and (2) man has rejected that revelation (vv. 21-23). In other words, the heathen are not condemned for failure to live up to a revelation they do not possess; they are condemned because they have failed to live up to the light they *do* have.

a. *God's revelation of Himself (vv. 19, 20).* Verses 19 and 20 declare that God *has* revealed Himself to all men, and they affirm the character of that revelation: "because that which is known of God is manifest in them; for God manifested it unto them. For the invisible things of him since the creation of the world are clearly seen, being perceived through the things that are made, even his everlasting power and divinity." "That which is [or, can *be*] known of God" is defined in verse 20 as "the invisible things" of God. Williams translates this, "His invisible characteristics"; Weymouth, "His invisible perfections." This concept is further defined as "his eternal power and divine nature"

---

[2] The KJV rendering suggests that what measure of truth the heathen have, they possess in their sin.

[3] Some interpreters (e.g., Murray) understand verse 19 not as introducing the reason or grounds for the revelation of God's wrath, but as explaining "how it can be said that men hinder the truth in unrighteousness" (I, 37).

(Weymouth, v. 20b). The latter expression, which is a translation of a word found only here in the New Testament, denotes divine nature and properties.[4] It sums up all the attributes other than power, such as wisdom and goodness. The two terms together point up the richness of the revelation; it is such that it gives to men an awareness of both the greatness and the goodness of God.

What is or can be known of God is "manifest in them."[5] The words speak of a manifestation in the minds and consciences of men. Williams renders it, "is clear to their inner moral sense." The NEB has, "lies plain before their eyes"; Knox, "is clear to their minds."

What is knowable of God is manifest in men because "God manifested it unto them" (v. 19c). By these words Paul emphasizes that the revelation of God in creation was the result of God's deliberate self-disclosure.

In addition to what has already been said, verse 20 brings out at least three other things about God's revelation of Himself. First, His invisible attributes — His power and divinity — "are clearly seen" "from the creation of the world" (KJV). These last words may be seen as denoting the source from which man derives his knowledge of the invisible God. This interpretation, reflected in the KJV rendering, is preferred by Gifford. Most modern scholars, however, think the phrase should be interpreted temporally — that is, "ever since the world was made" (cf. ASV). The thought is that God's self-revelation has been continuous from the beginning of time. "Are clearly seen" is the translation of a single Greek word. Some understand it in the sense of mental perception; others of physical sight. (See Cranfield, p. 115.)

Second, these invisible things of God have been clearly seen since the creation of the world because they are "perceived through the things that are made." "Perceived," like "clearly seen," is variously interpreted, some understanding it as mental perception (cf. NEB, "visible . . . to the eye of reason"), others as physical perception. Cranfield, who takes both "seen" and "perceived" to refer to physical sight, understands the sentence as a whole to be "a paradoxical assertion that God's invisible attributes are actually seen in, and through, His creation" (p. 115). "The things that are made" are the created things observable to man's senses.

Third, these tokens of the power and divinity of the Creator leave the beholders "without excuse" for their failure to recognize Him in His handiwork. Probably the phrase should be read as a result clause, though Gifford insists on purpose. "God's *purpose*," he writes, "was to

---

[4]A similar word, used in Colossians 2:9, denotes the essence of deity, divine personality.

[5]Barrett prefers to understand this in the sense of "*among* them." Cranfield also prefers this idea, rendering it "in their midst" (p. 113). Cf. Mrs. Montgomery's translation.

leave nothing undone on His part, the omission of which might give men an excuse for sin" (p. 64).

b. *Man's rejection of God's revelation (vv. 21-23)*.

Verses 21-23 tell of man's rejection of the revelation of the Creator's eternal power and divinity. Two things are brought out. First, men's rejection of God was deliberate. Although they knew God — that is, possessed such knowledge of Him as should have elicited praise and gratitude — "they glorified him not as God, neither gave thanks" (v. 21a). That is, they did not give to Him in thought, affection, and devotion, the place that is rightfully His as God and did not express to Him in word and deed the gratitude the creature owes his Creator. "Glorified" is a translation of a word occurring five times in Romans, and is used here of the response which men owe to God as Creator and Lord of life. When we glorify God we obviously do not augment or add to His inherent splendor and majesty; rather, we glorify Him when we acknowledge His divine perfections and give to Him the honor and praise that are His due. Cranfield thinks that the word in a context such as this includes the attitudes of humble trust and obedience.

Second, man's rejection of God was degrading. Having stated man's failure to make a positive response to God (v. 21a), the apostle proceeds to give a description of the resulting religious perversity exhibited in their lives. They "became vain in their reasonings, and their senseless heart was darkened" (v. 21b). "Became vain[6] in their reasonings"[7] suggests that they went astray in their thinking, that their thoughts turned to worthless things, that their reasonings were destitute of any fruitful thought. Norlie renders it, "they busied themselves with silly speculations about [God]." The NEB has, "all their thinking has ended in futility"; *Jerusalem Bible*, "they made nonsense out of logic."

The darkening of their hearts represents a degression. Having become vain in their reasonings, they were, by following their vain thoughts, led into a lower depth of spiritual darkness. "Heart" often refers to the whole inner being — the seat of intellect, will, and emotion. Jesus spoke of the heart as that from which evil thoughts proceed (Matt. 15:19). Some understand it here to refer to "moral sense." Paul's use here of the word "senseless" — interpreted variously as "without under-

---

[6]"Became vain" is the translation of a verb which occurs only here in the New Testament. It belongs to a word group, however, which is quite prominent in the Bible. One of the words in this group, translated "vanity" is applied to an idol (cf. Jer. 2:5). Moule understands "vain" here to mean "*wrong*," morally as well as mentally" (p. 61).

[7]The word translated "reasonings" usually has a bad connotation in the New Testament. In the KJV it is rendered "imaginations" (here), "reasoning" (Luke 9:46), "disputings" (Phil. 2:14), "doubting" (1 Tim. 2:8), and most often "thoughts" (Matt. 15:19; 1 Cor. 3:20). In the present passage it denotes "the false notions which men formed for themselves of God in opposition to the truth set before them in His works" (Gifford, p. 64).

standing," "misguided," "stupid," "uncomprehending," "unintelligent"[8] — suggests that by "heart" he meant mainly the intellectual element of the inner life. (For a similar use, see Mark 2:6,8.) "Was darkened" is vividly rendered in the NEB as "plunged in darkness." Barrett aptly remarks: "Once man had fallen from his true relation with God, he was no longer capable of truly rational thought about him" (p. 37).

Verses 22 and 23 are a further description of the degeneracy of the pagan world. Reference is made first to their folly. While professing "to be wise, they became [showed themselves to be] fools" (v. 22; cf. 1 Cor. 1:21). The language probably suggests moral obtuseness, not mere intellectual deficiency. Next, the apostle charges that this folly of the pagan world was expressed in their exchanging the worship of God for that of idols. They forsook "the glory[9] of the incorruptible God," whom they should have worshiped, for images resembling mortal men or even birds, beasts, and snakes (v. 23). This, in turn, led to other palpable acts of folly (as will come out in vv. 24-32).[10]

3. The execution of God's wrath (1:24-32)

Verses 19-23 have told of the pagan world's rejection of God. Verses 24-32 now tell of God's consequent rejection of them. Man's sin was his abandonment of God; God punished man by abandoning him. Three times in these verses there occurs the statement, "God gave them up" (vv. 24,26,28). There is in this phrase an unmistakable pang of sorrow (cf. the Prodigal's father), but there is as well a note of judgment. Robertson writes that to him the words "sound . . . like clods" falling on a coffin (p. 330).

Many understand the essential meaning to be that God withdrew all restraint and left pagan man to his self-determination and self-destruction (cf. Acts 14:16; 17:30). Gifford, pursuing this line of thought,

---

[8]The Greek word, according to some, suggests inability to see connections and consequences. In Matthew 15:16 Jesus used it of the disciples.

[9]In extra-biblical literature, the primary meaning of the Greek word for "glory" was "opinion." From this primary meaning it came to have such secondary meanings as "repute" (i.e., the opinion which others have of one) and "glory." In the New Testament it is regularly used in the sense of "splendor" and "majesty."

[10]Paul's argument in verses 19-23 points up two significant truths: First, man's religious development, contrary to much modern thought, has been downward. "Heathenism," wrote Meyer, "is not the primeval religion out of which men gradually advanced to the knowledge of the true God; but it is the consequence of falling away from the primitive revelation of God in His works" (quoted by Gifford, p. 64). Similarly, Sir Williams Ramsay wrote: "For my own part, I confess that my experience and reading show nothing to confirm the modern assumptions in religious history, and a great deal to confirm Paul. Wherever evidence exists, with the rarest exceptions, the history of religion among men is a history of degeneration" (The Cities of St. Paul, p. 17).

Second, man must worship someone or something. As has been said, "When God is pushed out the back door, an idol comes in the front door."

writes that "All history shows that God did not deal with other nations as He did with His chosen people, raising up prophets and sending warnings and chastisements directly and visibly from Himself to restrain or recall them from idolatry and impurity" (p. 65). Cranfield thinks the repetition of the statement is so emphatic that it must be interpreted as a deliberate and positive judicial act of God (p. 120). Similarly, Murray concludes that the giving over is not to be "reduced to the notion of non-interference with the natural consequences of sin" (I, 44). The words, he feels, must mean a positive infliction of divine retribution.

The thrice-repeated use of "God gave them up" may mark three stages[11] in the carrying out of the wrath of God against the heathen world.

a. *Abandoned to uncleanness (vv. 24,25).* God gave them up to follow the desires of their own hearts; that is, He let them do what they wanted to do (v. 24a). "Lusts" is translated from a word which, though sometimes having a neutral meaning, more often than not suggests a desire for something forbidden. That is its meaning here. The phrase "in the lusts of their hearts" does not express that *to which* they were given over. Rather, it describes the moral condition *in which* they were living when God gave them up. That to which God gave them over, in accord with their own desires, was "uncleanness," and this in turn led to the dishonoring of their bodies (v. 24b). The rendering of TCNT sums up the thought of verse 24: "Therefore God abandoned them to impurity, letting them follow the cravings of their hearts." The Greek word for "impurity" ("uncleanness," ASV) usually suggests sexual aberration, immorality. God, it should be observed, did not cause their impurity; He *did* abandon them to the natural consequences of the lusts at work in them.

The reason for this judicial abandonment is stated in verse 25: "for that[12] they exchanged the truth of God [cf. v. 18b] for a lie, and worshipped and served the creature rather than the Creator." "Lie," which is modified by the definite article in Greek, refers to idolatry. The NEB brings this out: "they have bartered away the true God for a false one."

---

[11]Robertson prefers not to think of this as three "stages" in the giving over. He sees the threefold use of "God gave them up" as simply "a repetition of the same withdrawal" (p. 330). He is essentially correct in his appraisal, but perhaps there is some degression to be noted in the apostle's repetition of the phrase. Another possibility is to see the first two uses of "God gave them over" as referring to the same thing (sexual impurity) and the third use as referring to something different (a reprobate mind).

[12]This is a translation of a Greek relative pronoun (*hoitines*) which has explanatory force. In the present context its meaning is more clearly expressed by rendering it "because" (see RSV, NEB).

b. *Abandoned to passions of dishonor (vv. 26,27)*. The second stage in the divine abandonment was God's giving men over to "vile passions." The Greek word for "passions" in this instance is different from that used for "lusts" in verse 24. It is used especially of sexual desire. Lenski understands the former word ("lusts") to denote a single evil desire; this word, on the other hand, denotes "a constant burning passion" (p. 112). The ABUV renders the phrase "shameful passions." Arndt and Gingrich translate it "disgraceful passions." A literal rendering is "passions of dishonor."

The actions described in verses 26 and 27, though similar to those of verses 24 and 25, represent a further degree of degeneracy. Whereas those verses spoke of impurity arising from natural passions, these tell of impurity arising from unnatural passions — sexual perversion. "Their women changed the natural use[13] into that which is against nature: and likewise also the men, leaving the natural use of the woman, burned in their lust one toward another, men with men working unseemliness" (vv. 26,27b). There may be significance in the apostle's choice of words. Instead of the usual words for "women" and "men," the Greek has terms which denote "females" and "males." "Burned in their lust" is vividly rendered by Montgomery as "were ablaze with passion." Knox has, "were burnt up with desire for each other." A literal rendering is "became inflamed." "Unseemliness" (v. 27), literally "the shameful thing," denotes obscenity.

The last part of verse 27 points up that such unutterable impurity brings its own punishment. Those guilty "are paid in their own persons the fitting wage of such perversion" (NEB).

c. *Abandoned to a reprobate mind (vv. 28-32)*. Because they did not seek to retain God in their knowledge, He gave them over to "a reprobate [disapproved] mind" (v. 28). Such a mind is a rejected, base, worthless mind — a mind incapable of making moral distinctions. The result was that the heathen did things not fitting and proper for people to do.

These unbecoming actions are listed in vivid detail in verses 29-31. One might compare the list in several translations to get the different shades of meaning that may be given to several of the words. For the most part they require no explanation. Martin Franzmann writes of them that they all have one thing in common: "they rend the fabric of society and make an agony of communal life" (p. 262).

The climax is reached in verse 32, where Paul writes: "who, knowing the ordinance of God, that they that practise such things are worthy

---

[13]The RSV expresses the essential meaning: "Their women exchanged natural relations for unnatural." Knox: " . . . exchanged natural for unnatural intercourse."

of death, not only do the same, but also consent with them that practise them." The opening pronoun ("who") is from a Greek word which is qualitative and explanatory. "Who are of such nature that, etc." expresses the idea. The content of the "ordinance [righteous decree] of God" is given in the words: "that they that practice such things are worthy of death." "Consent with" is variously understood. Some see in it the idea of delighting in; others, applauding or congratulating; still others, approving, and so on. But whatever precise meaning one sees here, these closing words, showing how deeply men need the interposition of God's saving activity, form a dramatic climax to Paul's indictment of the pagan world.

B. The Wrath of God Upon the Jew (2:1-3:8)

Paul has vividly depicted the deep guilt of the Gentiles, thus establishing their need for the righteousness of the gospel. Now he turns to the case of the Jews[14] and shows that they as well as the Gentiles have failed to attain a righteousness which is acceptable before God.

Sanday and Headlam call attention to the rhetorical skill with which Paul makes the transition from Gentile to Jew, likening it to Nathan's manner in confronting David. The Jew is addressed in veiled language at first (vv. 1-16) and then (v. 17) confronted openly with a "Thou art the man."

In establishing his case against the Jew, Paul's argument moves along three lines. First, he expounds the nature of God's judgment, especially insisting on its impartiality (2:1-11) and its universality (2:12-16). Second, he shows that the Jew has failed to live up to his privileges (2:17-29). Third, he closes the discussion with a consideration of anticipated Jewish objections to his argument (3:1-8).

1. The nature of God's judgment (2:1-16)

The Jew's privileges and superior morality tended to make him a critic of the pagan, whose religious position was less favored than his.

---

[14]Many interpreters feel that in verses 1-16 the apostle advances propositions applicable to both Jews and Gentiles. Referring to the description of the degradation of pagan life given in 1:18-32, Gifford, for example, writes: "But there were some among the heathen and many among the Jews to whom this description could not be applied in its strongest *external* feature of blind idolatry and heathen vice. They had not lost all knowledge of the true nature of God; they did not practise, still less applaud, the grosser forms of vice; their moral sense was keen enough to condemn the sins of others: yet they too must be brought to feel themselves guilty before God" (p. 71; cf. Barrett, p. 43).

Bruce expresses the opinion that even in this section Paul was thinking chiefly, if not exclusively, of the Jewish critic. Cranfield thinks "the probability that Paul is already thinking of the Jew in 2:1 is very strong" (pp. 138,139). Murray, while admitting that there is something to be said for the more general application of verses 1-16, thinks there are weighty reasons for limiting it to the case of the Jews. He mentions, among other things, the propensity of the Jews to judge the Gentiles for their religious and moral degeneracy.

Now the critic must be made to see that he himself does not escape the wrath of God.

The apostle begins with *a general charge of guilt*: "Wherefore thou art without excuse, O man, whosoever thou art that judgest: for wherein thou judgest another, thou condemnest thyself; for thou that judgest dost practise the same things" (v. 1). The thought is as follows: (1) You give assent to the righteous ordinance of God (v. 32) and judge others for the sins they commit; (2) you are equally guilty of sin against God (cf. 2:17ff.); (3) therefore you condemn yourself and are, like the Gentiles, without excuse.

At verse 2 Paul begins his *statement of the nature of God's judgment*. Two ideas are stressed:

a. *Verses 2-11 stress the impartiality of God's judgment*. The three key phrases are in verse 2 ("the judgment of God is according to truth"; verse 6 ("who will render to every man according to his works"; and verse 11 ("there is no respect of persons with God").[15] These three phrases all point up essentially the same truth, namely, that at the final judgment no one will enjoy a "most favored nation" status.

Paul begins with an affirmation: "And we know that the judgment of God is according to truth against them that practise such things" (v. 2).[16] The word rendered "we know" means to know as a matter of principle. The "we" likely means Paul and his fellow Jews. "Judgment" here is not the act of judging, but rather the judicial verdict, "the condemnatory sentence" (Murray, I, 57). "Truth," which here means something like reality, suggests that God will judge in accord with the true moral condition of men. Thus, the meaning is that God judges rightly, justly, fairly; there are special privileges for none.

Verses 3 and 4, by means of two rhetorical questions, graphically point up the attitude of the unbelieving Jew. The first question (v. 3), which implies an emphatic negative answer, suggests that they felt they were exempt from divine judgment, doubtless because of their descent from Abraham (Matt. 3:8,9; cf. Gifford, p. 72). The second question (v. 4) implies that they treated with contempt the wealth of God's goodness and forbearance, which suspended the infliction of His wrath upon them in the present age. His seeming indifference to their sin, due entirely to His patience and goodness, was not meant to be (as they thought) license to do evil, but rather an inducement to repent.

In verse 5 the apostle abandons rhetorical questions and directly arraigns the Jew. He has resisted the repentance which God's goodness

---

[15]The statement of verse 11 serves as a summary of the entire paragraph contained in verses 1-11.

[16]Barrett puts this statement in quotation marks and thinks Paul represents it as the utterance of an imaginary objector (cf. Montgomery's translation).

was calculated to produce and has instead become obstinate and impenitent in heart. Accordingly, he is treasuring up for himself a store of wrath to be executed in the (eschatological) day of wrath. That "day," called also the day of the "revelation of the righteous judgment of God," is further identified in verse 16 as "the day when God shall judge the secrets of men."

At that time God "will render to every man according to his works" (v. 6). This verse brings out two important aspects of God's judgment: (1) its universality ("every man"; cf. vv. 9,10) and (2) the criterion by which it will be carried out ("according to his works"). The mention of "works" reiterates the principle stated in other terms in verse 2b, namely that God's judgment will be administered in strictest justice. Deeds, not position or privilege, will be the determining factor.

Verses 7-10 expand upon the principle stated in verse 6 and apply it to two types of persons. These two kinds of persons are the righteous (those who "by patience in well-doing seek for glory and honor and incorruption," v. 7) and the wicked (those who "are factious, and obey not the truth, but obey unrighteousness," v. 8). Two different rewards are named: For the righteous there will be eternal life (v. 7), glory, honor, and peace (v. 10); for the wicked there will be wrath and indignation (terms descriptive of God's displeasure), tribulation and anguish (expressions which describe their punishment in terms of their experience (vv. 8,9).[17]

Verse 11 sums up all that Paul has said in verses 2-10 with the assertion that "there is no respect of persons with God." That is, He shows no partiality, has no favorites.

b. *Verses 12-16 stress the universality of man's accountability to God.* The essential teaching is that all are accountable to God for judgment — whether they are Jews (who possess the law of Moses) or Gentiles (who without the written law do by nature [instinct] at least some of the things which are stipulated in the law). Meyer writes that the moral nature of the Gentiles, "with its voice of conscience command-

---

[17]Paul's teaching here has been interpreted by some to be a contradiction of the main thesis of this epistle, namely, that by works no man shall be justified. But one must not imagine that Paul is here teaching salvation by works. *Judgment according to works* is to be distinguished from *salvation on account of works.* It is the former that is here taught. Bruce states it well: "While, for Paul, forgiveness and eternal life are utterly of God's grace, divine judgment (as uniformly in the Bible) is always passed according to what men have done" (p. 88). Godet similarly writes: "Justification by faith alone applies to the time of entrance into salvation through the free pardon of sin, but not to the time of judgment. When God of free grace receives the sinner at the time of his conversion, He asks nothing of him except faith; but from that moment the believer enters on a wholly new responsibility; God demands from him, as the recipient of grace, the fruits of grace. . . . The reason is that faith is not the dismal prerogative of being able to sin with impunity; it is, on the contrary, the means of overcoming sin, and acting holy; and if this life-fruit is not produced, it is dead, and will be declared vain" (Godet, pp. 117,118).

ing and forbidding, supplies to their own ego the place of the revealed law possessed by the Jews" (quoted by Murray, I, 73,74). The point is that there is a valid standard for judgment for every person. The standard for the Jew will be the law of Moses; the standard for the pagan (i.e., anyone who does not have "law" or "gospel") will be the law of conscience and nature. In other words, each person will be judged on the basis of the revelation he has, not on the basis of a revelation he does not possess. These two standards are not contradictory, but are essentially the same. The difference is in the manner in which they are mediated and in the degree of fullness which characterizes them.

Two questions arise in connection with verse 16. First, how is the verse related to what precedes it? Answer: Perhaps it is best to see verses 14 and 15 as parenthetical and connect verse 16 with the thought of verse 13. Second, what is the import of "according to my gospel"? It cannot mean that Paul's gospel will be the universal rule of judgment. If this were the meaning, the statement would contradict the previous argument of the apostle, namely, that those who "sinned without the law shall also perish without the law." "If specially revealed *law* is not the criterion in such cases, how much less could specially revealed *gospel* be" (Murray, I, 77). The phrase probably means that the gospel as preached by Paul teaches that God will judge men *through Jesus Christ*.

The mention of the "secrets of men" being brought into judgment shows how penetrating and thorough that judgment will be, dealing not simply with overt acts but also with inward thoughts and motives.

2. The Jew's failure to live up to his privileges (2:17-29)

Having set forth the nature of, and the universal accountability of men to, the judgment of God, Paul now, for the first time, specifically names the Jew and exposes his failure under the law. In a stunning indictment, he shows that the Jew, no less than the Gentile, *knew* the truth, *rejected* it, and therefore stood *condemned* before God (cf. 2:1). The entire discussion is a sort of exposition of the principle enunciated in verse 13, that "not the hearers of the law are just before God, but the doers of the law shall be justified."

The Jew boasted especially of two things: (1) his possession of the law (vv. 17-24) and (2) the rite of circumcision (vv. 25-29). Paul shows that these two things, indicative of the superior privilege of the Jew and the two things that marked him as a Jew, in and of themselves only compound the guilt of the Jew.

a. *The Jew's possession of the law (vv. 17-24).* In verses 17-24 the apostle discusses the Jew's possession of the law and its attendant privileges. Possession, he argues, is not enough. The law demands practice, and this the Jew has failed to carry out. The Jew, as someone has said, saw the law as his protection; Paul affirms the instrument of his condemnation.

Structurally the passage divides itself into three parts: (1) Verses 17-20 contain a supposition in which the boasted privileges of the Jew are catalogued and his assumed superiority over others is at least momentarily admitted. (2) Verses 21,22, by "a series of pungent questions," bring out "the flagrant inconsistency between profession and practice" (Gifford, p. 77). (3) Verse 23 forms a kind of summary of the full argument contained in the preceding verses, and this is reiterated and confirmed in verse 24 by a quotation from Isaiah 52:5.

b. *The rite of circumcision (vv. 25-29)*. The apostle insists that the rite of circumcision is of value only if it represents heart circumcision. Here, writes Haldane, Paul "pursues the Jew into his last retreat" and strips him of the last refuge to which he usually resorted. There was a rabbinic saying to the effect that "Circumcision is equivalent to all the commandments of the law." Circumcision, Paul teaches, is only an outward seal of a covenant relationship with God. Personal righteousness is the real expression of what the covenant means.

Verse 25a anticipates the objection raised by the Jew in 3:1. "Circumcision," says Paul, "indeed profiteth, if thou be a doer of the law." The thought appears to be that if one fulfills the conditions of faith and obedience involved in the practice of the law, circumcision is a true seal of God. "But if thou be a transgressor of the law, thy circumcision is become uncircumcision" (v. 25b).

In verse 26 "the uncircumcision" which keeps "the ordinances, [i.e., the moral requirements] of the law" would appear to be a description of Gentiles who receive Christ. In Godet's words, the reference is "to those many Gentiles converted to the gospel who, all uncircumcised as they were, nevertheless fulfil the law in virtue of the spirit of Christ, and thus become the *true* Israel, *the Israel of God*, Gal. 6:16" (p. 130).

Verses 28 and 29 reveal what it is that makes one a true Jew and what constitutes true circumcision. The true Jew is he who is one inwardly, not he who only makes outward profession. And true circumcision is also inward — circumcision of the heart, "by the Spirit, not by the written code" (v. 29a, NIV). The last part of verse 29 ("whose praise, etc.") alludes to the root meaning of the name Judah, from which "Jew" is derived (cf. Gen. 29:35; 49:8).

3. *Jewish objections to Paul's teaching (3:1-8)*

In these verses Paul meets and answers supposed Jewish objections[18] to the argument advanced by him in chapter 2, especially verses 17-29. In those verses the apostle has insisted that mere possession of the law does not exempt one from judgment, and that fleshly circumcision is worthless apart from that inward condition of heart of which it was intended to be the outward seal. Thus, it appears that he has virtually reduced the Jew to a position of equality with the Gentile.

In answering the objections Paul admits the advantage of the Jew, but at the same time insists that if God's character as righteous Judge of the world is to be maintained the Jew cannot be exempted from the judgment. Thus the anticipated objections become the occasion for affirming both the justice and faithfulness of God.[19]

The apostle's "straw man" brings forward three objections. Each is put in the form of a question.

a. *First objection (vv. 1,2)*. The question, raised in verse 1, asks what (in light of Paul's teaching) is the advantage of the Jew or the profit of circumcision. The assumption is that one may infer from Paul's teaching that the Jew has no advantage over the Gentile and that there is no profit in circumcision. The assumption, however, is wrong. Paul's argument was not intended to prove the equality of Jew and Gentile "in respect of privilege but in respect of *reality of guilt*, and of *need of a Divine justification*" (Moule, p. 77).

Paul's answer (v. 2) therefore affirms that the Jews do have an advantage — "Much every way!" (cf. 9:4,5). Chiefly, their advantage consisted in their being entrusted with the oracles (the very words) of God (cf. Ps. 147:19,20). The reference is to the entire written revelation which we know as the Old Testament. "Entrusted" suggests that possession of the utterances of God was not only a great privilege (i.e., something which benefited the Jews), but also a weighty responsibility (i.e., something having reference to other peoples). As Gifford puts it, the divine oracles "were a trust committed to the Jews for the common benefit of mankind" (p. 82). Moule speaks of the Jews as " 'the keepers of Holy Writ' for the world" (p. 77).

---

[18]The style is typical of this letter (cf. 2:1,2; 6:1,15; 7:7, et al). It is as though the apostle were face to face with a heckler who from time to time interrupts his arguments with questions and objections. In this way Paul anticipates the arguments of his opponents and answers them.

[19]The problems raised in 3:1-8 are more fully discussed in chapters 9-11. It is a characteristic of the Roman letter that the apostle will introduce a topic for brief and summary treatment, then later pick it up and give it fuller discussion (cf. righteousness — 1:17; 3:21ff.; law — 3:20; 7:1ff.; the Jew — 3:1-8; chapters 9-11, etc.).

b. *Second objection (vv. 3,4)*. The question (v. 3) asks whether God has failed because some have not believed.[20] "Shall their want of faith make of none effect the faithfulness of God?" The question assumes that Paul's doctrine of condemnation nullifies the promises of God. This appears to be the thought: If some do not believe, so what? In view of Israel's possession of the oracles of God, what difference does it make if some of the Jews are lacking in faith? Does their lack of faith destroy the validity of God's Word and nullify His own faithfulness to the Jewish race?[21] Will He fail in His purpose? This question is given full treatment in chapters 9-11.

Paul's answer, given in verse 4, is in three parts. First, he repels with horror the suggestion of unfaithfulness on God's part: "God forbid" (v. 4a; NEB, "Certainly not!"). Second, he affirms that God's truth is absolute and inviolable: "Yea, let God be found true, but every man a liar" (v. 4b). Murray calls this "an arresting way of placing in the forefront the indefectible faithfulness of God to his Word" (I, 95). The idea is that God's truth "cannot be impaired, even if man's falsehood is universal." More than that, "God's truth is the only truth; it will be found in the end that He alone is holy and righteous, and every man, in himself, unholy and unrighteous" (Gifford, p. 83). Moule offers a paraphrase: "Rather should we admit any charge of untruth against man, than the least against God" (p. 78). Denney expresses the sense thus: "When the case is stated between God and man there can only be one conclusion: let God come out . . . true, and every man a liar" (p. 603). There is perhaps the suggestion that man's lack of faith, so far from nullifying God's faithfulness, is really only a foil against which the faithfulness of God stands out more conspicuously. Third, he enforces his argument by a quotation from the Old Testament which speaks of God's righteousness over against man's sinfulness. The passage cited is a part of David's confession (Ps. 51:4).[22] Paul, by using it, seems to say that David saw the truth of what has just been affirmed. "His main thought was . . . that he would even own the very worst against himself, that God might be seen to punish him justly" (Moule, p. 78).

c. *Third objection (vv. 5-8)*.

The question (v. 5a) is whether God, if the Jews' unrighteousness makes more manifest His righteousness, is fair in inflicting punishment

---

[20]The unbelief in view is the unbelief of the Jews of Paul's day.

[21]The "faith of God" (v. 3, KJV) obviously does not mean our faith in God, but rather God's own *faithfulness*.

[22]Murray has a helpful paragraph on the difficulty of Paul's appeal to David's statement, which was made in a context quite different from that of the apostle's argument. See p. 95 of his commentary.

for their sin. If under these circumstances He condemns them for being unrighteous, does that not make Him unrighteous? Stated otherwise, the thought is this: If the Jews' sin commends (exhibits, sets off more clearly) God's righteousness, He then is obligated to exempt them from judgment. This claim of impunity on the objector's part represents a perversion of the truth stated in verse 4.

Paul's answer (vv. 5c-8) is in four parts: First, he apologizes for even mentioning an objection which he finds repulsive. "I speak," he says, "after the manner of men" (v. 5c); that is, "I am using a human analogy" (cf. Weymouth). Murray thinks the apology refers to the foregoing questions, by the use of which the apostle was "accommodating himself to the human mode of interrogation and reasoning." This is Paul's way of saying that the questions, in reality, "are impertinent and out of place. For God's justice is not something that can be called in question" (I, 99). Thus, the parenthetic words have, as Cranfield observes, "the effect of underlining Paul's repudiation of the [objector's] thought" (p. 184). Second, he repels the thought with horror ("God forbid," v. 6a; Moffatt: "Never!"). Third, he shows the objector's reasoning to be absurd, for on this principle God could not punish anyone (v. 6) and unthinkable standards of personal conduct would prevail (vv. 7, 8). Fourth, Paul affirms that the condemnation of people who reason and act in this manner is deserved ("whose condemnation is just"; v. 8).[23]

C. The Wrath of God Upon the Whole World (3:9-20)

With these verses the apostle brings to a close his assessment of human need. The chief emphasis appears still to be on the Jew, but the argument broadens in scope so that it becomes a sort of summary of all that has been written in the preceding section (1:18-3:8). The burden of the paragraph then is that the whole world lies under the condemnation of God. This is argued first from the universality of sin and guilt (vv. 9-18) and secondly from the operation of the law (vv. 19,20).

1. The universality of sin (3:9-18)

By the words "What then?" (v. 9a) Paul means, "What conclusion are we to draw from the foregoing argument?" This is expanded by the question "are we better than they?" (v. 9a). Both the translation and the import of this latter question are much disputed. The uncertainty centers on the reference in "we" and the meaning of the verb. Moule

---

[23]Verses 7 and 8 are essentially a restatement of the objection and answer given in verses 5 and 6. These two verses (5 and 6) view the matter, so to speak, from God's perspective. Verses 7 and 8 restate it from man's side, as it were.

thinks the pronoun refers to Paul and his fellow Christians. The thought then is, Are we Christians — apart from Christ — any better than they (the Jews)? He sees the question with its answer as "a repudiation of the thought that he has been speaking from a pedestal. . . . As if he had said, 'Do not think that I, or my friends in Christ, would say to the world, Jewish or Gentile, that we are holier than you. . . . Apart from Him who is our peace and life, we are in the same condemnation' " (*Expositor's Bible*, p. 85). Most interpreters understand "we" to embrace Paul and his fellow Jews.

There is much more debate over the meaning of the Greek behind the word "better." Some take the verb as a passive and interpret it to mean "excelled by"; that is, Are we Jews excelled by them (the Gentiles)? Are we worse off than they? Weymouth, following this line of interpretation renders it, "What then? Are we Jews at a disadvantage?" Lightfoot, who championed this interpretation, explains the meaning: "'What then,' argues the Jew, 'do you mean to tell me that others have the advantage over us?' St. Paul's answer is, 'Not at all. We said before that Jews and Gentiles all were under sin. But if we do not give them any advantage over you, neither do we give you any advantage over them. Your Scriptures show that you are not exempted" (*Notes on the Epistles of St. Paul*, p. 267). Cranfield, while admitting that the word is used nowhere else in this way, understands it to be a middle having active force. His translation is, "Do we Jews have an advantage?" The KJV, TCNT, ASV, NASB, and NIV suggest the same understanding of the verb. Knox's rendering states the matter in a neutral way: "Well, then, has either side the advantage?"

Paul's reply is in two parts. First, he makes an assertion: "No, in no wise: for we before laid to the charge both of Jews and Greeks, that they are all under sin"[24] (v. 9b). Cranfield thinks "No, in no wise," which translates two Greek words (*ou pantos*), should read "Not in every respect" or "Not altogether." This, he thinks, is better suited to the context. (See 3:2, where Paul has asserted that the Jew does have a great and important advantage.) While the Jew has a real advantage, he is not at an advantage in every respect. "There is," Cranfield explains, "at least one respect in which they [the Jews] are at no advantage — the matter of sinfulness, of having no claim on God in virtue of their merit" (p. 190).

"Under sin" may suggest the guilt of sin (Coneybeare), being under the control of sin (Goodspeed, TCNT), or the condemnation which sin brings (Phillips). Perhaps the phrase is general enough to include all of

---

[24]This is the first occurrence in Romans of the Greek word (*hamartia*) translated "sin." Paul prefers the singular form and almost personifies it, thinking of it as a power which controls man (cf. Goodspeed's rendering).

these ideas. Taylor's paraphrase seems to touch the central idea: "we have already shown that all men alike are sinners."

Second, Paul supports his assertion of the universality of sin and need by an impressive catena of Old Testament quotations (vv. 10-18), the first of which (v. 10) seems to be a summary of all that follows (vv. 11-18). These quotations, which Cranfield describes as having been "constructed with considerable care and artistry" (p. 191), are drawn chiefly from the Book of Psalms. The quotation found in verses 15-17, the only one not taken from the Psalms, comes from Isaiah. Some of them are verbatim quotations, but several reproduce only the sense of the original.

The passages quoted speak of the degradation of character (vv. 10-12), of speech (vv. 13,14), and of conduct (vv. 15-18). One should notice the mention of the various organs of the body: throat, tongue, lips, mouth, feet, eyes. Together they show that "from whatever aspect man may be viewed, the verdict of Scripture is one of universal and total depravity" (Murray, I, 102).

Only a few of the words and phrases of this paragraph require explanation. "None that understandeth" (v. 11a) perhaps means there is no right apprehension of God. "None that seeketh, etc." (v. 11b) may mean there is no desire to worship the true God. "Have all turned aside" (v. 12a) means they have left the way of life prescribed by God. "Are . . . become unprofitable" (v. 12b), which is translated from a Greek word meaning to become bad, suggests uselessness, serving no good purpose. The ancients used the word of milk that had turned sour. "Together" (v. 12b) points up that there are no exceptions — to a man they have gone bad. To say that the throat is "an open sepulchre" (v. 13a) is to suggest that man's inward person is corrupt, that what proceeds out of his mouth is as offensive as the stench of an open grave. "Used deceit" (v. 13b) indicates a tense which depicts a habit of life. "Cursing" (v. 14) reflects impiety, irreverence toward God; "bitterness" (v. 14), malignity toward men.

The language of verses 15-17 suggests that the conduct of men is so murderous and violent that wherever they go they leave a path of misery and woe. (Compare the trail of a devastating tornado.)

Verse 18 may give the underlying cause of all of these expressions of sin: Men are not actuated by any regard for the will of God, nor do they have any reverence ("fear") for His person. Murray observes that in the Bible "the fear of God is the soul of godliness and its absence the epitome of impiety" (I, 104). No indictment, he says, could be more inclusive and decisive than that given by these words.

2. *The operation of the law (3:19,20)*[25]

The Jew might object that the Scriptures just quoted by Paul were originally spoken of the Gentiles (though the Isaiah passage, cited in verses 15-17, is distinctly directed against the unrighteousness of Israel). But Paul, in verses 19 and 20, denies their plea and affirms that the operation of the law (Scripture) is such that *their* guilt, as well as that of the Gentile, is patent.

Three things are to be observed in these two verses: First, whatever the law (Scripture) says, it says to "them that are under [lit., 'in' i.e., in the realm of the authority of] the law" (v. 19a). The quotations might aptly describe pagan men, but the words are first of all a condemnation of the Jew, in whose Bible the words were written.[26] Everything in the O. T. (including those things that are said about Gentiles) "is indeed addressed in the first instance to the Jews and is intended for their instruction. They should accept them, therefore, as applying first and foremost to themselves" (Cranfield, p. 196). Second, what the law says is intended to stop every mouth and bring all the world under God's judgment. Law, to be sure, lies heaviest on Israel (v. 19a); yet it binds the whole world; it shuts *every* mouth. If the Scriptures prove that the Jews are under the guilt and control of sin, there can be no question about the condition of the Gentiles. "That every mouth may be stopped" (v. 19) is a vivid way of saying that every person, before God's righteous judgment, will be reduced to silence, deprived of all excuse. All the world's being "brought under the judgment of God" may mean that all mankind are "answerable to God." The NEB has "exposed to the judgment of God." Cranfield says the language conveys the picture of "men standing at God's bar, their guilt proven beyond all possibility of doubt, awaiting God's sentence of condemnation" (p. 197). Third, the reason why every mouth shall be stopped and all the world made accountable to God is stated in verse 20: "because by the works of the law shall no flesh [the term denotes man in his frailty and sinfulness] be justified in his [God's] sight; for through the law cometh the knowledge of sin." The

---

[25]Since the word "law" in this passage must allude to the foregoing citation of Scripture, it must be understood as including the entire O. T. revelation. This is the view which has traditionally been advocated.

[26]One's first impression, and the interpretation reflected above, is that the words, "them that are under the law," refers only to the Jews. Murray feels, however, that the subsequent mention of the utterances of the law being intended to stop every mouth and make "the whole world" liable to God suggests that Gentiles as well Jews are referred to. He understands Paul to mean that the Gentiles are "under [lit., in] the law" in the sense that they are "in the sphere within which the law of which Paul had quoted samples had relevance." Although they did not possess the written revelation of the O. T. and in that sense were "without the law," they were nonetheless "not outside the sphere of the judgment which the Old Testament pronounced" (I, 106,107).

final clause teaches that the law was never intended to be a vehicle of salvation, but rather an instrument to show men how desperately they need salvation — to give "the knowledge of sin."[27]

For Further Study

1. Read Romans 1:18-3:20, looking for references to the ideas of wrath, punishment, judgment, etc.

2. Use a concordance to study the wrath of God in other portions of the New Testament. Write out in your own words the essential teachings about divine wrath in each passage which deals with it.

3. Read in a Bible dictionary articles on Law, Jew, Sin, Gentile, and Judgment.

4. Read Luke's account of Paul's sermon preached in Athens (Acts 17:22-31) and the account of the message preached at Lystra (Acts 14:15-17). Is there anything in these sermons that is similar to the thought of Romans 1:18-32?

5. Read Philippians 3:1ff. Does this passage relate in any way to what Romans 2:1-3:8 says about the condition of the Jew?

---

[27]The idea of law giving the knowledge of sin is developed more fully in 7:7ff.

Chapter 4

The Righteousness of God:
The Doctrine of Justification
(Romans 3:21-5:21)

Paul has shown the revelation of the wrath of God (1:18-3:20); now he will set forth the revelation of the righteousness of God (3:21-5:21). The former passage has unfolded man's need of justification (the divine righteousness); the present passage proclaims God's provision for that need. Bengel speaks of it as the opening of "a more pleasant scene" (p. 48).

The discussion begins with a summary statement in which Paul briefly, but powerfully, describes the divine method of justification (3:21-31). This is followed by a discussion of Abraham's justification, introduced as an Old Testament example of the divine method by which men become right with God (ch. 4); a statement of the blessed results of being made right with God (5:1-11); and a profound treatment of the grounds upon which God makes men right (5:12-21).

A. A Summary of the Divine Righteousness (3:21-31)

It has been said that if one misunderstands this passage he runs the risk of misunderstanding the entire Roman epistle. Luther called it "the chief point, and the very central place of the Epistle and of the whole Bible." Calvin declared that "there is not probably in the whole Bible a passage which sets forth more profoundly the righteousness of God in Christ." Cranfield, calling attention to the centrality of the passage for the entire epistle, says "it reads like a solemn proclamation" (p. 199).

The opening words of verse 21 pick up the thought introduced at 1:17 ("For therein is revealed a righteousness of God . . .") and repeat it in slightly altered form: "But now apart from the law a righteousness of God hath been manifested, etc." The word "But" marks the contrast between the revelation of the wrath of God (1:18) and the manifestation of the righteousness of God. The adverb ("now"), though taken by some interpreters as having only logical force, is to be interpreted temporally. It marks, as Gifford says, "the contrast between the times of the old and new dispensations" (p. 88).

"The righteousness of God" (KJV) is better rendered without the definite article, as in ASV: "a righteousness, etc." This righteousness is that which has already been mentioned in 1:17. Mrs. Montgomery renders it here "a righteousness coming from God"; Williams, "God's way of giving men right standing." The essential idea is that of a status of righteousness before God which is His free gift. It is this righteousness which is the subject of discussion from this point through 5:21.

This righteousness, Paul affirms, has now been "manifested." The word conveys the thought of being brought to light. The idea, made clear by the context, is that God's righteousness has been brought to light "in historical reality in the person of Jesus Christ" (Gifford, p. 89). The tense of the verb (perfect) affirms that the manifestation is complete, but that its results are a continuing reality. "Stands manifested" might express the meaning. (Compare 1:17, where a present tense verb is used.)

The remainder of the paragraph (especially through verse 26) sets out the characteristic features of this divine righteousness.

1. It is "apart from the Law" (3:21a)[1]

That is, the righteousness of God — His way of giving men right standing with Himself — is in no way dependent on the law, is not earned by fulfillment of its requirements.

The latter half of verse 21 shows that, although the divine righteousness is apart from works of the law, it is not a novel thing nor is it contradictory to the law. Indeed, both "the law and the prophets" bear witness to it. Here "the law and the prophets" sums up the entire Old Testament revelation. This testimony of the Old Testament is seen in all the types, promises, and prophecies of Christ, for "to him bear all the prophets witness, that through his name every one that believeth on him shall receive remission of sins" (Acts 10:43). It may be remembered that Jesus, "beginning from Moses and from all the prophets," explained to the Emmaus disciples all "the things concerning himself" found "in all the Scriptures" (Luke 24:27; cf. Luke 24:44). There is then a distinct continuity between the old dispensation of law and prophets and the new dispensation inaugurated by the advent of the Messiah.

2. It is "through faith in Jesus Christ" (3:22)

---

[1] It is debated whether the phrase "apart from the law" is to be read with the verb "hath been manifested" (see Gifford, Cranfield) or as a description of "the righteousness of God" (see Williams' translation). Either way, it follows that the righteousness itself is apart from the law. If the construction with the verb is followed, the fact is inferred; if the words are construed with the noun, the fact is affirmed.

That is, men come to experience the righteousness of God (justification) through faith in Christ. Those words reiterate the "from faith to faith" of 1:17. Gifford speaks of faith as "the rightful disposition of the creature toward his Creator." It is, he says, the soul's "lowliest 'confession of sin,' and the only homage it can render to God" (p. 89).[2]

Faith here is specifically defined as to its object, "Jesus Christ."[3] Thus, it is not a nebulous "faith-in-God" concept, but a well-defined and particularized faith — "in Jesus Christ."

The addition of the words "unto all them that believe," which on the surface appear to be redundant, is intended to emphasize that faith-righteousness is effectual for *all* believers. Thus, the words "through faith in Jesus Christ" emphasize that it is *only* through faith that the divine righteousness is attainable; "unto all them that believe" emphasizes that this righteousness is *always operative* where there is faith, regardless of who the believing person is. That this is the force of these words is confirmed by the statements which follow: "for there is no distinction [in the method of salvation for Jew and Gentile]; for all have sinned, and fall short of the glory of God" (vv. 22b, 23). This means that the *method* of justification is the same for all because the *need* of all is the same; Jews and Gentiles alike stand bankrupt before God.

"Have sinned" (aorist tense) sums up the entire history of the race.[4] "And" expresses a consequence: "and so." "Fall short," a present tense verb, emphasizes the present and continuing effect of sin in the lives of men: they *habitually* fall short of the glory of God. The verb, which means "to fall behind," "to be inferior," "to lack," "to want," "to be destitute of," appears to point in this context more to a condition than to an action. Some interpreters think there is special significance in Paul's use of the middle voice of the verb. Thus, Gifford writes that "men not only come short of [the idea of the active form of the verb] but suffer want . . . and feel themselves destitute of [the idea of the middle] 'the glory of God' " (p. 89).

The meaning of "the glory of God" is much debated. Essentially the phrase denotes the visible brightness and splendor emanating from the perfection of God. It can denote, in a passage such as this, the approval of God (cf. John 12:43). This is the view preferred by some, for example,

---

[2]Some recent interpreters have argued that the Greek *pisteos* should here be rendered "faithfulness," and maintain that it is the faithfulness belonging to and exhibited by Christ that is in view. It is better to retain the more usual meaning of trust in and commitment to Christ.

[3]The KJV rendering "faith of Jesus Christ," is a very literal rendering of the Greek, but it is somewhat misleading. "Jesus Christ" in the Greek is an objective genitive and is correctly rendered "in Jesus Christ."

[4]The tense is probably what grammarians call a "constative" aorist. It does not refer to the idea of "race sin" in Adam, but simply contemplates the fact of human sin in its entirety and states it in "summary" fashion.

Calvin, Hodge, and Denney. If this latter interpretation is followed, the meaning of coming short of the glory of God is obvious. If we retain the meaning of "splendor," etc., the coming short of God's glory may be variously explained. Murray, for instance, thinks the meaning is that men, because of their sin, "come short of reflecting the glory of God, that is, of conformity to his image (cf. I Cor. 11:7; II Cor. 3:18; 8:23)" (p. 113). Gifford understands it in the sense of man's failure to attain to the glory (i.e., excellence) for which man was intended. He points to the use of the same phrase in 5:2, where the justified person's hope of sharing in the glory of God suggests that this was the God-intended destiny of man.[5] The present verse then simply states that man, because of his sin, fails to attain that destiny.[6] This is the interpretation which seems to have most to commend it.

3. It is freely bestowed: "being justified freely by his grace" (3:24a)

The chief exegetical problem of these words is to ascertain the exact connection of the participle ("being justified") with the context; it does not appear to be grammatically related to anything that has preceded. One possibility is to understand verses 22b and 23 as parenthetical; then the participle may be construed (at least in sense) with the words of verse 22a ("unto all them that believe"). The word is used in its full forensic sense: "to declare righteous," "to acquit" of guilt.

The gratuitous nature of justification is brought out in two expressions: "freely" and "by his grace." The former suggests "at no cost" (i.e., to the believer), "gift-wise." Moffatt: " . . . justified for nothing." "By his grace" adds emphasis to this thought, grace denoting "undeserved favor" (Gifford: "free, unbought love"). The combination of the two phrases, which support and confirm one another, heightens the thought.

4. It is made possible by the death of Jesus (3:24b-26)

Verse 24a has declared that our justification comes at no cost to us; the present passage shows that it was procured at great cost to God, namely, the death of His own Son: "The price," writes Murray, "magnifies the marvel of the free grace" (I, 115).

The death of Christ is represented in these verses under three figures: redemption, propitiation, and vindication. The first of these is stated in verse 24b: "through the redemption that is in Christ Jesus." The root meaning of the Greek word for "redemption" is a releasing

---

[5]Cranfield has essentially the same interpretation. He sees an allusion to "that share in the divine glory, which, according to Jewish thought, man possessed" before he fell into sin and "which will be restored in the eschatological future" (p. 204).

[6]A comparison of various translations indicates the wide variety of interpretations assigned to this passage. Some of these may be seen in *The NT from 26 Translations*.

brought about by the payment of a price. The TCNT uses the term "deliverance"; NEB, "liberation." Conybeare's translation employs the word "ransom." There is, indeed, this idea in the Greek word[7] (cf. Matt. 20:28; Mark 10:45; Eph. 1:7; Titus 2:14), though one need not subscribe to the view put forth by Origen to the effect that Christ's death was a ransom paid to Satan for the release of those held captive by him.

Second, the death of Christ is represented in terms of a propitiation (v. 25a). The root meaning of the Greek word is that of placating an offended god. A secondary meaning is the removal (expiation) of the thing causing the offense. Christ's death is both propitiatory and expiatory, but the emphasis of this passage seems to be on the former idea. The meaning then is that Christ's death as propitiatory averts the wrath of God from the sinner.[8]

It is not certain whether the Greek word should be read as an adjective or as a noun. In the former instance the meaning would be that God set forth Christ "as propitiatory covering" (Rotherham), "a propitiatory sacrifice" (Conybeare) or "offering"; or simply that God set Him forth "as propitiatory." As a noun, the word may mean either "means of propitiation" (cf. TCNT) or "place of propitiation," the latter being its most frequent connotation. Gifford understands the passage to affirm that God set forth Christ "as a propitiatory," and explains this to mean "mercy seat" (p. 91). Indeed, in twenty-one of the twenty-seven occurrences of the word in the Septuagint, it is used of the mercy seat, that is, the lid of gold above the ark of the covenant. And in the only other occurrence of the word in the New Testament (Heb. 9:5), it has the same sense.

"Set forth" is translated from a Greek word which in the papyri frequently meant "set forth *publicly*." Thus, there may be in it here the notion of "a public exhibition" (cf. NASB, "displayed publicly"). The TCNT brings this out by rendering it, "For God set him before the world." It is significant that it was *God* — the context implies God the Father — who thus set forth Christ. This makes the concept of propitiation entirely different from pagan notions of appeasing the gods. In Christianity the God whose holy nature required the propitiatory sacrifice is Himself the One who provided it.

The words "in [by] His blood" are better construed with "propitiation" than with "faith" (cf. ASV, RSV, NEB, NASB). If the Greek phrase is

---

[7]See Sanday and Headlam; Leon Morris, *The Apostolic Preaching of the Cross*; Murray; and Barrett.

[8]Dodd has advocated the idea of expiation, arguing that hardly a trace of the thought of appeasement attaches to the word as it is used in the Greek translation of the Old Testament. For the view advocated in the present work, see Morris, *The Apostolic Preaching of the Cross*. Cranfield says that "We may set aside as unlikely to be correct . . . the various suggestions . . . which are expressly intended to exclude the idea of propitiation" (p. 216).

interpreted instrumentally (i.e., "through" or "by") the meaning is that it was by the shedding of His blood that Christ became a propitiation for our sins. The rendering of ASV and others seems to represent blood as the element *in* which lies the inherent power of Christ's death. Some interpret the phrase to mean that the propitiation *consisted* in the shedding of Christ's blood. In contexts such as this, "blood" calls attention to the sacrificial character of Christ's death.

"Through faith," which is parallel to "in [by] his blood" and (like that phrase) a modifier of "propitiation," is inserted to show that the propitiatory sacrifice of Christ is effective only for believers. This is because faith is the means by which the benefits of Christ's death are appropriated.

Third, the propitiatory death of Jesus is represented as a vindication. It was intended "to show his [God's] righteousness because of the passing over of the sins done aforetime, in the forebearance of God" (v. 25b). The general sense is that the death of Christ served to vindicate God's past dealings with the sins of the race. His forbearance — the word speaks of His temporary suspension of wrath — had for a time appeared to obscure in the apprehension of men His perfect righteousness. His justice, it seemed to them, slumbered in the face of wicked deeds which obviously deserved punishment. The cross, however, stands as the divine vindication of the righteousness of God in reference to His treatment of sins committed in the foregoing ages of the world.

The phrase translated "to show" is a combination of a preposition and a noun which more literally may be rendered "as an exhibition" or "as a demonstration." Both *Modern Language* and Goodspeed bring out in their translations the idea of vindication. The "righteousness" of God in this context must be understood in the sense of an attribute of God — His justice (cf. 3:5). The word for "passing over," wrongly rendered "remission" in KJV, occurs only here in the New Testament. It suggests letting sins go unpunished — not the revocation of punishment (which "remission" suggests) but the *suspension* of punishment (cf. NIV). The meaning is that God did not exercise the full measure of His wrath upon the guilty persons but rather exercised "forbearance." The idea is the same as that found in Acts 14:16 and 17:30. The "sins" in question are not those of believers before their conversion but rather *"the sins of the world before Christ"* (Meyer, quoted by Gifford, p. 92). Conybeare renders it "the former sins of men in the times that are gone by."

The KJV represents verse 26 as a mere resumption of the thought of verse 25, but it is better to see it as adding yet another facet to the truth of that verse. God passed over (i.e., suspended judgment upon) the sins committed by earlier generations, and He did this in view of the exhibition of His justice "at this present time." The reference in these last words is to the time subsequent to the death of Christ. The righteousness (justice) of God, partially obscured in former ages, has now, in this present time, been clearly manifested and exhibited. The present era, initiated by the incarnation and passion of Christ, is a time of critical decision. The "passing over" is "at an end, and man must accept the full remission . . . of sin, or expose himself to the judgment of a righteous God" (Schaff, quoted by Gifford, p. 93; cf. Acts 17:30).

Verse 26b gathers into a brief statement the two purposes the preceding verses have given of the setting forth of Christ as a propitiation: (a) "that he [God] might himself be just" and (b) that He might be "the justifier of him that hath faith in Jesus." The former phrase, which picks up the thought of verses 25b and 26a, reaffirms the justice of God; God is Himself righteous. The latter phrase, which reiterates the idea underlying verses 24 and 25a, reaffirms that God is the author of righteousness to those who believe. Perhaps the central truth of verse 26b is that the propitiatory death of Christ makes possible the justification of the sinner without compromising the moral character of God. He would not be just in remitting sin unless some account were taken of sin. The sacrifice made at Calvary enables Him to be righteous ("just") even when declaring righteous ("justifying") those who put faith in Jesus.

5. It involves far-reaching consequences (3:27-31)

These verses draw out some of the "grand results" of Paul's representation of the righteousness of God (the grace-method of justification). Three things are emphasized: First, the gospel method of justification excludes all boasting and gives glory to God only (vv. 27,28). In Paul's use of the word "glorying" (v. 27), there may be special allusion to the boasting of the Jew mentioned in 2:17,23 — what Moule calls "the boasting of the Jew in his pride of privilege" (p. 87).[9] We should not, however, rule out the possibility that Paul was thinking generally of the boasting of all men — that is, their claim of human merit as a ground of acceptance with God. Such boasting, Paul says, is "excluded" (v. 27a). The Greek verb is in the aorist tense, which in this place has the force of "shut out once for all," that is, "by one decisive act" (Sanday and Headlam, p. 95). This exclusion of human boasting is effected not by a law of works, but by "a law [i.e., principle or system] of faith" (v. 27b).

Second, the gospel method of justification puts Jews and Gentiles on the same footing before God (vv. 29,30). The argument of these verses is that if God is one (a cardinal belief of the Jew), He is God of both Jews and Gentiles. And since there is but one God to whom all men are

---

[9] In Greek the definite article appears before the word "glorying," lending some support to Moule's interpretation.

responsible, the means of justification must be the same for all men —
whether they are Jews or Gentiles.

Third, the gospel method of justification establishes the true purpose of the law (v. 31).[10] Gifford thinks "law," which in Greek is without
the article, denotes neither the law of Moses nor the O.T. Scriptures,
but "that which is common to all law, its essential character and principle" (p. 95). It is perhaps better to see the word as referring primarily to
the Mosaic law. "Make of none effect" is the translation of a word which
is characteristic of Paul, found no fewer than twenty-five times in his
epistles, and only twice elsewhere. Its literal meaning is "to render
inactive," but here it is used in the sense of rendering invalid, "to
abrogate," "to abolish." Knox translates, "Does that mean that we are
using faith to rob the law of its force?"

Paul rejects the thought with a strong denial, "God forbid!" Then
he asserts, "we establish the law." The thought appears to be that the
faith system announced in the gospel sets up the law, makes it stand
firm, because it puts the law upon its proper base.[11] So far from making
the law void, the righteousness of faith fully vindicates and establishes it.

B. An Example of the Divine Righteousness (4:1-25)

Abraham's experience[12] of justification is recounted by Paul as both
an example and a proof, from Scripture, of the teaching which he has
unfolded in 3:21ff. His argument forms a kind of commentary on the
ideas of "apart from the law" (3:21), "witnessed by the law and the
prophets" (3:21), and "through faith" (3:22).

The experience of Abraham had crucial significance for Paul's argument. Of all the righteous men of Old Testament times, none could
surpass him. God Himself spoke of him as "Abraham my friend" (Isa.
41:8). It has been well said, then, that "the case of Abraham was the
centre and stronghold of the whole Jewish position" (Sanday and Headlam, p. 98). Accordingly, it was most appropriate for Paul to demonstrate that, in his case, the principle of faith-righteousness, not
human merit, was at work.

Four statements sum up the apostle's argument.

1. *Abraham's justification is explained by faith, not works (4:1-8)*

---

[10]It is debated whether verse 31 is the conclusion to the argument of 3:21ff. or the
introduction to the discussion of chapter 4. For the latter view see Sanday and Headlam, p.
96 (cf. also the punctuation of ASV).

[11]Davidson and Martin understand the meaning to be that the law is not "side-stepped."
They explain that God, in saving men through faith, "is not being soft or sentimental. His
justice is satisfied" (p. 1022).

[12]The experience of David (vv. 6-8) is brought in almost incidentally as a corroboration
of the principle at work in Abraham's justification.

Paul introduces this matter with a question which perhaps is to be thought of as raised by an imaginary opponent of his doctrine: "What then shall we say that Abraham, our forefather, hath found [in the way of acceptance and privilege] according to the flesh?" (v. 1). The word "then" points back to the discussion of 3:21-31. In light of that, what is to be said about Abraham?

The chief exegetical problem of verse 1 is to determine whether "according to the flesh" is to be construed with "hath found" (as in ASV) or with "our forefather" (KJV). If the former construction is correct, then "flesh" may be interpreted ethically; and the import of the question is as follows: "What shall we say that Abraham has gained by *his natural powers unaided by the grace of God?*" (Sanday and Headlam, p. 98).[13] If "according to the flesh" is construed with "forefather," then the phrase simply describes the fatherhood of Abraham in terms of natural generation. The sense is: "What then are we to say about Abraham, our forefather by natural descent? How did he gain his position of favor with God?"

One must avoid dogmatism in making a decision between these two, for strong arguments may be made for either. Perhaps the former construction is to be preferred. If this is done, then verse 2a should not be thought of as answering the question of verse 1, but rather as giving a reason for asking it. "Whereof to glory" is the translation which suggests *grounds* for boasting. Perhaps a period should be placed immediately after "glory." The remainder of the verse, the thought of which is highly condensed, is clearly paraphrased by *The Living Bible:* "But from God's point of view Abraham had no basis at all for pride."

Paul proves this by showing in the following verses that the patriarch was *not* justified by works but by faith (i.e., reliance upon and trust in the Lord). He first *cites the Scripture* (Gen. 15:6) which tells of Abraham's justification (v. 3). This text (the first explicit reference in the Bible to God's act of justifying) says nothing about works, speaking only of Abraham's faith. He "believed God, and it [his faith] was reckoned unto him for righteousness." "Reckoned," an accounting term, means that Abraham's faith was credited to his account for righteousness. "Righteousness" means "right standing with God" (Williams).

Next (vv. 4,5), Paul *shows that the language employed in Genesis 15:6 involves the principle of gratuitous justification*, that is, justification which is in no way based on human merit. If a man does a piece of work,

---

[13]Conybeare, who (like Sanday and Headlam) sees "according to the flesh" as a modifier of "hath found" interprets the meaning of the phrase differently: "What, then, can we say that our father Abraham gained *by the fleshly ordinance?*" Moule takes "according to the flesh" to be equivalent to "in respect of his own independent works and merits" (p. 89).

his pay is a matter of debt, not a gift of grace. But when one simply trusts God, it is a matter of grace that his faith is counted as righteousness.

Finally, Paul *shows that the principle of justification by faith,* exemplified in the experience of Abraham, *is reiterated and confirmed by the words of David* (vv. 6-8). The quotation, taken from Psalm 32, is David's exclamation of joyful relief at the assurance of forgiveness. Paul, in introducing the quotation, speaks of David's pronouncing "the blessedness" of the person "unto whom God reckoneth righteousness [i.e., whom God justifies] apart from works" (v. 6). The quotation speaks of "iniquities" being "forgiven," of "sins" being "covered," and of "sin" not being "reckoned." Thus the blessedness of which David speaks belongs not to the man who lays claim to good works but to the one who admits to being a sinner.

2. Abraham's justification was not dependent on the rite of circumcision (4:9-12)

The patriarch became partaker of the blessings cited in the preceding verses when he was justified by faith, and this justification came to him while he still lived "in uncircumcision." Thus the order in his spiritual experience was faith, justification, circumcision. Paul's argument is especially pertinent in view of the fact that ritual circumcision among the Jews had its origin in the experience of Abraham. The nature and conditions of the rite must in all cases be interpreted in light of its nature and condition in the case of Abraham.

From the fact that Abraham's justification preceded the initiation of the rite of circumcision two conclusions may be drawn: The first concerns *the universality of the by-faith method of justification.* In the experience of Abraham we see the justification of an uncircumcised (Gentile) believer, not of a circumcised (Jewish) person. Godet therefore writes: "It is not for believing Gentiles to enter by the gate of the Jews, but for the Jews to enter by the gate of the Gentiles" (p. 174). The second, which shows the relation of Abraham's circumcision to his faith, concerns *the true meaning of circumcision.* It was not merely a mark of racial identity. It was a "sign" and "seal" of the righteousness of faith. Perhaps one should not make a sharp distinction between these words. The thought is that "he received the sign of [consisting in] circumcision [as], a seal of the righteousness," etc. Circumcision, then, was an outward sign or seal of an inward condition secured by faith. It "did not confer, but confirmed . . . righteousness" (Griffith-Thomas, I, 175).

Verses 11b and 12 may be closely related to the statement of verse 11a, the idea being that the purpose of Abraham's circumcision was to mark him out "as the divinely appointed father of the promised seed" (Gifford, p. 103). Moule thinks verses 11b and 12 express the purpose of the entire thought of verses 9-11a: "It was divinely ordained that Abraham's justification should precede his circumcision, and so that his circumcision should not *convey* but *attest* his justification — in order that his relationship to *all* the believing, Gentiles and Jews, might stand clear of the circumcision-covenant" (p. 92).

3. *Abraham's justification was apart from law (4:13-17)*

He was, in fact, justified some 400 years before the law was given through Moses. It might appear, in light of this fact, that no one would argue that law had anything to do with Abraham's experience. Contemporary Judaism, however, taught that Abraham enjoyed God's favor because he fulfilled *by anticipation* all the requirements of the law.

Verse 13 states the proposition that is developed in this paragraph: "For not through the law was the promise to Abraham or to his seed that he should be heir of the world, but through the righteousness of faith." "The promise" is defined by the words "that he should be heir of the world." However, there is no promise in Genesis expressed in exactly those words. Perhaps Paul's words should be taken as a comprehensive statement summing up all the promises received by Abraham: that he should have numerous descendants, that One of those descendants would be the Messiah through whom all the world would be blessed, and that through the Messiah Abraham's descendants would have world-wide dominion (cf. Gen. 12:3,7; 13:15,16; 15:1,5,18; 17:8,19; Gal. 3:8).

"Through the law" is more accurately rendered "through law," for there is no article in Greek. Sanday and Headlam, among others, see significance in this and interpret it as denoting "any system of law" (p. 110). For Murray it is "law as commandment demanding obedience" (I, 141). Moule, however, sees no significance in the absence of the article, explaining that such a construction "is quite natural where the thing is conspicuous and well known" (p. 93).

In Galatians 3 Paul interprets "seed," a collective singular, as referring primarily to Christ and secondarily to the people of Christ. Some interpreters think that in the present passage "seed" must refer, not specifically to Christ but to all those who are the spiritual descendants of Abraham (cf. Rom. 4:16,17).

Verses 14 and 15 state why the promise could not be of law. In the former (v. 14) two things are specifically said: First, to make the promise depend on law is to make faith "void," that is, useless. Second, to make the promise depend on law is to nullify the promise, rule it out altogether. (The Greek word means literally "put out of work.") Verse 15 explains why this is so: "for the law worketh wrath." That is to say, law brings men under the condemnation of God and thus produces an effect which is the opposite of that intended by the promise. Thus, there is a natural antithesis between law and promise. One is founded on justice, the other on grace. The two, therefore, are incompatible; they move in different spheres.

Verse 15b explains *how* the law works wrath: "where there is no law, neither is there transgression." Stated positively, this means, "Wherever there is law there is transgression. It is only where there is no law that there is no transgression" (cf. 5:13). *The Living Bible* expresses the sense: "The only way we can keep from breaking laws is not to have any to break!"

Moule sees significance in the use of the word "transgression" rather than "sin." The latter, he explains, "is wherever the Fall is; 'transgression' is a narrower word; the 'overstepping' of a definite condition" (p. 94).

Verses 13-15 have stated and proved that the promise is not, and cannot, be of law. In verse 16a Paul concludes that the promise must therefore be of faith — and of faith that it might be a matter of sheer grace. "Promise, faith, and grace stand together on one side: law, works, and merit on the other" (Gifford, p. 105).

Verses 16b and 17 affirm the divine purpose in this promise-faith-grace arrangement: It is "that the promise [which here essentially denotes salvation] may be sure to all the seed." Were the promise dependent upon law, it could not be sure to any; for none could earn it by obedience to law. "Sure" is the translation of a Greek word which in this context has in it the notion of being made firm, of being reliable, dependable, certain. The RSV uses the word "guaranteed." Abraham's "seed" are his spiritual descendants — Jews and Gentiles.

4. *Abraham's faith was typical of the Christian's faith (4:17-25)*

This paragraph may be divided into two parts: Verses 17-22 describe the character of Abraham's faith; verses 23-25 show that his faith is a type of the Christian's faith.

a. *The character of Abraham's faith (vv. 17-22).* The focal point of the discussion of Abraham's faith has to do with its object. Three ideas are put forth: First, the God in whom he believed is a God who gives life to the dead (v. 17b). It was only because he knew God to be this kind of God that Abraham could have believed the promise that he would be the father of many nations. From a human point of view, its fulfillment was indeed as impossible as raising the dead. Second, Abraham believed in a God who "calleth the things that are not, as though they were" (v. 17b). These words are understood by most interpreters (e.g., Cranfield, Barrett) to mean that He calls nonexistent things into being. The allusion is obviously to the birth of Isaac, the child of promise. Meyer,

Gifford, Sanday and Headlam, and others take the meaning to be that God summons or commands nonexisting things as though they did exist, that is, "as if they were as much present and obedient to His word as things that be" (Gifford, p. 106).

"In hope believed against hope"[14] (v. 18) is what grammarians call an oxymoron, that is, a combination of contradictory terms used to heighten the effect of the statement. Chrysostom interpreted the phrase to mean "past hope of man, in hope of God"; Theodoret, "past hope according to nature, but in hope of the promise of God" (quoted by Gifford, p. 106). The TCNT has, "With no ground for hope . . . sustained by hope." Goodspeed uses the phrase, "hoping against hope."

Third, Abraham's faith was placed in a God who, contrary to nature, could give procreative powers to his aged servant's body (vv. 19-22). The patriarch's body, so far as the begetting of children was concerned, was as good as dead. Deadness also characterized Sarah's womb. But Abraham, fully aware[15] of his and Sarah's physical inabilities, looked away from himself and focused his attention upon the promise of God. Then, in a great exercise of faith, he gave glory to God, being fully convinced that God was able to do what he had promised. "Giving glory to God" in this context means that Abraham recognized and relied upon God's faithfulness and power.

Moule observes that this passage contains a suggestion as to *why* God prescribes faith as the condition of justification. "Faith," he explains, "is an act of the soul which looks wholly away from 'self' (as regards both merit and demerit) and *honours the Almighty and All-gracious in a way not . . . in the least meritorious.*" Thus, faith brings the creature to the Creator "in the one right attitude — complete submission and confidence" (p. 97). Paul, then, fittingly states: "Wherefore [for this reason] also it [faith] was reckoned unto him [Abraham] for righteousness" (v. 22).

b. *Abraham's faith as typical of the Christian's faith (vv. 23-25).* The relevance of Abraham's experience for the situation of the Christian is now stated. The point is that the Christian's faith (since it is faith in "him who raised Jesus Christ our Lord from the dead") is essentially like that of Abraham.[16] The patriarch's case, then, was not recorded on

---

[14]Lit., "beyond hope . . . in hope."

[15]KJV reads "he considered *not* his own body, etc." Most recent translations, following a different text, omit the negative. Cf. Moffatt: "His faith never quailed, even when he noted the utter impotence of his own body, etc."

[16]Several points of similarity between the Christian's faith and Abraham's faith may be easily derived from this passage: (1) He believed in God; we also believe in God. (2) Abraham's faith was in a God who gives life to the dead; our faith is in the God who raised Jesus, etc. (3) Abraham's faith concerned the messianic promise; our faith touches this promise at the point of its fulfillment in Jesus.

account of its personal interest only, but "for our sake also," as a typical instance of justifying faith. The suggestion is that not only was *Abraham* justified by faith, but all who believe after the pattern of his faith will also similarly be justified.

"For our trespasses" and "for our justification" — the Greek preposition is the same in both phrases — may be interpreted either *prospectively* (i.e., Christ died "with a view to making atonement for our trespasses" and He was raised "with a view to our justification" [i.e., that our justification might become an accomplished fact]) or *retrospectively* (i.e., Christ died "on account of our trespasses" and He was raised "on account of [i.e., because He had accomplished] our justification").[17] A third possibility is to take the first occurrence of the preposition ("for") as retrospective ("on account of") and the second as prospective ("with a view to").

To sum up, Romans 4 has shown that Abraham was justified by faith, not works, while he was in uncircumcision; that the promise of heirship was received by faith; and that the faith exercised by Christians is of the same character as the faith of Abraham.

C. The Results of the Divine Righteousness (5:1-11)

The commentaries are not in agreement as to how this passage fits into its context.[18] Two approaches in particular may be mentioned. One sees the passage as having to do with the effectiveness of the by-faith method of justification. This is the view of Godet, who sees 5:1-11 as presenting the certainty of final salvation for the justified. Similarly, Stifler thinks the entire fifth chapter answers the question, "Will faith save at last, and will it save all, both Jew and Gentile?" That is, "What assurance does this faith in Christ's work give one for the future?" (p. 87). Other interpreters, however, understand 5:1-11 as setting forth the results or fruit of justification. Perhaps we should see both of these emphases in the passage, for the whole thing is indeed permeated by both a note of assurance and a note of exultation.

---

[17]For an exposition of the "retrospective" view, see Godet, pp. 184,185. Most interpreters think the preposition in both its occurrences must be interpreted prospectively. Denney wisely cautious against "over precision" in handling the passage.

[18]Cranfield mentions the "truly remarkable variety of suggested titles" for the entire fifth chapter (p. 255). Many interpreters (including Bengel, pp. 61,62; D. Brown, p. 44, Nygren, p. 188; and Cranfield, pp. 252-254) understand the second major division of the letter to begin here. Nygren, for example, says that up to this point (1:18-4:25) the apostle has expounded the phrase "he who is righteous by faith." Now (chs. 5-8) he will discuss the last two words of the Habakkuk text: "shall live." ;These chapters, then, are a description of the life into which the justified are brought. It is, as Nygren sees it, a life free from the wrath of God (ch. 5), free from sin (ch.6), free from law (ch.7), and free from death (ch.8).

The more traditional approach understands chapter 5 to be more closely related to that which precedes it than to the chapters which follow it. One strong argument for this is the linguistic affinity between chapter 5 and chapters 1-4. A study of the frequency of use of such words as "righteous," "justify," "righteousness," "righteous ordinance," "glory" (or "boasting") will point this up.

The passage begins with "therefore," suggesting that in it Paul is drawing inferences from the doctrine which has been unfolded in the preceding chapters. Sanday and Headlam observe that every line of it "breathes St. Paul's personal experience, and his intense hold upon the objective facts which are the grounds of a Christian's confidence" (p. 119).

"Being justified" (better, "having been justified") takes up and builds upon the last word ("justification") of chapter 4. The tense of the participle in Greek is aorist, the time reference being to the moment of conversion.

The remainder of the passage unfolds three of the gracious results of the believer's justification. These are as follows:

1. *Peace with God (5:1)*[19]

Paul begins with the affirmation that we, having been justified, now "have[20] peace with God." The present tense of the verb points up that we have this peace now, as an immediate and abiding possession. "Peace with God" speaks of a relationship with God, not subjective feelings or a state of mind. The latter Paul elsewhere calls "the peace *of* God" (Phil. 4:7). The phrase used in this passage ("peace *with* God") means that as justified persons, believers have been brought into a state of favor and acceptance with God. They are no longer at war with God, no longer are objects of the divine wrath. They are now sons of God, reconciled, restored, and beloved. (Compare 5:11, "we have now received the reconciliation.")

"Through whom also we have had our access by faith into this grace wherein we stand" (v. 2a) is not to be interpreted as a second and further result of justification. It simply elaborates upon the thought of verse 1. He through whom we have peace is the One "through whom we have had our access . . . into this grace wherein we stand." Four terms in the statement deserve mention. One, the word "access" is more exactly rendered "introduction." It was used by the ancients of one's introduction to a royal court; "the idea," explain Sanday and Headlam, "is that of introduction to the presence-chamber of a royal monarch" (p. 121). Its

---

[19]Cranfield questions that the passage represents peace as a *consequence* of justification. He understands the thought to be that "God's justification of sinners of necessity involves also their reconciliation, the removal of enmity, the establishment of peace" (pp. 356,357). He also feels that peace is the one dominant concept running through all of 5:1-11. There is much to be said for this, in light of the repetition of the statements of verses 1,10, and 11.

[20]There is strong textual evidence for reading "let us have" instead of "we have." Internal considerations, however, argue convincingly for "we have." If the subjunctive ("let us have") is accepted as the true reading, the meaning would be "let us go on [pres. tense] enjoying the peace we now have."

use here was doubtless intended to evoke the thought of the believer's high privilege. Moreover, it implies that we could not come to God in our own strength but only through an introducer (Christ). Two, the tense of the verb rendered "have had" is such as to show that our introduction into "this grace" of acceptance with God is prior to the experience of peace with God. Three, "this grace," which speaks of a state of grace or favor, is another way of denoting our justification, the state of acceptance with God. Denney calls it "the new spiritual atmosphere in which the believer lives as reconciled to God" (p. 823). Four, "wherein we stand" emphasizes that the favor into which Christ has brought us is an abiding and unchanging status.

2. Joyful hope (5:2-8)

Not only do we have peace; we also "rejoice in [lit., 'on the basis of'] hope of the glory of God" (v. 2b).[21] "Rejoice" is the translation of a word which bespeaks a joy outwardly expressed as well as inwardly felt — "not merely the inward joy of the heart, but the grateful and confident utterance of the lips" (Gifford, p. 110). It combines the ideas of exultation and triumph and denotes, as Cranfield says, "exultant rejoicing, jubilation" (p. 259).

The object of this exultant rejoicing is our "hope of the glory of God." "Hope," a word found three times in verses 2-5 and elsewhere in Romans at least ten times, may be defined as sure and certain confidence. "Expectation" or "confident anticipation" might well express its meaning. Three things are here said about it: First, it is hope "of the glory of God";[22] that is, Christians, as a result of their being made right with God, have confident expectation of *sharing* in the glory of God. Of this glory "man was, from the first, designed to partake (I Cor. xi 7), but by sin all men *'come short'* or suffer loss of it (iii. 23). . . . In presenting this *'glory of God'* as an object of the believer's *hope*, the Apostle points to its *future* perfection in the glorification of our whole nature, body, soul, and spirit" (Gifford, p. 110). Sanday and Headlam identify "the glory" as "the Glory of the Divine Presence (Shekinah) communicated to man," explaining that the believer has partial experience of it now, but in the life to come his "whole being will be transformed by it" (p. 121). Similarly, Cranfield defines glory as "that illumination of man's whole being by the radiance of the divine glory which is man's true destiny but which was lost through sin" (p. 260). The present passage implies that it will be restored when our redemption is made complete at the coming of Christ. Moule interprets "the glory" to be a general designation of "the

---

[21]Our statement assumes that verse 2b is coordinated with the leading affirmation of verse 1 ("we have peace with God").

[22]On this phrase, see the discussion of 3:23.

eternal bliss of the justified." It is the glory "of God" because it is bestowed by Him. The present statement, he points out, "is a brief anticipation of ch. viii" (p. 100).

Second, this hope is actually enhanced, not destroyed or negated, by present tribulations (vv. 3,4). "We rejoice [exult] in hope," "but we also rejoice [exult, triumph] in our tribulations."[23] "Tribulations" is the translation of the Greek word *thlipsis*, which primarily denotes "pressure." Vine says it may be used of "anything which burdens the spirit" (p. 39). Here it depicts the pressure put upon the believer by a godless and hostile world. It is variously translated as "tribulation" (KJV, ASV), "sufferings" (NIV), "afflictions" (ABUV), "troubles" (Moffatt), and so on. Paul's teaching is that we not only bear and endure these tribulations, we actually rejoice (glory, exult) in them. They are, as Cyril of Alexandria put it, "the nurse of our hope in the world to come" (quoted by Gifford, p. 111). Cranfield writes that they are "part of the discipline by which [God] teaches us to wait patiently for His deliverance" (p. 261).

The thought, however, may not be that we rejoice in tribulations, or in the midst of tribulations themselves, but that we rejoice because we know that beneficial results flow from them when they are met by faith. Tribulation, when endured in the strength of God, produces "stedfastness" ("patience," KJV; "fortitude," Montgomery; "endurance," Goodspeed; "brave persistence in good works . . . and an abiding hope of final victory which no present dangers may disturb," Gifford; "perseverance," NIV). Steadfastness, in turn, produces "approvedness"[24] ("strength of character," TCNT; "ripeness of character," Weymouth; "tested character," Williams). This approvedness or tested character produces (is ground for) "hope" (confidence, expectation). This, Gifford explains, is because tested, approved character in its nature is "a pledge of perseverance to the end" (p. 111).

Third, the believer's hope is one that can never disappoint him or put him to shame (vv. 5-8). The reason for (and proof of) this is that our hope is founded on our experience of the unfailing love of God. This love, explains Paul, "hath been shed abroad [lit., 'poured forth,' like an overflowing stream in a thirsty land][25] in our hearts through the Holy

[23]Gifford has a beautiful comment: "No sooner has the Apostle pointed to *the glory of God,* as a light shining afar to cheer the believer on his course, than he thinks of the contrast between that bright distance and the darkness that lies around him here.

"To weaker faith earthly sorrows might seem to dim the heavenly light: but to him hope shines out brighter through the gloom" (p. 111).

[24]The Greek word represented by "approvedness" may suggest (1) the process of proving or testing (as the testing of metals), or (2) the effect of testing, namely, approval or approvedness. The latter is the meaning of the word in the present passage.

[25]The Greek word for "shed abroad" was perhaps chosen by Paul to suggest "unstinted lavishness" (Cranfield, p. 263). The same word is used in Acts 10:45 of the pouring out of the Holy Spirit.

Spirit which was given to us"[26] (v. 5b). That is to say, it is through the indwelling Spirit that God's love for us has been brought home to our hearts and realized in us.

Further encouragement to believe that the hope founded on our experience of the love of God cannot fail is evidenced by the greatness of that love (vv. 6-8). God "commendeth" His love to us in that He gave His Son for us while we were still in a condition of helplessness and ungodliness. "Commendeth"[27] here suggests giving proof of, demonstrating, establishing. Perhaps the thought is that the death of Christ sets His love before us in all its greatness. It is indeed unlike anything else in the world, bestowed as it is on the helpless ("weak," v. 6), the "ungodly" (persons in revolt against the authority of God, v. 6), and "sinners" (those who have missed the mark of righteousness, v. 8). The point in all of this is that God's love is love for the undeserving.

3. *Assurance of final and complete salvation (5:9-11)*

This passage emphasizes a notion that underlies the statement of the preceding verses (2-8), for there the apostle has shown that the believer's hope of glory *cannot fail* because it is founded on God's love — a love exhibited in the death of Christ on the cross. Here the argument is drawn out more fully and stated with even greater clarity. The apostle reasons from the greater to the lesser, the idea being that in the initial experience of justification the greatest obstacle to our eternal bliss has been overcome. *That* having been settled, we may now *much more* expect final salvation from the wrath to come.

A threefold contrast is drawn in these verses: (a) a contrast between our *present* justification and our *future* (final) salvation (v. 9); (b) a contrast between our former (preconversion) *hostility* ("enemies") toward God and our present state of *reconciliation* (v. 10); and (c) a contrast between the *death* of Christ, from which justification and reconciliation flow, and the *life* of Christ in (or by) which our final (complete) salvation is secured (vv. 9, 10). We shall be saved by (or in) His life because we have become partakers of that life. There may also be the suggestion of what is stated clearly in Hebrews 7:25: "Therefore he is able to save completely those who come to God through him, because he always lives to intercede for them" (NIV).

Verse 11, by the words "and not only so," alludes to the future salvation growing out of our reconciliation (v. 10) and then points up that

---

[26]Gifford writes: "If we ask how the Holy Spirit pours out the love of God in the heart, we may find the answer in our Lord's words: 'He shall testify of Me:' 'He shall glorify Me; for He shall take of mine and shall shew it unto you.' Christ is the fountain from which God's love is poured forth in the heart" (p. 112).

[27]The present tense should not go unnoticed. The great proof of God's love is said to be the event of the cross (a past happening), but it stands as a continuing evidence of God's attitude toward us.

in addition to this future salvation we "also" have a present rejoicing. The word rendered "rejoice" is the same as that found in verse 2b, and (like it) includes the notion of exultation and triumph. This rejoicing is "in God" and is made possible "through our Lord Jesus Christ, through whom we have now received the reconciliation" (at-one-ment; cf. KJV).[28]

D. The Grounds of the Divine Righteousness (5:12-21)[29]

This paragraph is one of the more difficult and controversial in Romans, and, as Nygren says, "Exegetes have hardly known what to do with it" (p. 20). Some modern interpreters, because of the difficulties, prefer to think of it as a sort of parenthesis within the letter. Even Luther, in his famous preface to this epistle, called the passage "an entertaining outbreak and excursion." But it is surely a mistake to view these verses as extraneous to the thought of the epistle. It is in fact one of the most important passages in the book. Nygren calls it "the high point of the epistle, in the light of which the whole is best to be understood" (p. 20). Indeed, he uses its thought as the key to his exposition.

Three matters call for consideration. First, it is important to understand the *object* of the passage, that is, its place in the scheme (argument) of the letter. John Brown thinks of it as a commentary on the phrase, "through the redemption that is in Christ Jesus" (Rom. 3:24). The apostle's object, he explains, is to show how completely justification is based on the redemptive work of Christ. To do this, Paul institutes "a comparison and contrast between the way in which man originally became guilty, through the sin of Adam, and the way in which mankind

---

[28]This (vv. 10,11) is one of four New Testament passages which treat the work of Christ under the figure of reconciliation. (The others are 2 Cor. 5:18ff.; Eph. 2:16ff., Col. 1:19ff.) The word suggests a change of relations between God and men and implies a previous state of estrangement and hostility. The New Testament teaches that it is man's sin that has caused the estrangement and that it is not God who is reconciled to man, but man who is reconciled to God.

Reconciliation, however, is not purely a subjective process. It was in some sense effected outside man before anything happened within him. This idea is especially suggested by the passage under consideration. A reconciliation that can be "received" must in some sense be an accomplished fact before men receive it. In other words, reconciliation is both godward and manward. The death of Jesus removes the offending sin from man's heart and turns away the divine wrath. Man receives or accepts what God has wrought.

[29]It is debatable whether 5:12-21 should be thought of as concluding the discussion begun at 3:21 or as introducing the material of chapters 6-8. Perhaps the passage looks both ways, rounding out the argument of the preceding passage and serving to introduce that which follows. Nygren, though not wanting to look upon the passage either as "epilogue" to what precedes or as "prologue" to what follows, says that in these verses "comes together all that Paul had discussed in the preceding chapters, both about the wrath of God and God's righteousness, and all that which he is about to present in the chapters that follow" (p. 207). Here, he says, "all the lines of [Paul's] thinking converge, both those of the preceding chapters and those of the chapters that follow" (p. 209).

become righteous — are justified — through the redemption in Christ Jesus" (p. 71).

Similarly, Hodge speaks of this section as "the illustration of the doctrine of the justification of sinners on the ground of the righteousness of Christ, by a reference to the condemnation of men for the sin of Adam. . . . As this idea of men's being regarded and treated, not according to their own merit, but the merit of another, is contrary to the common mode of thinking among men, and especially contrary to their self-righteous efforts to obtain the divine favour, the apostle illustrates and enforces it by an appeal to the great analogous fact in the history of the world" (p. 71).

Stifler sees in this passage a further proof "that justification by faith gives a sure hope of the glory of God. The proof is found in the likeness of Adam and Christ in relation to those who are in them respectively. As Adam's one sin never fails to bring death, so Christ's one righteous act in behalf of sinners never fails to bring the opposite award to those who are in Him" (pp. 94,95). Barrett expresses a similar conception of the passage, pointing out that in 5:1-11 "Paul argued that justification and reconciliation carry with them the certainty of future salvation." Here, he observes, Paul "supports the same conclusion by a different method," showing that "we can be as sure that we shall share in the consequences of Christ's acts as that we do already share in the consequences of Adam's" (p. 110).

Godet, who interprets 1:18-3:20 as setting forth universal condemnation and 3:21-5:11 as setting forth universal justification, understands the present passage as comparing "these two vast dispensations by bringing together their two points of departure" (p. 199).

Dargan understands this passage as answering a question that might naturally arise from the preceding discussion of the great sacrificial act of Christ as the means of our deliverance from sin. The question is: "How could one act of one person, even though a divine Person, avail as a sacrifice and atonement for all sin of all men?" Dargan feels that Paul's discussion in the present passage "shows that there is analogy in the history of the origin of sin and death. If these came in through one act of one man, so also could their antidote come in through one act of one man" (p. 52; cf. Dodd, p. 100; Barclay, *Expository Times*, Vol. 70, p. 172).

Murray thinks the object of this passage is to demonstrate "that the divine method of justifying the ungodly proceeds from and is necessitated by the principles in terms of which God governs the human race. God governs men and relates himself to men in terms of solidaric relationship" (pp. 179,180).

Second, and closely related to the foregoing, is the essential *teaching* of the passage. This may be stated as follows: The principles operating in the justification of believers "in Christ" are the same as those operating in the condemnation of the race "in Adam." The general truth (Gifford calls it the "master-thought of the whole passage," p. 115) being taught is that of the solidarity and unity of the race — the unity of the many in the one — both in sin and death, and in righteousness and life. "In God's sight," wrote Thomas Goodwin, "there are two men — Adam and Jesus Christ — and these two men have all other men hanging at their girdle strings" (quoted by Bruce, p. 127).

The heart of the passage is stated in verse 18. Because of the solidarity of the race one act of one man (Adam) brought sin and its penalty upon all the human race. On the other hand, one act of one man (Christ) counteracted this and made righteousness and life available to all mankind. Adam stood for the race in the matter of sin and death; Christ stands for the race in the matter of righteousness and life. We all are "in Adam" and under the consequences of his deed by natural descent. We are "in Christ" and experience the consequences of His redemptive deed by faith (cf. 1 Cor. 15:22; 2 Cor. 5:14).

Denney feels that the key to the passage is the expression "much more." We have lost something through our relation to Adam; we have gained "much more" in Christ. And if the loss is certain, "much more" is the gain certain. Christ's death does not merely reverse the effects of Adam's sin; it rather overpowers them by greater gifts. Godet suggests the same: "With a boldness of thought with which it is scarcely possible to imagine, Paul discovers, in the extension and power of the mysterious condemnation pronounced in Adam, *the divine measure* of the extension and power of the salvation bestowed in Christ, so that the very intensity of the effects of the fall becomes transformed . . . into an irresistible demonstration of the greatness of salvation" (p. 201).

The passage deals only incidentally with Adam, sin, and death; its main theme is Christ, righteousness, and life. Adam and his deed are brought in as an illustration; Christ is the subject. One therefore should not spend so much time considering what this passage teaches about sin and death that he fails to see the glory and wonder of the redemption which it proclaims.

Third, it is important to consider the *structure* of the passage. It may be set forth as follows:

1. *Verses 12-14 contain a comparison between Adam and Christ*[30]

---

[30]The comparison is begun in verse 12 but is actually broken off before it is completed. That is to say, the "as" of verse 12 is not followed by a corresponding "so." The brokenness of the statement is denoted in ASV by a dash at the end of verse 12. The KJV represents verses 13-17 as a parenthesis, suggesting that the comparison begun in verse 12 is picked up, restated, and completed in verse 18 and 19. (See Cranfield, p. 273, who accepts the KJV punctuation as correct.)

They are alike in that they both stand at the head of the human race and the deeds of both have far-reaching effects upon the race.

Verse 12. The "therefore" with which the verse begins points up the fact that there is a logical connection between the passage under consideration and the discussion which precedes it. It is debated whether the word draws a conclusion from only verse 11, or from 5:1-11, or from 3:21-5:11. We should avoid dogmatism on the matter; at any rate, it is not a question of profound significance.

The first part of the verse affirms that it was "through one man" (Adam) that both sin and death[31] entered into the world (i.e., had their beginning in the human race). As Cranfield says, "Sin's entry meant also the entry of death, which followed sin like a shadow" (p. 274). In the second half of the verse it is asserted that death "passed [through] unto" (i.e., penetrated, pervaded) the entire human race — and this because "all sinned." Death, writes Murray, "*entered* through the sin of *all*" (I, 182).

"All sinned" is the most sharply debated statement of the verse and has indeed "given rise to an enormous volume of discussion" (Cranfield, p. 274).[32] Sanday and Headlam call it "the *crux* of this difficult passage" (p. 134). Out of the many interpretations that have been proposed, there are at least three that deserve mention.

First, there is the view that "all sinned" means that all have actually and personally sinned — *independently of Adam and on their own initiative.* Most of the Greek commentators understood it in this sense, as for example Theodoret: "Not on account of his forefather's sin, but on account of his own, each man received the doom of death" (quoted by Gifford, p. 117). Because it was advocated by Pelagius, this often is designated as the Pelagian interpretation. This interpretation runs counter to the whole argument of Paul and must surely be rejected. (a) It contradicts the clear and unambiguous statements which follow in verses 15, 16, 17, 18, and 19. (b) It does not harmonize with verses 13 and 14, which are intended to prove the main statement of 5:12, namely, that the penal consequences of Adam's sin passed through to all men. (c) It is inconsistent with the parallel which Paul draws between Adam and Christ, or else it hopelessly confuses his argument. To hold to this position and yet preserve the analogy between Adam and Christ the idea would be as follows: If all men die because they personally sin (as this interpretation affirms), all men are saved because of their own personal deeds of righteousness. This is patently contrary to all Pauline teaching

---

[31]The reference is primarily to physical death, as is clear from the connection with verse 14 (cf. Gen. 3:19).

[32]Most modern scholars are agreed that the Greek phrase (*eph' Loi*) which introduces "all sinned" should be translated "because" (or "for that"), not "in whom."

and indeed to the whole gospel. (d) It is inconsistent with the facts of human experience. It is not true that all die because they have personally sinned. Death is more extensive than personal transgression, the most obvious instance being the death of infants.

Second, there is the view that "all sinned" means that all men sin actually and personally *as a result of the corrupt nature inherited from Adam.* Cranfield, a proponent of this view, explains that "their sinning is related to Adam's transgression not merely externally, as being an imitation of it, but also internally, as being its natural consequence, the fruit of the desperate moral debility and corruption which resulted from man's primal transgression and which all succeeding generations of mankind have inherited" (p. 278). This interpretation is also advocated by Sanday and Headlam, who argue that it (in distinction from the preceding view) does not sever the connection between Adam and his posterity. "If they sinned, their sin was due in part to tendencies inherited from Adam" (p. 134). Cranfield adds: "While men did not sin in Adam in Augustine's sense, they certainly do sin in Adam in the sense that they sin in a real solidarity with him, as a result of the entail of his transgression" (p. 278).

Barclay thinks this interpretation is undoubtedly the most acceptable to the modern mind, "but equally undoubtedly," he adds, "it is not what Paul meant" (*Expository Times*, Vol. 70, p. 173). The main argument which can be adduced as an objection to it "is that the parallel which Paul is drawing between Adam and Christ requires that, as Christ is alone responsible for our salvation, so too Adam must alone be responsible for our ruin" (Cranfield, p. 278).[33] Murray observes that the view is also "inconsistent with the repeated affirmation of verses 15-19 to the effect that condemnation and death came to reign over all by reason of the one sin of the one man Adam" (I, 184).

Third, there is the view that "all sinned" refers not to men's sinning in their own persons but *to their sinning in Adam.*[34] According to it, "all men literally and really sinned in Adam. . . . Adam is not simply the representative of mankind; . . . every individual man sinned in the sin of Adam, and is personally involved in that sin" (Barclay, p. 173). Barclay calls this "the *realistic* interpretation" (p. 173), and thinks that no other does justice to Paul's thought. Murray, who subscribes to it, sums it up as follows: "For some reason the one sin of the one man Adam is

---

[33]Cranfield replies to this objection by asserting that "it is surely enough for the justification of the analogy that in both cases the act of one man has far-reaching consequences for all other men: it is not necessary that the ways in which the consequences follow from the acts should also be exactly parallel" (p. 278). This, however, hardly seems to be a satisfactory answer.

[34]It should be observed that Paul does not explain *how* all sinned; he simply states the *fact.*

accounted to be the sin of all" (I,185). The most conclusive argument for this interpretation is the fivefold assertion in verses 15-19 that condemnation and death issue from the *one sin* of the *one man* Adam. Among those who hold to this view, in addition to Barclay and Murray, are Bengel, Gifford, Dargan, Lagrange, and Bruce.

Verses 13,14. The essential statement of these verses is that "death reigned . . . over them that had not sinned after the likeness of Adam's transgression." That is to say, death reigned over those who did not overtly violate an expressed commandment of God. "They did not sin *like* Adam, but *in* him; and fell *with* him."

The purpose of these verses is to enforce and prove the main statement of verse 12; namely, that the penal consequence (death) of Adam's sin passed through to all men. They do this by pointing to a particular period in human history — the period between Adam and Moses. During this time men died, but it could not have been for their own sin. "Sin," indeed, "was in the world; but sin is not imputed [brought into account] when there is no law" (v. 13).

This latter statement may mean that though there was sin in the world before the Mosaic law was given, it did not take the form of transgression, and therefore was not taken into account. That is, the sin men committed was not charged against them. It therefore could not have been the cause of their dying. Yet they did indeed die, and since death is the penal consequence of sin the sin charged against them must have been the sin of Adam. This is the view of Godet, Gifford, Dargan, and others.

Murray offers a different interpretation. He argues that it is not consonant with Paul's teaching nor with the import of the whole Bible to understand this passage to mean that "although there may be sin yet it is not *imputed* as sin when there is not a law. This," he continues, "would contradict 4:15. Apart from the provisions of justifying grace, which are not in view in this verse, when sin is *not imputed* it is because sin does not exist" (I,188,189). Murray then concludes that the reference in this passage is to infants, imbeciles, and all people who were "outside the pale of special revelation" (I,190). Other interpreters who follow the line of thought preferred by Murray limit the reference only to infants and imbeciles.[35]

Paul refers to Adam as "a figure of him who was to come." The "coming One" is of course the Messiah, who in one respect is the antitype of Adam. For just as Adam's one act brought death to all who are "in" him, so Christ's one act brings life to all who are "in" Him.

---

[35]Murray's interpretation naturally gives rise to the question of why Paul selected this one segment of history to support his thesis. For his answer see p. 190 of his commentary.

2. *Verses 15-17, which introduce points of contrast between Adam and Christ, drive home the vast dissimilarity between the two heads of the race*

Having suggested a parallel between them in verses 12-14, the apostle proceeds now to show some respects in which the parallel breaks down. Both Adam and Christ stand at the head of the human race and so extend the influence of their acts to all. But there are profound and far-reaching differences in those acts.

Verse 15a shows that the two acts differ in *quality* or nature. Adam's was a deed of sin, a false step, a going astray (Greek, *paraptoma*). Christ's was a deed of grace (Greek, *charisma*).[36] Verse 15b affirms that if (as is true) the race has suffered because of Adam's deed of sin "much more" will it be benefited because of Christ's deed of grace. Murray speaks of this as "the abundant plus which emanates from the grace of God" (I, 193).

Verse 16 shows that the two acts differ in their *originating point and in their mode of operation*. To state it otherwise, there is a contrast in the two men (Adam and Christ) and in the circumstances of their acts. Adam was a sinner; Christ is Savior from sin. Divine judgment (the judicial sentence) started from *one trespass* of one man (Adam) and issued in condemnation. The free gift (Greek, *dorea*) started from the *many trespasses* of the whole race and issued in justification (acquittal, a declaration of righteousness). In the case of Adam "there is expansion outwards, from one to many"; in the case of Christ "there is contraction inwards; the movement originates with many sins which are all embraced in a single sentence of absolution" (Sanday and Headlam, pp. 140, 141). Murray writes that "the sentence needed only the one trespass to give it validity and sanction. . . . But the free gift . . . is of such a character that it must take the many trespasses into reckoning. . . ." (I, 196).

Verse 17 gathers up and carries on the ideas expressed in the two preceding verses. Specifically, it relates that the two acts differ in *the consequences which flow from them*. Through Adam's deed a sentence came unto condemnation (v. 16), the many died (v. 15), death reigned (v. 17). "Reigned," in this context, suggests universal, even tyrannical sovereignty. Through Christ's deed, on the other hand, they who receive His grace receive acquittal (v. 16) and reign in life (v. 17). It is the

---

[36]We are interpreting *charisma* as referring to Christ's redemptive work for men. Cranfield prefers to think that Paul had in mind "the gracious gift of a status of righteousness before God" (p. 284).

contrast between the reign of death and the reign of life which is the new element introduced in verse 17.

The difference in expression is worthy of note. In the one instance "death" reigned; in the other the justified themselves reign "in life." It is also to be observed that the blessing here promised is not to all unconditionally, but only to those who "receive" the gift of righteousness which is offered.

3. *Verses 18-21, after the long parenthesis begun at verse 13, pick up the principal elements of the comparison between Adam and Christ and draw the argument to a conclusion*

Verse 18 is a summary or recapitulation of verses 12-17. The Greek is so condensed that the verse has not a single verb. Cranfield characterizes it as "a kind of note-form" (p. 289). "Trespass" obviously refers to Adam's disobedience which led to his fall and the fall of the race. Godet, Gifford, Sanday and Headlam, and others interpret "act of righteousness" as the act of justification. Cranfield understands it as denoting the obedience of Christ's entire life; others, perhaps better, take the reference to be to His atoning death. "Justification," the Greek of which denotes the *act* of justification, may here include the status resulting from that act. "Of life" may then be a genitive of identity. Viewed in this manner the whole phrase is equivalent to "the justification which is [or 'consists in'] eternal life." Another possibility is to see "of life" as a descriptive (attributive) genitive, suggesting that justification *leads to* eternal life.

Verse 19 explains and gives a confirmation of the statement contained in verse 18. Specifically, it indicates the connecting links between Adam's disobedience[37] and the condemnation of the many, and between Christ's obedience and the possession by the many of a right standing before God. "Through the one man's disobedience the many were made [constituted, set down as] sinners" and, corresponding to this ("even so"), "through the obedience of the one shall the many be made [constituted, set down as] righteous." As the "disobedience" of Adam was one act, we must understand the "obedience" of Christ to be the one great act of His submission to death (cf. Phil. 2:8). It is well to remember, however, that this death in its atoning power presupposes a sinless life.

The most crucial question arising from this verse concerns the inclusiveness of the phrase "through the obedience of the one shall the many be made righteous." Taken in its most literal sense, it could teach

---

[37]Adam's sin is designated as transgression (v. 14), trespass (vv. 15, 17, 18), and as disobedience (here).

universalism. This, however, runs counter to express teachings elsewhere in this epistle. It is therefore generally held that we must restrict "the many" to those who are believers. In other words, personal agency or response on the part of the individual is assumed.[38]

Verses 20,21. Paul has set forth the sin of Adam and the atoning deed of Christ as the controlling factors in human history. The question naturally arises: "What was the purpose of the law? How does it fit into the scheme of things discussed in the preceding verses?" Moreover, verse 16 contrasts the one offense of Adam with "many trespasses." Whence came the many trespasses?

Verse 20a answers these questions: "And the law came in besides, that the trespass might abound." "Came in besides [i.e., alongside]" suggests coming in to the side of a state of things already existing (cf. Conybeare, "the law was added"; Moffatt, "slipped in"). Moule thinks Paul's term represents the law as a kind of "afterthought in the great plan" (p. 110). Sanday and Headlam explain that Paul "regarded Law as a 'parenthesis' in the Divine plan: it did not begin until Moses, and it ended with Christ" (p. 143). Denney understands the thought to be that the law, "as an accessory or subordinate thing," entered into a situation already created by sin. "It has not," he adds, "the decisive significance in history which the objective power of sin has" (p. 631). "That" may mean either "in order that" (expressing purpose)[39] or "so that" (expressing result). Dargan, who prefers the former, explains that the purpose of the law was "to make existing sin appear in all its enormity and universality as a trespass against law, and so be judged by the law. The poison was in man through Adam's fall. The law brings the poison to light, and judges it" (p. 58). Gifford, who also proposes the idea of purpose, explains that God's intention in giving the law was that sin (which already existed) might take the definite form of transgression of a known law. "It is not," he explains, "*the ultimate purpose* of the law, but only an intermediate purpose, a mean to an end; the ultimate purpose is '*that grace might reign through righteousness*' (v. 21)." Therefore, on the deepest level the law did not "frustrate, but further, the end contemplated in the work

---

[38]Some contend that we must assume personal agency of the individual in both cases; that is, both in condemnation through Adam and in justification through Christ. They argue that if Paul teaches universal condemnation because of Adam's deed (apart altogether from personal sin), then he must also here teach universal salvation because of Christ's work (apart altogether from a personal response to that work). But, in reply to this, all that we must suppose is that the persons involved ("all men . . . all men" [v. 18]; "the many . . . the many" [v. 19]) have a connection with the two heads of the race. The connection with Adam, which all have, is natural. To be a member of the human race is to be related to him. The connection with Christ, however, is spiritual, and only believers have that (cf. 1 Cor. 15:22). Murray expresses the sense: "All who are condemned, and this includes the whole human race, are condemned because of the one trespass of Adam; all who are justified are justified by the righteousness of Christ" (I,203).

[39]This is the view to be preferred, but it obviously does not express an all-inclusive purpose of the law. Other indications of purpose are given in Gal. 3:17-25; 2 Cor. 3:6-11; 1 Tim. 1:8-11.

of Christ" (Denney, p. 631). Cranfield understands "abound" to mean not only that sin became more clearly manifest as sin, but also that it was made more sinful. The law, "by showing men that what they are doing is contrary to God's will gives to their continuing to do it the character of conscious and willful disobedience" (p. 293). Robertson, who interprets "that" as expressing result, understands Paul to mean that the giving of the law resulted in the multiplying and stimulating of sin. Denney explains "abound" similarly: "The offence is multiplied because the law, encountering the flesh, evokes its natural antagonism to God, and so stimulates it into disobedience" (p. 631).

The law, by thus causing the trespass to abound, made more evident the need of mankind for redemption.

Verses 20b, 21 teach that grace, by its superabundance, overpowered the reign of sin and death. For "where sin increased, grace increased all the more, so that, just as sin reigned[40] in death, so also grace might reign through righteousness to bring eternal life through Jesus Christ our Lord" (NIV). This statement, which is a fitting summation of both the similarities and the dissimilarities set forth in the preceding verses, is solemnly triumphant. Denney describes it as having "almost the value of a doxology" (p. 631). Adam, whose name loomed large in the opening verses of the paragraph, now drops out of sight, and in his place stands "Christ Jesus our Lord."

The key terms of verse 21 are "sin," "death," "grace," "righteousness," and "life," and the order in which they occur may not be without significance. "Grace," someone has said, "rises highest in the middle; the two conquering giants, sin and death, at the left; the double prize of victory, righteousness and life, at the right; and over the buried name of Adam the glory of the name of Jesus blooms."

For Further Study

1. Read Romans in a modern translation making note of every reference to Righteousness, Justify, Justification, and similar terms.

2. Study each reference to these terms and state in your own words the essential teaching of each passage about them. Consider the terms separately — first, righteousness; then justify, etc.

3. Read Romans 3:21-5:21, watching for recurring words and phrases.

4. Read Genesis 1-3; 12-15.

5. Using a concordance, check the references to Justify in the Book of Galatians and compare these with Romans. Do the same for the words Law and Faith (or Believe).

6. Use a Bible dictionary to study Abraham, Promise, Reconciliation, Righteousness, Justification, Grace, Faith, Hope, Glory, Adam, Death, and Life.

---

[40]Observe that in verse 14 death was represented as the tyrant; here sin is the tyrant and death is the sphere of its dominion. Probably "death" is here to be interpreted as physical death, as in verses 12 and 14. But the term may include all the penal consequences of sin.

Chapter 5

The Life of God:[1]
The Doctrine of Sanctification

(Romans 6:1-8:39)

With the opening of the sixth chapter the thought of Romans takes a new turn. In the preceding chapters (following a brief *introduction* in which the apostle introduced himself and his gospel, gave certain necessary explanations to establish rapport with his readers, and announced the theme of his letter [1:1-17]), Paul has shown that the unrighteousness of man brings him under the *wrath of God* (1:18-3:20), and that God has met man's need by providing *a divine righteousness* based upon the redemptive work of Christ and apprehended through faith (3:21-5:21). The section closes with the assertion that there is now an entirely new order of things in which abounding grace reigns through righteousness unto eternal life through our Lord Jesus Christ.

Thus with the close of chapter 5, Paul's exposition of the doctrine of justification stands complete; chapters 6-8 will discuss the believer's new life.[2] The traditional theological term to describe this phase of redemption is "sanctification" (progressive righteousness), though many modern commentators prefer the word "salvation." Even though interpreters are not agreed on the term to use, there is general agreement that 6:1-8:39[3] treats the new life in Christ and that it has to do with the moral results of justification. Bruce entitles it "The Way of Holiness."[4] In a superficial way, the section is like 12:1ff., but it is markedly different. Chapters 12-15:13 are in the nature of a practical appeal.

---

[1]The reference is to the life of God *in the believer* (cf. Eph. 4:18).

[2]The word "life" (Greek, *zoe*) occurs eight times in these chapters.
[3]Some understand this unit to begin at 5:1; others at 5:12.
[4]See Godet, Dodd, Sanday and Headlam, Nygren, and Cranfield.

Chapters 6-8 are more decidedly theological. Cranfield thinks of them as setting forth "the theological basis of the Christian's moral obligation."[5]

Three levels of thought, corresponding to the three chapter divisions, may be discerned: (1) the believer and sin (ch. 6), (2) the believer and the law (ch. 7), and (3) the believer and the Spirit (ch. 8). These three units show, respectively, that the new life of the believer is a life *characterized by holiness, freed from the law*, and *indwelt by the Spirit*.

A. A Life Characterized by Holiness (ch. 6)

The whole of chapter 6 shows that justification by faith, as set out in the preceding chapters, in no way encourages a life of sin. So far from affording a pretext for sin, it is in fact "the only sure foundation of practical holiness" (Gifford, p. 125).[6] The discussion is built around two questions inserted by Paul in anticipation of objections which he felt someone might bring against his doctrine.

1. The first question and its answer (6:1-14)

The question, which sets before the reader a false inference that Paul recognizes one might draw from his teaching, is stated in verse 1: "What shall we say then [i.e., What conclusion shall we draw from the foregoing discussion]? Shall we continue in sin, that grace may abound?" Note the expression "continue *in* sin." To do this is to remain under its power, to let it continue to be the element in which we live and move

---

[5]The relation between 1:18 - 5:21 (justification) and chapters 6-8 (sanctification) is variously explained, and it is a matter of considerable importance. Indeed, Godet thinks that an understanding of the true relationship of these two concepts is "the key to the Epistle. . . . and even to the whole Gospel" (p. 231). Three views may be mentioned: One makes sanctification the *condition* of justification. Those who follow this interpretation propose that the relation between justification and sanctification may be expressed by the conjunction "but." Godet, who dissents from this view, paraphrases: "No doubt you are justified by faith; *but* beware, see that you break with the sin which has been forgiven you; apply yourselves to holiness; if not, you shall fall into condemnation again." To put it otherwise, interpreters who see this as Paul's line of thought understand the apostle to be here entering upon a discussion of the *preservation* of salvation. "According to this view, salvation consists essentially of justification, and sanctification appears solely as the condition of not losing it" (Godet, p. 231). This interpretation is contrary to the whole tenor of Paul's thought.

A second theory, which perhaps is most widely accepted, makes sanctification the *corollary* of justification. Its advocates hold that the relation between justification and sanctification may be expressed by a "therefore." "You are justified freely; *therefore*, impelled by faith and gratitude, engage yourselves now to renounce evil, and do what is well-pleasing to God" (Godet's paraphrase, p. 231).

The third view teaches that sanctification is neither the condition nor the corollary of justification. Godet states it well: "The real connection between justification and Christian holiness, as conceived by St. Paul, appears . . . to be this: justification by faith is the *means*, and sanctification the *end* . . . justification is to be regarded as the *strait gate*, through which we enter on the *narrow way* of sanctification, which leads to glory" (pp. 233-234). There is truth in both the second and the third interpretations.

[6]Cranfield thinks of the word "holiness" as the key word of chapter 6.

and have our being, to let it be the moral atmosphere of our existence.[7]
The question follows logically from the two closing verses of chapter 5,
where the apostle appears to say the more sin, the more grace.[8] It might
be raised either by a person craving for sinful license or by one who
opposes the doctrine of gratuitous salvation because he feels that continuance in sin is its logical outcome. It is noteworthy that Paul in
answering the question does not in the least modify what he has said
about the gratuitous nature of our pardon.

The *answer* is in two parts. First, by exclaiming "God forbid!" (v.
2a), the apostle repels with horror at the thought of a believer continuing in sin. (This expression, denoting indignant denial, was used earlier
to reject the slander that Paul taught that we are to do evil that good may
come [Rom. 3:8].) One who would suggest such a thing reveals not only a
basic misconception of the apostle's teaching but also a profound misunderstanding of divine grace.

Second, Paul shows that a believer's continuance in sin is a moral
impossibility, because justification involves union with Christ (vv. 2b-
14). This union is such that it involves both death to sin (vv. 2b-4a) and
participation in a new state of being which is life (vv. 4b-11). This makes
it grossly incongruous for the Christian to live a life of sin (vv. 12-14).
Our discussion of the text revolves around these ideas.

a. *Union with Christ means death to sin (vv. 2b-4a).* In the expression "We who died to sin" (v. 2b), the relative pronoun is both qualitative ("who are of such nature") and explanatory. Justified people are of
such a nature that continuance in sin is excluded. They are people who
have died to sin. Therefore, their relation to sin has been broken.[9] They
have been released from its power and influence, and it is morally
impossible for them to continue in it. This does not mean that sin is
entirely extirpated from the believer's heart and that he lives a life of
sinless perfection. Godet explains that "death to sin is not an absolute
cessation of sin . . . , but an absolute breaking of the will with it, with its
instincts and aspirations" (p. 238).

The tense of the Greek verb for "died" is aorist, pointing to a
particular event of the past. The reference may be to the death of Christ,
at which time believers *in essence* died with Him (cf. Moule); or Paul
may have been thinking of the believer's conversion, at which time he

---

[7]Lightfoot, however, sees a somewhat different notion. Instead of "continue in," he
understands the Greek to mean "cling to." Moule interprets it to mean "not mere
continuance, but *perseverance in will and act*" (p. 111).

[8]Some interpreters (e.g., Godet) understand the question to look back over the entire
discussion of justification as given in chs. 1-5.

[9]Compare the ideas of dying to the law (Rom. 7:4; Gal. 2:19) and of being crucified to the
world (Gal. 6:14).

actually died to sin. Godet probably is correct in explaining that although the Christian's break with sin is "gradual in its realization," it is "absolute and conclusive in its principle" (p. 238).

Believers' baptism is a symbolic representation of this death to sin. "Or are ye ignorant that all we who were baptized into [in relation to][10] Christ Jesus were baptized into [in relation to] his death? We were buried therefore with him through baptism into death" (vv. 3,4a). The "or" which introduces the question suggests this sequence of thought: If you do not understand the assertion just made about the believer's death to sin, are you unaware of the meaning and symbolism of the initiatory rite by which you confessed your faith and identified yourself with the people of God? The very form of the ceremony (burial in water) sets forth in dramatic fashion the believer's participation in the sacrificial death of Christ.

To say that "we have been buried" with Christ is an emphatic way of expressing the truth that we have *died* with Him, for "burial is the seal to the fact of death" (Cranfield, p. 304).

b. *Union with Christ means participation in new life (vv. 4b-11).* The symbolism of baptism not only depicts the believer's death with Christ, but also his participation in Christ's resurrection life. In fact, we were buried in baptism for the express purpose of rising again. The immersion is only momentary; the believer is immediately raised up from his watery grave, an experience symbolic of Christ's rising from the dead. The rite is carried out in this manner because just as "Christ was raised from the dead through the glory [power][11] of the Father," we also are to "walk[12] in newness of [i.e., newness which consists in][13] life" (v. 4b).

Verse 5 is a confirmation of the statement of the preceding verse. The thought is that one who shares in the death of Christ inevitably shares also in His resurrection life. "For if we have become united with

---

[10]Cranfield concludes that the Greek of this phrase is not to be distinguished in meaning from passages which speak of being baptized "in the name of" Christ. "All that Paul wishes to convey . . . is simply the fact that the persons concerned have received Christian baptism" (p. 301). Robertson thinks the translation "into" makes Paul say that the believer's union with Christ was effected by baptism. This, he says, was not Paul's idea, "for Paul was not a sacramentarian. . . . Baptism is the public proclamation of one's inward spiritual relation to Christ attained before baptism" (p. 361).

[11]The "glory" of God is His manifested excellence. It includes, but is more comprehensive than, the power of God. Cranfield defines glory here as "the power of God gloriously exercised" (p. 304). By using "glory" instead of "power" Paul may here suggest that the supreme excellence of God is displayed in the power which brought Jesus from the dead (cf. John 11:40).

[12]"Walk" is an ingressive aorist, suggesting "begin to walk." The word is frequently used in the Bible to denote one's conduct.

[13]"Newness of life" is an emphatic way of saying "new life."

him in the likeness of his death, [then certainly] we shall[14] be also in the likeness of his resurrection." The *imagery* in this verse is that of one plant being grafted in to another (cf. KJV), but the *idea* is that of being vitally connected. Moule says that "coalescence," not "implanting," is the idea (p. 113). We, as believers, are vitally and inseparably connected with Christ both in death and in life. The "likeness of his death" is our death to sin; the "likeness of his resurrection" is the newness of life imparted to us.

Verse 6 introduces yet another truth relative to Paul's argument; namely, "that our old man [the former, unregenerate self,[15] Gal. 2:20] was crucified[16] with [Christ], that the body of sin [the body as conditioned and controlled by sin; the sinful body] might be done away [rendered powerless, made dead in relation to sin], so that we should no longer be in bondage to sin" (that is, that our service to sin should be terminated). This, Paul says, is a thing that believers "know" by experience.

Verse 6 has represented the believer as a slave who is crucified and dies with Christ in order that his enslavement to sin may cease. Verse 7 is probably to be interpreted as illustrating or confirming this by citing a proverbial statement[17] borrowed from ordinary human experience (cf. NEB). The essence of it is that "death puts an end to all bondage" (Gifford, p. 128), cancels all claims. Bruce, following this line of thought, interprets Paul to mean that "Death pays all debts, so the man who has died with Christ has his slate wiped clean, and is ready to begin his new life with Christ freed from the entail of the past" (p. 139). Godet infers from the verse that the believer can no longer serve sin in the doing of evil, "any more than the slave deprived of his body by death can continue to execute the orders formerly given him by his wicked master" (pp. 246, 247).

Verse 8 expresses Paul's certain belief that death to sin is followed by new life. "Shall . . . live" does not refer (at least not exclusively) to the future resurrection state, but rather to participation in the resurrection life of Christ here and now.

Verse 9 states the ground of the certitude expressed in the preceding verse. The believer's confidence that he shares in Christ's resurrection life rests on the knowledge that Christ is alive forevermore. Having been raised from the dead, He "dieth no more; death no more hath

---

[14]The future refers not to future resurrection but to the certainty of moral resurrection.

[15]Cranfield uses the expression "our fallen human nature, the whole self in its fallenness" (pp. 308-309).

[16]The tense is aorist, pointing to a single definite act of the past (cf. v. 2).

[17]Murray, who dissents from this view, sees "he that hath died" as a direct reference to the believer as one who has died with Christ. "Is justified" is then understood in the sense of being "quit" of sin. The analogy, he says, is that of "the kind of dismissal which a judge gives when an arraigned person is justified. Sin has no further claim upon the person who is thus vindicated" (p. 222).

dominion over him." The rising of Christ from the dead, unlike that of Lazarus, was not a mere extension of His natural life. Lazarus was raised only to die again. Christ was raised to endless life, and because of that His "death has become the death of Death" (Chrysostom, quoted by Gifford).

Verse 10 confirms the fact of Christ's endless life. Death has no further claim on Him, "For the death that he died, he died unto sin once; but the life that he liveth, he liveth unto God." In saying that Christ died "unto sin" Paul means that He died *in relation to* sin. He was the altogether sinless One, yet bore the sin of the race "in his own body on the tree," suffering for sinners the full penalty of their transgression against God. "Once" means "once for all," emphasizing that Christ's death was so unique and decisive that it can never be repeated, nor does it need to be. To say that His risen life is life lived "unto God" is to say that Christ's resurrection life has about it the quality of eternity.

Verse 11, which sums up the two streams of thought which run through this paragraph (death with Christ, life with Christ), is in the form of an urgent appeal: "Even so reckon [i.e., regard] ye also yourselves to be dead unto sin, but alive unto God in Christ Jesus." The meaning is that just as Christ died once for all to sin, the believer is to regard himself, by virtue of his union with Christ, as forever dead to the dominion of sin; and just as Christ lives endlessly unto God, the believer, who shares Christ's life, is to regard himself as forever alive to God. To "reckon" does not mean to pretend to be, but to recognize that we are, dead to sin and alive to God.

c. *Union with Christ is incongruous with a life of sin (vv. 12-14).* The preceding verses have presented, as it were, the godward side of our experience through faith — union with Christ. These verses, which insist on the duty of moral effort, represent the manward aspect of our experience. Our conduct must demonstrate that we are in reality what we "reckon" ourselves to be — namely, dead to sin and alive to God. These verses, which are transitional, conclude the discussion begun at verse 1 and introduce the discussion of verses 15-23.

They contain a threefold command (vv. 12,13), a promise (v. 14a), and an explanation (v. 14b). The *command* is built around three verbs having imperative force. Two are negative: "Let not sin therefore *reign* in your mortal body . . . .: neither *present* your members unto sin as instruments of unrighteousness" (vv. 12,13a). Both verbs are present imperatives, suggesting that we must not let sin *go on reigning* and must not *go on presenting* our members to sin. "Stop letting sin reign" and "stop presenting" may express the ideas. "Therefore" (v. 12a), which points back to the preceding verses (particularly v. 11), shows that these commands are logically involved in the facts stated in those verses. "In your mortal body" (v. 12a) identifies the body as the "special field for the action of sin" (Moule, p. 117). The "members" (v. 13a) of the body are such things as hands, eyes, tongue, and so forth. Weymouth uses the word "faculties"; Goodspeed, "the parts of your bodies." "Instruments" (v. 13a) may suggest the general idea of "tools" (Beck, Sanday and Headlam, Cranfield, et al.), but the Greek word may have the more particular sense of "weapons." Montgomery's rendering brings this out: "Do not continue to present any part of your body to sin to be used as a weapon of unrighteousness." Gifford expresses it as follows: "Sin fights for the mastery; it calls out an army of the lusts of the body, and seeks to use the members, hand, eye, or tongue, as weapons wherewith the lusts may re-establish the rule of unrighteousness" (Gifford, p. 130).

The positive command is to "present yourselves unto God, as alive from the dead, and your members as instruments [weapons, tools] of righteousness unto God" (v. 13b). The verb ("present") in this instance is aorist, suggesting an action to be undertaken decisively and with a sense of urgency. Do it "once for all." Robertson: "do it now and completely" (p. 363).

Verse 14a could be interpreted as having imperative force ("sin must not have dominion over you"), but it is better to see it as a *promise*: "Sin shall not have dominion over you." It thus gives invigoration and incentive for carrying out the commands of verses 12,13. We must not become discouraged in our struggle with sin, for though weak in ourselves, we have the help of God; and joined as we are to Him, our efforts shall not fail and sin shall not gain mastery over us. It may "tempt and harass and ensnare, it will still be a powerful, dangerous, and too often victorious, enemy; but it shall have no authority over you" (Gifford, p. 130).

Verse 14b, which is explanatory, states the reason why sin shall not exercise lordship over believers: "for ye are not under [the regime of] law, but under [the regime of] grace." "Not under law," a matter to be pursued in greater detail in chapter 7, is variously interpreted. Many take it to mean that for believers the authority of the law has been abolished, the last phrase suggesting that grace, a new authority, has superseded it (cf. Montgomery and *Modern Language*). Cranfield thinks that statements such as those found in 3:31; 7:12,14a; 8:4; 13:8-10 argue against this interpretation. He therefore contends that since the opposite of grace is condemnation, or disfavor, "not under law" means "that believers are not under God's condemnation pronounced by the law" (p. 320). But whatever the precise meaning may be, the statement in the present context doubtless alludes to the inability of law as a principle of holiness. In contrast, "grace" sums up all the provisions of redemption in Christ. We may conclude then that to be under law is to be a servant of sin and therefore under condemnation, but to be "under grace" is to be justified and to have the assurance that sin will not and can not lord it over us. In that position, we have the resources necessary for carrying out the righteous ordinances of God.

2. The second question and its answer (6:15-23)

In 6:1-14 the dominant thought has been that of the believer's union with Christ (in death to sin and newness of life.). This union, Paul teaches, rules out a life of sin. In the present paragraph the Christian life is considered in terms of service. That service, Paul shows, is an exclusive thing demanding total commitment. The gist of the entire section is that though the Christian is not under law, he is not free to commit sin. He comes under a new and higher obligation, doing slave-service to righteousness and to God.

The *question* which introduces the discussion is stated in verse 15: "What then? shall we sin, because we are not under law, but under grace?" Paul knew that the assertion of verse 14b was capable of being misused, and by this question he anticipates the false deduction that one might draw from it. He imagines an opponent arguing, "Well, then, since the law, which commands us not to sin, no longer wields its authority over us, we therefore may sin with impunity."

The question is much like that found in verse 1, and, as there, the inference here is immediately rejected by "God forbid!" But there are also differences. For one thing, the *motivations* involved are different. Verse 1, alluding to the truth of 5:20, draws the false inference that one should continue in sin so as to make grace abound the more; the present verse, alluding to the statement of verse 14b, draws the false inference that acts of sin no longer matter because of our new status under grace. In the former, one sins that grace may abound; in the other, one sins in hope of impunity. The *tenses* of the principal verbs are also different. Verse 1 employs a present tense, denoting continuous, habitual action. Verse 15 employs an aorist tense, suggesting a single act, or occasional acts, of sin. Robertson expresses the sense: "Surely, the objector says, we may take a night off now and then and sin a little bit 'since we are under grace'" (Robertson, p. 364).

The *answer* to Paul's question is set forth in verses 16-23. It begins with a statement (v. 16) from which two important principles emerge: (1) Men are slaves of whatever power they obey. (2) Only two alternatives present themselves: servitude to sin, which results in (eternal) death; or servitude to obedience, which results in "righteousness." The latter word may refer to inwrought righteousness; or it may have forensic force and refer to the final verdict (final justification) at the judgment. Cranfield thinks that since the word is set over against death, it is equivalent to eternal life.

The statement of principle is followed by a burst of thanksgiving to God (vv. 17,18). A striking contrast is drawn between what the Romans had been ("ye were") in the past, and what they had become ("obedient"; "free from sin"; "servants of righteousness") by the grace of God. The tense of "were" (v. 17a) is imperfect: "used to be." "Became" (v. 17b) is aorist, indicating a point in time (i.e., their conversion experience).

"Form of teaching" (v. 17b) denotes the pattern or standard of apostolic instruction, with perhaps an allusion to its ethical implications. The statement that the Romans had been "delivered" unto, that is, handed over to, this form of teaching is unusual. It may emphasize the completeness of their commitment to the gospel. Conybeare renders it, "the teaching whereby you were moulded anew."

In verse 19a Paul apologizes for comparing the doing of righteousness to slave service. The paraphrase of *The Living Bible* expresses the sense: "I speak this way, using the illustration of slaves and masters, because it is easy to understand." This apology is followed (v. 19b) with an appeal for such dedication of our members as will issue in progressive righteousness (sanctification).

Verses 20-22 enforce this appeal in two ways. First, there is the assertion that one cannot, at the same time, be the slave of sin and the slave of righteousness (v. 20). Second, there is a contrast drawn between the harvest of shame reaped from the Romans' previous servitude (v. 21) and the fruit of their present servitude (v. 22): growth in holiness now and ultimately eternal life. This does not mean that the service of righteousness is "the procuring cause of Life Eternal, but only the training for the enjoyment of what is essentially a Divine gift" (Moule, p. 122). Eternal life, we are taught elsewhere, already belongs to the believer, at least in germ (cf. 1 John 5:13). In its fullest sense, it is the "end" of all our experience with God.

Verse 23, in a succinct statement, gathers up the main drift of the passage. Sin, which is personified, is thought by some interpreters to be here represented as a general who pays wages[18] to his soldiers. By others the imagery is thought to be that of sin as a slave-owner who pays an allowance to his slaves. Lightfoot, however, interprets in a slightly different way. Sin, he thinks, is represented throughout verses 12-23 as a sovereign (v. 12), who demands military service of his subjects, levies from them a quota of arms (v. 13), and gives them death as their soldier's pay (v. 23).

Set over against death as the wages of sin is "eternal life," described as "the free gift of God." "Free gift" is the translation of a word

---

[18]The Greek word was often used of a soldier's pay or rations.

(*charisma*) which was sometimes used of the bounty given out to soldiers on special occasions. Gifford comments that "Sin only pays hard wages, but God gives of His free grace what no service could earn" (p. 133).

This triumphant statement which concludes chapter 6 should be compared with the similar note of triumph with which chapter 5 closes.

B. A Life Characterized by Freedom From the Law (ch. 7)

Chapter 7 might be thought of as an exposition of the assertion of 6:14: "Sin shall not have dominion over you: for ye are not under law, but under grace." The words "ye are not under law" seem to require explanation, and with that matter chapter 7 is concerned. Deliverance from sin (ch. 6) and deliverance from law (ch. 7) are such closely connected facts that, as Godet writes, "the one is the complement of the other" (p. 263).

It is to be observed also that there is a remarkable parallelism between what chapter 6 says about sin and what chapter 7 says about the law. Nygren (p. 268) sets this out graphically by comparing 6:1 (sin) and 7:1 (law); 6:2 ("died to sin") and 7:4 ("died to the law"); 6:4 ("that we might walk in newness of life") and 7:6 ("that we might serve in newness of the spirit"); 6:7 ("he who has died is freed from sin") and 7:6 ("we have been discharged from the law, having died to that wherein we were held"); and 6:18 ("having been set free from sin") and 7:3 ("free from the law"). From such a comparison it is clear that "Paul's thought in chapter 7 follows a course similar to that in chapter 6. The same categories are used, being simply applied to different matter" (Nygren, pp. 268,269).

The thought of the chapter is presented in two distinct paragraphs. Verses 1-6 assert the *fact* of the believer's freedom from the law; verses 7-25, inserted in answer to an objection which Paul felt someone might bring against his teaching, explain the *character* of the law.

1. *The believer's freedom from the law (7:1-6)*

Previously (6:14) Paul declared that the believer is no longer "under the law." He did not, however, expand upon or give any validation of his assertion. He simply stated the fact. Here he returns to the idea and explains how this release from the law has been effected.

The passage contains an introductory question (v. 1), an illustration (vv. 2,3), and an application (vv. 4-6).

The *question* (v. 1), which seems to be connected logically with the thought of 6:14, expresses the principle that the power and authority of law is terminated by death. It binds a person for so long a time as he lives, but once the man has died, law has no more power over him. The form of the question ("Or are ye ignorant . . . ?") as well as the parenthesis which is contained in it ("for I speak to men who know the law")[19] both suggest that the apostle assumed that his readers had understanding of this principle.

The principle expressed in verse 1 is *illustrated*[20] in verses 2 and 3 by reference to marriage. Paul cites the case of a wife who, by the death of her husband, has been freed to marry another. "While he liveth" she is bound by law to continue in union with him. But if and when he dies, she is "discharged [the word is the same as that translated "done away" in 6:6] from the law of the husband[21]" and is legally free to contract another marriage. The key words are "while he liveth," and the main thought is that death dissolves legal obligation.

The principle stated in verse 1 and illustrated in verses 2,3 is now *applied* to the case of the believer and the law (vv. 4-6). The thought is somewhat inverted, for in the illustration the husband dies; and the woman (who represents the believer) lives. If the parallel were preserved, the application would affirm the death of the law. However, the application affirms, not that the law has been made dead to believers, but that believers "were made dead[22] to the law through the body of Christ[23]" (v. 4a). Perhaps we should not look for an exact correspondence of ideas. The main point is that believers have been released from the law, and this release has been effected by a death which is just as decisive as that of the husband in the illustration. The law has not died, but believers (by their union with Christ in His death) have died to it.

The purpose of our death to the law is twofold. The immediate purpose is that we "should be joined to another, even to him who was raised from the dead." The ultimate purpose (which grows out of our union with Christ) is "that we might bring forth fruit unto God" (v. 4b).

Verse 5 contrasts the fruits of our unregenerate life with those of our life in union with Christ. "In the flesh" denotes our unregenerate state, "flesh" being used not in a physical but in an ethical sense. "Sinful passions" comes from a Greek construction which literally reads "the passions of sins." Some prefer to retain this literal rendering and interpret the phrase to mean the passions *which lead to* and find expression

---

[19]"The law" here refers to the Mosaic law, with which both Jews and Gentiles within the Christian community were acquainted. Paul's statement, therefore, really has little significance in deciding whether the readers of this letter were mainly Jewish or mainly Gentile.

[20]"For," the opening word of verse 2, means "for example."

[21]The "law of the husband" is the law which *concerns* the husband.

[22]"Were made dead" is a translation of a term which more literally means "were put to death." Gifford says it "indicates a violent death, namely the crucifixion of the old man with Christ (vi. 6)" (p. 135).

[23]The "body of Christ" is His natural body which was nailed to the cross for us.

in sins. In either case, the refe⸻ ... to sin as principle. "Through t⸻ ... ⸻ulated and intensified ⸻ ... of the law, "in t⸻ ... ⸻e our hearts, so ⸻ ... ⸻lds, "break for ⸻ ... the restraints o⸻

Verse 6 ⸻ ... ⸻ormer condition "in the flesh" (v. ⸻ ... ⸻e ("in the flesh") we were in captivity to th⸻ ... ⸻n we were held"). But now we have been discharge⸻ ... from the law by[24] having died to it. The result ("so that") is that we now "serve in newness of the spirit,[25] and not in oldness of the letter."

There is a double contrast in these last words: "newness" and "oldness"; "spirit" and "letter." Gramatically, "of the spirit" is either genitive of identity ("newness which is, consists of, the Spirit"), or ablative of source ("newness which comes from the Spirit"). "Of the letter" probably is to be interpreted as a genitive of identity ("oldness which consists of the letter"), and letter refers to the written law (cf. 2 Cor. 3:6).

2. The character of the law (7:7-25)

A sensitive Jew, reading Paul's argument in 5:20; 6:14; and 7:1-6, might conclude that the apostle has placed the law and sin in the same category. Indeed, he might assert that Paul's statements leave the impression that the law is actually evil, that in some way it is identified with sin. Paul, anticipating this objection to his teaching, raises the question, "What shall we say then? Is the law sin?" (v. 7a). "Sin" in this instance may be an emphatic way of saying "sinful." Paul indignantly denies the inference ("God forbid") and proceeds to deal with this misunderstanding of his teaching. In short, he shows that the inference drawn from his teaching is unfounded. The law, he argues, can neither justify (7-13) nor sanctify (14-25); but it is not evil.

In the process of refuting his imaginary opponent, Paul expounds the true character and function of the law. This he does by setting out the operation of the law (1) in reference to the unbeliever (vv. 7-13) and (2) in reference to the believer (vv. 14-23). Verses 24 and 25 form (3) a conclusion to the discussion.

---

[24]"Having died" is a translation of a participle which explains the *means* by which the action of the main verb ("discharged") was effected.

[25]ASV uses lower case letters "spirit," but the word is better taken as a reference to the Holy Spirit.

a. *The law and the unbeliever (vv. 7-13).* As one reads 7:7-25 he cannot help but notice the prominence of the first person singular pronouns. In the ASV, "I," "me," "my" appear no fewer than forty-six times. This gives rise to a question: Is Paul's use of the first person singular rhetorical, representative, or autobiographical?[26] We prefer to think of it as autobiographical, agreeing with Bruce that this is "the most natural way" to interpret it (p. 148). Three stages in Paul's preconversion relation to the law are presented: (1) the period of ignorance and innocence, (2) the period of awakening to his inability to keep the law, and (3) the period of "deadness" and condemnation.

The burden of the entire unit is that although the law is not evil, it is indeed powerless to give man a right standing before God. Its function, as seen in the experience of Paul, is quite otherwise. The line of thought, in outline form, is as follows:

(1) The law reveals sin, brings the knowledge of it, exposes it for what it really is (v. 7). "I had not known sin," writes Paul, "except through the law" (v. 7b; cf. 3:20). "Sin" here denotes not the *act* of sinning but the *principle* of sin in the heart. "Knowing" sin, in this context, denotes primarily a practical, experiential conviction of sinfulness. The gist of the statement, then, is: "Apart from the law, I would not have known sin *in its true character*, as rebellion against the will of God, and would not have been convicted of my guilt in this regard." Perhaps there is the added notion of the law as bringing to Paul an awareness of the strength and virulence of sin as a principle of evil within. D. Brown, who sees this as the main sense of the statement, writes that law was not needed to reveal to Paul the *existence* of a sinful propensity within his heart, "but the dreadful nature and desperate power of it the law alone discovered" (p. 71).

---

[26]Cranfield, in discussing verses 7-13, lists six "main suggestions" which have been proposed. His own conclusion is that we have here "an example of the general use of the first person singular." He goes on to explain, however, that Paul's choice of this mode of speech is here "due not merely to a desire for rhetorical vividness, but also to his deep sense of personal involvement, his consciousness that in drawing out the general truth he is disclosing the truth about himself" (pp. 343,344).

Moule hears the voice of "the personal Paul" throughout 7:7-25. The apostle, he thinks, is here "speaking to all of us, as in some solemn 'testimony' hour." In verses 7-13 "Paul takes us first to his earliest deep convictions of right and wrong, when, apparently after a previous complacency with himself, he woke to see — but not to welcome — the absoluteness of God's will. He glided along a smooth stream of moral and mental culture and reputation till he struck the rock of 'Thou shalt not covet,' 'Thou shalt not desire,' 'Thou must not have self-will.' Then, as from a grave, which was, however, only an ambush, 'sin' sprang up; a conscious force of opposition to the claim of God's will as against the will of Paul; and his dream of religious satisfaction died" (*Expositor's Bible*, p. 191). Moule concludes then that 7:7-11 is for certain Paul's personal account of his pre-Christian experience. The tenses are all past, and the experience described was one of conviction, "with only rebellion as its issue."

The latter part of verse 7 shows that it was the tenth commandment which first aroused this conviction (or awareness of the power) of sin within Paul. "For I had not known coveting, except the law had said, Thou shalt not covet." "Coveting" is to be understood in the sense of lust, any illicit desire. As D. Brown observes, Paul saw in the tenth commandment "the prohibition not only of desire after *certain things* there specified, but of 'desire after *everything divinely forbidden*'; in other words, all 'lusting' or 'irregular desire' " (p. 71).

(2) The law arouses and awakens sin (vv. 8-11). Bruce observes that "Prohibitions, as a matter of common knowledge, tend to awaken a desire to do the thing that is forbidden; the smoker may forget how much he wants to smoke until he sees a sign which says 'No Smoking' " (p. 147). And in this connection, someone else tells of the person who objected to the reading of the ten commandments in public worship because it "put ideas into the minds of the young"!

In the statement "apart from the law sin is dead" (v. 8b), the verb is not expressed in Greek and must be supplied by the translator. "Is dead" suggests that Paul is stating a general principle. Perhaps, since the whole discussion is historical and personal, it would be better to supply "was." The idea then is that apart from the law sin was a dormant principle in Paul's life. Sin was in him, but it was inert, inactive; and he was not aware of its virulence and power. Then when the commandment not to covet came to his consciousness, the very sin which it forbad was roused to activity. "Sin [i.e., the principle of sin; 'indwelling sin'], finding occasion, wrought in [him] through the commandment all manner of coveting" (v. 8a). "Occasion" is the rendering of a word which was used of the starting point or base of operation for a military expedition. Here it may denote something like "opportunity" (NEB). "All manner of coveting" indicates all kinds of illicit desires.

In saying that he "was alive apart from the law once" (v. 9a), the apostle means that there was a time when he was not conscious of resistance to and alienation from God. D. Brown paraphrases it: "In the days of my ignorance, when . . . a stranger to the law, I deemed myself all right, in good standing before God" (p. 72). Some take the reference to be to the time of Paul's childhood, before conscience awoke and moral responsibility came. Others see the statement as pointing to the time when he was a proud Pharisee, living a complacent, self-righteous life without a sense of conviction for sin (cf. Phil. 3:4-6). The former is perhaps the better view.

"When the commandment came" (v. 9b) speaks of that time when the commandment against covetousness first came home to his consciousness. It was then that "sin revived" (that is, was aroused to activity, sprang to life) and Paul "died" (that is, realized his desperate condition, his condemnation before God). He was spiritually dead before, but was not conscious of his deadness. Now, through the instrumentality of the law (specifically, the tenth commandment), he came to realize his true condition.

(3) The law, in spite of its role of arousing and awakening sin, was not in itself to be blamed for Paul's "death" (vv. 12,13). He concludes that "the law [in its entirety] is holy, and [specifically] the [tenth] commandment holy, and righteous, and good" (v. 12). The fault belongs to sin, which is so evil that it turns to man's harm what was meant for his good. All of this brings out more clearly the true nature of sin — its "exceeding sinfulness."

Verse 13 opens with a question: "Did then that which is good become death unto me?" That is to say, "Did then the blame for my death rest with the law?" The question is called forth by the statement in verse 10 that the commandment which was intended for life was found by Paul "to be unto death." The inference of the question is summarily dismissed with "God forbid!"

The remainder of the verse teaches the truth of the matter: It was sin, by making use of that which is good (the law), that worked death (condemnation) to Paul. This fact is expanded and explained by two purpose clauses. First, it is stated that sin wrought death in order that its true nature might be seen — "that it might be shown to be sin." The thought is that sin's perversity, "its enormous turpitude," is evident in its turning a good thing (the commandment) into an instrument of death. The second purpose clause restates this idea, but in stronger language: "that through the commandment sin might become exceeding sinful." The meaning seems to be that by its abuse of the law the gravity of sin was tragically heightened. NEB: "And so, through the commandment, sin became more sinful than ever."[27]

b. *The law and the believer (vv. 14-23).* Jowett quotes another who calls this passage "the most terrible tragedy in all literature, ancient or modern, sacred or profane." Then, quoting the same author, he says, "set beside the seventh of Romans all your so-called great tragedies . . . are . . . so much sound and fury, signifying next to nothing. . . . The seventh of Romans should always be printed in letters of blood. Here are passions. Here are terror and pity. Here heaven and hell meet — for their last grapple together for the everlasting possession of that immortal soul, till you have tragedy indeed; beside which there is no other tragedy" (*Great Pulpit Masters,* Vol. 5, p. 71).

---

[27]Godet sums up verse 13 by showing that it contains three ideas: "(1) sin slays by that which is good; (2) *that* thereby it *may accomplish* an act worthy of its nature; (3) *and that* thereby (final end) this nature *may be manifested* clearly" (p. 279).

The use of the first person singular is here, as in 7:7-13, a problem. We conclude that here, as in the earlier passage, Paul speaks autobiographically. That is to say, Paul is describing his own experience. And yet, as Griffith Thomas observes, "It is not an experience which is his only, but one that is characteristic of all men in like circumstances" (p. 41).

It is much debated whether the experience recounted is that of Paul as an unregenerate or as a regenerate person.[28] Interpreters who take the former position point especially to verse 14, "I am carnal, sold under sin," and affirm that this could hardly be said of a Christian.[29] Those who take this to be the experience of a regenerate person point to verse 22, "I delight in the law of God," and argue that an unconverted person would hardly speak in this manner. A similar thought is expressed in verse 25b: "So then I of myself with the mind, indeed, serve the law of God." Murray comments that the verse referred to "means subjection of heart and will, something impossible for the unregenerate man" (I, 258). Furthermore, these interpreters see significance in the consistent use of the present tense throughout the passage, contending that they weigh heavily against the view that the reference is to Paul's pre-Christian experience. Cranfield, for instance, writes that "the use of the present is here sustained too consistently and for too long and contrasts too strongly with the past tenses of vv. 7-13 to be at all plausibly explained" as historical presents.[30] As further proof that this is the experience of Paul the Christian, he adds that "a struggle as serious as that which is here described, can only take place where the Spirit of God is present and active (cf. Gal. 5:17)" (p. 346).

---

[28]See Anders Nygren (pp. 284ff.) for a brief survey of the different approaches to this passage.

[29]Griffith Thomas sees the unit as describing "a man who is trying to be good and holy by his own efforts and is beaten back every time by the power of indwelling sin." It is, he continues, "the experience of any man who tries the experiment, whether he be regenerate or unregenerate." Thomas then concludes that it is best to regard the passage as giving "a picture of a Jew under law, not of a Christian under grace." The conflict which is represented "is not between the two natures of the believer, but refers to the effect of law on a heart that recognises its spirituality" (pp. 42-44). Denney concludes that "it is the experience of the unregenerate, but read with regenerate eyes," interpreted in a regenerate mind (p. 641).

[30]See Cranfield, pp. 344,345 for a fuller discussion of this matter. He distinguishes at least seven possibilities. All but two of these he sets aside as failing to do justice to the text. The two he thinks best are: (1) That the passage is "autobiographical, the reference being to Paul's present experience as a Christian" and (2) that the passage "presents the experience of Christians generally, including the very best and mature." Cranfield lists, as accepting one or the other of these views, Methodius, Ambrose, Ambrosiaster, Augustine, Aquinas, Luther, Calvin, Barth, Nygren, Barrett, and Murray. He thinks the question whether one accepts the first or second is "relatively unimportant," but he himself is inclined toward the second (pp. 344,345). His exposition of the entire passage (7:7-25) is based on the assumption that "Paul is not just speaking about his own experience, but is taking himself as representative, first (in vv. 7-13) of mankind generally, and then (in vv. 14-25) of Christians" (p. 341).

Moule, who (like Cranfield) sees this as the experience of a regenerate person, offers this modification: It is, he explains, "St. Paul's confession, not of a long past experience, not of an imagined experience, but of his own normal experience always—*when he acts out of character as a regenerate man*" (*Expositor's Bible*, pp. 194,195; author's italics). In other words, the passage describes the experience of a Christian, but it is not Christian experience as God intends it to be.

The central lesson to be learned from this section is that the law can tell us what to do, but it cannot impart the power needed by us to carry out its injunctions. It can enlighten the Christian conscience, but it cannot produce holiness of life. "As indwelling sin was too powerful for the law to control while we were under it," so in our converted state our ability to carry out the righteous demands of the law "is due, not to the law itself, but wholly to the gracious renovation of our inner man" (D. Brown, p. 73).

Godet, it seems to us, correctly analyzes the passage by dividing it into three cycles, each of which closes with a sort of refrain: verses 14-17; verses 18-20; verses 21-23. "It is," he says, "like a dirge; the most sorrowful elegy which ever proceeded from a human heart" (p. 282). We will not attempt a detailed exposition of the paragraph but will simply call attention to several points of special interest.

Verse 14b ("I am carnal, sold under sin") is, as was mentioned above, the most difficult part of this passage for those who subscribe to the view that Paul is describing his experience as a Christian. Moule gets around the difficulty by interpreting "I" (emphatic in Greek) to mean "I, apart from Christ." For David Brown it is the sinful principle which still indwells the Christian.[31] Calvin resolves the problem by including verse 14 with the preceding paragraph, in which Paul tells of his experience as an unregenerate man. No one of these interpretations is entirely satisfactory.

The literal meaning of the Greek word for "carnal" is "fleshy," that is, made of flesh. Rotherham renders it "creature of flesh." The word, however, has an ethical quality here and may rightly be understood in the sense of "fleshly." To be fleshly (carnal), however, is not the same as being "in the flesh" (8:8) or "after the flesh" (8:5).

"Sold under sin" is not to be interpreted as though the apostle were saying he had abandoned himself to sin. Murray understands the phrase

---

[31]"The 'I' here is of course not the regenerate man, of whom this is certainly not true; but . . . neither is it the unregenerate man — from whose case the apostle has passed away. It remains, then, that it is *the sinful principle in the renewed man*, as is expressly stated in ver. 18" (p. 73).

to mean that the apostle "is subjected to a power that is alien to his own will" (p. 261).[32] The verses which follow appear to confirm this view.[33]

In verse 15 "know" (KJV, "allow") means "approve." "Flesh" (v. 18) is used ethically of the unregenerate nature. "Sin" (v. 20) may denote the principle of sin.

"Law" (v. 21) may be legitimately interpreted either as the Mosaic law or in the sense of a rule or principle of action (cf. NEB). Moule, who understands it in the former sense, takes Paul to mean that in regard to the law his will is with it, his action against it.

The assertion of verse 22 is one of the strongest arguments for interpreting this entire passage as referring to Paul the Christian. "I delight in" may be translated, "I have a sympathetic pleasure in" (cf. Rotherham). Conybeare renders it, "I consent gladly"; Williams, "I approve"; NASB, "I joyfully concur with." The "inward man" is variously interpreted. D. Brown paraphrases it "from the bottom of my heart" (cf. TCNT). Others see the phrase as denoting the regenerate self. Williams has "my better inner nature"; *Living Bible,* "my new nature." Murray, following Gifford, sees the phrase as denoting "inmost spirit," "the centre of his personality"; and thinks it approximates (if it is not identical with) the "mind" of verses 23, 25 (p. 265). Compare Weymouth: "In my inmost self all my sympathy is with the law of God."

In verse 23 "law" means principle. The "law of my mind" is then the principle which my (regenerate) mind (self) approves.

c. *Conclusion (vv. 24,25).* In verse 24 there is what Gifford calls "a wail of anguish and a cry for help" (p. 143).[34] Some see only despair in Paul's words, and therefore they feel the verse cannot possibly express the feeling and experience of a Christian. Verse 24, however, should not be interpreted as a cry of despair but of earnest longing for deliverance. The word rendered "wretched" indicates distress, affliction, or suffering, but it does not necessarily denote hopelessness.

"Who shall deliver me . . . ?" is here the expression of an earnest longing for something which Paul knew was surely coming (cf. 8:23).

---

[32]Moule, who paraphrases "sold under sin" to mean "sold" so as to be under sin's influence, raises the question as to *when* Paul was sold under sin. His answer: "At the Fall and in Adam" (p. 131).

[33]Cranfield's statement is helpful, pointing out that "The more seriously a Christian strives to live from grace, and to submit to the discipline of the gospel, the more sensitive he becomes to the fact of his continuing sinfulness." He then cautions that Paul's words are not to be taken as an "encouragment . . . to wallow complacently in our sins" (p. 358).

[34]Cranfield thinks such a cry is "characteristic of Christian existence. . . . The farther men advance in the Christian life, and the more mature their discipleship, the clearer becomes their perception of the heights to which God calls them, and the more painfully sharp their consciousness of the distance between what they ought and want to be and what they are" (p. 366).

"The body of this death" is the physical body. It is called the body of "this death" because the body, the stronghold of sin, is destined to succumb to death.

Verse 25a provides the triumphant answer to the longing of the preceding verse. It is an exclamation expressing Paul's confident assurance of ultimate deliverance. The agent in this deliverance is not expressly mentioned, but the fact that gratitude is offered to God "through Jesus Christ" implies that He is the One who brings the longed-for redemption.

Verse 25b is a summing up of the entire argument begun at verse 14.

C. A Life Indwelt by the Spirit (ch. 8)

The majesty and splendor of this chapter are apparent to every reader. Godet, quoting Spener, writes that "if holy Scripture was a ring, and the Epistle to the Romans its precious stone, chap. viii would be the sparkling point of the jewel" (p. 295). Significantly, it begins with *no condemnation* and ends with *no separation*.

Throughout chapter 8, Paul is, in a sense, still defending (as he was in chs. 6 and 7) his doctrine of faith-righteousness against objections. The chapter is, however, more than a mere defense; it is really a summing up of all that has preceded it and as such is a fitting climax of the entire argument of chapters 1-7.

Gifford looks at chapter 8 as depicting the "nature of the deliverance anticipated in St. Paul's triumphant thanksgiving in vii. 25" (p. 146). Barrett reminds us that Paul is "still speaking of justification and its consequences. Among these consequences, hardly mentioned in the epistle up to this point . . . is the gift of the Spirit" (pp. 154,155). We are considering it as the presentation of another (indeed, the crowning) aspect of the life of God in the believer. That life has been shown to be a life of holiness in union with Christ (ch. 6) and a life of freedom from the law (ch. 7). Now (ch. 8) it is depicted as a life indwelt by the Holy Spirit.[35] The idea, at least in part, is that the Christian life is "a life animated, sustained, directed and enriched by the Holy Spirit" (Stott, p. 84).

Attention is called to the connection between chapters 7 and 8 by many interpreters. Moule calls it "a connexion at once of contrast and of complement." The contrast is seen in the unrelieved sternness of chapter 7 (except for the brief exclamation of thanks at the close) and the revelations of triumph in chapter 8. The one is to the other "as an almost

---

[35]This is the way in which many commentators view the chapter. See, for example, Godet, p. 294; Moule, *Expositor's Bible*, pp. 203ff.; Murray, p. 274; Cranfield, p. 370; et al.

starless night . . . [is] to the splendour of a midsummer morning"
(*Expositor's Bible*, p. 203). Chapter 8 complements the earlier chapter
by its numerous references to the Spirit. In Romans 7:7-25 there is not a
single reference to the Holy Spirit, but in chapter 8 the Greek word for
"Spirit"[36] occurs twenty-one times, more frequently than in any other
single chapter of the New Testament.

Chapter 8 may be divided into four subsections, each of which gives
some facet of the believer's life in the Spirit. Victory (vv. 1-11), sonship
(vv. 12-17a), hope (vv. 17b-30), and security (vv. 31-39) are the dominant
concepts.

1. *A life of victory (8:1-13)*

Defeat seems to permeate nearly all of chapter 7, but here the
apostle (picking up the note sounded in 7:25a) shows that the indwelling
Spirit brings to the believer's life unbounded power for conquest and
victory. The argument in the passage is closely knit, and the syntax is
sometimes difficult to unravel. Two principal thoughts, however, may
be clearly discerned. These are the believer's triumph (1) over sin (vv.
1-8) and (2) ultimately over death (vv. 9-13).

a. *Victory over sin (vv. 1-8)*. The "therefore" of verse 1 may draw
an inference from all that precedes; more likely, it gathers up and draws
an inference from the discussion of 6:1-7:25. It is equivalent to saying,
"The conclusion of the matter is this."[37]

Our victory over sin is stated in two ways: First, there is for us now
"no condemnation" (v. 1). Condemnation is the opposite of justification.
"No" condemnation means that God has acquitted believers of guilt and
has lifted the judicial sentence under which they formerly lived. Second, we have been set free "from the law of sin and of death" (v. 2). That
is, we not only are no longer under condemnation; we have been
delivered from the bondage of indwelling sin. D. Brown speaks of this as
release "from the enslaving power of that corrupt principle which carries
death in its bosom" (p. 79). "For," with which verse 2 begins, indicates
that the statement of the verse is a confirmation of what is affirmed in
verse 1. That is to say, the evidence that we are free from condemnation
is that "the law [principle, regulating power] of the Spirit of life in Christ

---

[36]It is a problem for translators whether this word should in each occurrence in chapter 8
be capitalized (cf., for example, v. 15, ASV).

[37]Gifford (p. 146) sees "therefore" as drawing an inference from 7:25, the thought being
"now that a deliverer has been found, this is what we may conclude." Godet sees 7:7-25.as
somewhat parenthetical, and understands "therefore" as taking up the thread of Paul's
exposition of Christian sanctification. He paraphrases as follows: "Since ye are dead to sin
and alive to God, and so subject to grace, and made free from the law, all condemnation has
disappeared" (p. 296).

Jesus" has freed us "from the law [principle, regulating power][38] of sin
and death" (cf. 7:23,25). The "Spirit of life in Christ Jesus" is of course
the Holy Spirit. He is the Spirit "of life" because He is the author of life.

How this victory over sin has been made possible is told us in verses
3 and 4: "What the law could not do [that is, condemn sin, break its
power], in that it was weak through the flesh [that is, because it had to
depend upon sinful human nature to carry out its precepts], God, [by]
sending his own Son in the likeness of sinful flesh and for sin, condemned sin [that is, broke its power; brought its authority to an end] in
[through] the flesh"[39] (v. 3). This condemnation of sin was to the end
"that the ordinance of the law [that is, the righteous demands of the law]
might be fulfilled [carried out] in us, who walk not after the flesh [our
fallen, sinful nature], but after the Spirit" (v. 4).

Verses 5-9 *expand* and *explain* more fully the emancipation from
sin enunciated in the first four verses of the chapter. The two phrases
which especially dominate the thought are "after the flesh" (vv. 4,5) and
"after the Spirit" (vv. 4,5). These should be compared with "the things of
the flesh" (v. 5) and "the things of the Spirit" (v. 5), "the mind of the
flesh" (vv. 6,7) and "the mind of the Spirit" (v. 6), "in the flesh" (vv.
8,9) and "in the Spirit" (v. 9). "Flesh" in each instance denotes the
sinful nature of man (NEB, "lower nature"). To be "after" the flesh, therefore, is to be governed and controlled by one's sinful nature. Goodspeed: "controlled by the physical." "After the Spirit" speaks, con-
versely, of life controlled by the Spirit.

In saying that "the mind of the flesh is death" (v. 6a), Paul probably
means that the tendency of the lower (unregenerate) nature is toward
death. The language may suggest an affinity between the lower nature
and death. At any rate, "death" is the end toward which the fleshly mind
moves; the mind of the Spirit, on the other hand, is toward "life and
peace."

b. *Victory over death (vv. 9-13).* Believers are "not in the flesh but
in the Spirit" (v. 9a); that is, they are no longer dominated and controlled
by the lower nature but are under the controlling influence of the Holy
Spirit. And this is because the Spirit of God dwells (has His home) in
them.[40] "And if Christ [by the indwelling Spirit] is in you [as is true of
every believer], the body is dead [that is, mortal; has the seed of physical

---

[38]Moule, giving a different interpretation, takes "the law" here to be the Mosaic law.
"It is the law of sin and death," he says, not because it is "sinful and deathful," but because
it is "sin's occasion" and "death's warrant" (*Expositor's Bible*, p. 211).

[39]"In the flesh" modifies "condemned," not "sin." "Flesh," which in this instance refers
to the flesh (body) of Christ, calls attention to the true human nature of the incarnate Son of
God.

[40]Note that the idea of being "in the Spirit" is interchangeable with that of having the
Spirit "dwell in" the believer.

death in it] because of sin [cf. 5:12ff.]; but the spirit[41] is life because of righteousness" (v. 10).[42] The meaning is that the inner spirit of the believer has been quickened — "is instinct with new and undying 'life'" (D. Brown, p. 83) — by the Spirit of God, and this is the assurance of the believer's future bodily resurrection. "Sin" may be the Adamic sin (cf. 5:12ff.) or personal sin. "Righteousness" appears to be used in the sense of justification.

Verse 11 brings out two additional thoughts: (1) that the resurrection of believers is dependent upon the resurrection of Christ and (2) that it is the Spirit who both raised Christ and will raise us.

Verses 12,13 may be seen as drawing an inference from the foregoing verses, namely, that we are obligated to live according to the Spirit. The idea is not expressly stated, but in affirming that we are *not* debtors "to the flesh, to live after the flesh," it is clearly implied that we *are* debtors to the Spirit, to live according to the Spirit. D. Brown paraphrases verse 12: "Emancipated from the tyrannous service of Sin into the service of Righteousness, we owe nothing now to the flesh; we disown its claims, and are deaf to its imperious demands" (p. 84). In verse 13, to "put to death" the deeds of the body is an equivalent to "reckon . . . dead" (6:11). The statement of the verse suggests that either we kill sin or it will kill us.

2. A *life of sonship (8:14-17a)*

Two ideas run through this paragraph: sonship and heirship. The former points to our present relationship; the latter is a promise of our future glory. The entire passage, however, may be seen as revolving around the thought of our sonship toward God.

In verses 14-16, we have the thought of the *assurance of sonship*. Three such assurances are given: The first may be defined broadly as spirituality, that is, the living of a life guided by and under the control of the Spirit of God (v. 14). It is noteworthy that the Spirit, who in the foregoing verses has been represented mainly in terms of a power by which believers conquer sin and death, is now thought of as a loving and personal guide. The second assurance of sonship toward God is the believer's confidence in approaching Him (v. 15). In our conversion we did not receive "the spirit of bondage" which engenders fear, but "the spirit of adoption" which leads us to cry "Abba, Father." The third ground of filial assurance is the witness of the Spirit (v. 16). The believer,

---

[41]Calvin, Moule, Murray, and Cranfield take this to be a reference to the Holy Spirit. See also the KJV.

[42]The NEB expresses the relationship of the various parts of this verse more accurately than ASV: "But if Christ is dwelling within you, then although the body is a dead thing because you sinned, yet the spirit is life itself because you have been justified."

when he cries "Abba! Father!"[43] in prayer, is giving witness to his sonship. Verse 16 affirms that the Spirit adds to this His own witness.[44]

Verse 17b points up a *privilege* which grows out of our filial relation to God. Since we are His children, we are "heirs of God" (cf. Gal. 4:7) and "joint-heirs with Christ." The main thought in the latter phrase is that we share in the glory which is Christ's (cf. John 17:22-24; also v. 17b, "glorified with him"). This thought introduces the idea which dominates verses 17b-30.

3. A life characterized by the hope of glory[45] (8:17b-30)

One purpose Paul had in writing this subsection was to encourage the Roman Christians in the midst of their sufferings. The thought of their future glory, he felt, would kindle their expectations and give them patience under trials. Gifford therefore entitles this paragraph, "The sources of comfort under the necessity of suffering" (p. 154).

Verse 17b, though grammatically related to the verses which precede it, serves to introduce the unit which follows. It suggests that sharing in Christ's sufferings is the *path to glory*. Three things are to be noticed: One, the Greek construction suggests that sufferings are to be expected. Two, these sufferings are shared *with* Christ. This does not mean that our sufferings in any way contribute to the expiatory and redemptive power of the sufferings of Christ. He alone bore the burden of our guilt and He by Himself accomplished our redemption. Underlying the thought is that of our vital union with Christ. Three, these sufferings are in a sense only the birth pangs which shall issue in glory. One should be careful not to interpret this verse as meaning that the Christian's suffering is meritorious. Rather, the thought is that our participation in Christ's sufferings is a part of the discipline by which we are prepared for glory. The glory itself is a free gift, but the capacity to enjoy it is imparted and enhanced through trial.

Verses 18-22 describe the *surpassing greatness of the glory* which awaits God's people. At least three indications of this are given: First, so great is the glory that it dwarfs our sufferings. The latter, in fact, are not even worthy of mention in view of the splendor which awaits the people of God (v. 18). "I reckon" (v. 18) is the translation of a word which is

---

[43]These words are found elsewhere in the New Testament in Mark 14:36 and Galatians 4:6.

[44]The RSV punctuation of verses 15b and 16 has much to commend it: "When we cry, 'Abba! Father!' it is the Spirit himself bearing witness with our spirit that we are children of God." This suggests that it is in prayer that the Spirit gives us witness to our sonship.

[45]Our exposition has pointed out Paul's development of the doctrines of condemnation (1:18-3:20), justification (3:21-5:21), and sanctification (chs. 6-8). Although our treatment includes 8:17ff. under the general heading of sanctification, these verses in reality deal with glorification, which is the culmination of the process of sanctification.

variously rendered in KJV by "think," "conclude," "suppose," "count." It denotes more than mere supposition or opinion. It here has in it the idea of a fixed conclusion arrived at after careful consideration. "Revealed" suggests that the glory already is realized in Christ (cf. v. 17b); we await its unveiling in our case. The Greek construction emphasizes the certainty of that revelation.

A second indication of the greatness of the glory which we confidently expect is that creation[46] itself is destined to share in it (vv. 19-22). These verses express what has been called Paul's "cosmic soteriology." The essential thought is that just as the whole universe has suffered because of man's sin, so it will share in the coming glory. We therefore can sense the "sympathetic longings" of creation for the future revelation of glory which we await (cf. v. 19). The drift of the passage is as follows: (a) Creation has been subjected to vanity (emptiness) (v. 20a). The Greek word for "vanity" is from a root denoting "seeking without finding," and so implies frustration. Murray thinks its use here points to "the lack of vitality that inhibits the order of nature and the frustration which the forces of nature meet with in achieving their proper ends" (I, 303). (b) This subjection of creation was through no fault of its own — "not of its own will, but by reason of him who subjected it" (v. 20b). The reference in the latter words ("him who subjected it") must be to God. Having originally placed creation under the dominion of man, God also subjected it to the consequences growing out of human sin. (c) Creation, though subjected to the effects of man's sin, will also partake of the benefits of man's deliverance. It therefore was subjected "in hope" — the word denotes strong expectation — that it would be "delivered from the bondage of corruption into the liberty of the glory of the children of God" (vv. 20b,21). (d) Even now creation is experiencing the birth pangs that will issue in a new day. The whole creation will eventually undergo a change corresponding to that which believers will experience (v. 22). This will make creation "the fit scene of the glory of God's children" (Gifford, p. 156). (e) Implied in all of this is that if creation exhibits expectation concerning the future, believers should do no less.

Verses 23-25 speak of the believer's *expectation of glory*. Not only is creation groaning and travailing in pain, but "ourselves also," although we already have "the first-fruits of the Spirit, even we ourselves

---

[46]The word "creation" simply denotes "the things created," and its precise meaning must be determined by its context. Here there are some necessary limitations which must be assumed; for example, unfallen angels (who obviously were not "subjected to vanity"); fallen angels (who do not share in the hope of glory); believers (for the whole passage distinguishes their longings from the longings of "creation"); and unbelievers, for if they are included the passage teaches universalism — a teaching contrary to numerous unambiguous statements of Scripture. Here then the word denotes creation as distinct from man and angels.

groan within ourselves, waiting for our adoption, to wit, the redemption of our body" (v. 23). "First-fruits" is an agricultural term denoting the first fruits of the harvest, thought of as a pledge of the full crop to come. "Of the Spirit" is a genitive of identity. The meaning is that the Holy Spirit within us is the first fruits (the God-given guarantee and the foretaste) of our full inheritance (cf. Eph. 1:13,14). Our full inheritance, that for which we yet wait, is spoken of as "our adoption," that is, that condition in which all the privileges and benefits of our status as sons of God will be realized. The "redemption of our body" is specified as the leading feature of this future adoption. By "redemption" we are here to understand the deliverance of our bodies from mortality and corruption. Perhaps the context emphasizes that although we already have the first fruits (the pledge, the foretaste) of the Spirit, we must await the resurrection of our bodies to receive the Spirit in all His fullness.

Verses 24 and 25 point to the past aspect of salvation ("were saved") but emphasize that that experience was characterized by hope. We were saved "in[not 'by'] hope." This hope (expectation) which is an ingredient in our salvation implies that there is more of God's bounty in store for us.

In verses 26-30, the emphasis is on *the pledge of the believer's glory*. Three things are cited as guarantees that we shall enter into that glory for which God destined His people: First, there is the help of the Holy Spirit (vv. 26,27). This is stated generally in verse 26a: "And in like manner the Spirit also helpeth our infirmity." "In like manner" perhaps suggests that in addition to the help which hope gives us in our state of weakness, there is also the help of the Spirit. "Helpeth" is a picturesque word implying that the Spirit stands over against us and pulls with us as we bear our burdens. Martha used the same word when she said of Mary, "Bid her therefore that she *help* me" (Luke 10:40).

After the general statement of the Spirit's help, his assistance in prayer is singled out as a specific example (vv. 26b,27). The idea is that in those times when our yearnings are too deep for words or when we really do not know how to pray in words but can only groan under the sense of need, the Holy Spirit prompts, and is in, these sighs or groans. We therefore must not be disheartened. Through our inarticulate groanings the Spirit Himself is interceding in our behalf. And the Father who searches and knows our hearts and who also knows the mind (the meaning, the desire, the preferences) of the Spirit, understands our longing sighs.

Second, there is the all-embracing purpose of God (vv. 28-30). These verses affirm our knowledge of the fact that in God's government of the world all things are made to contribute to the welfare of His people. "We do know that God causes all things[47] to work together for the good of those who love him" (v. 28, TCNT). Goodspeed renders it, "We know that in everything God works with those who love him . . . to bring about what is good." The statement has nothing to do with blind chance or fate. It is the work of a loving God in behalf of His people.

Two expressions describe God's people: They are those who love Him; they are those who are called according to His purpose. Only those who fit these two qualifications can legitimately claim the promise of Romans 8:28.

The specific "good" which is denoted, is spelled out in verses 29 and 30. In short, it is that God's people shall become more Christlike, "conformed to the image of his [God's] Son." These two verses also define the purpose (v. 28) of God. The key words are "foreknew," "foreordained," "called," "justified," and "glorified." The first word ("foreknew") suggests more than knowing something in advance. Williams translates it "set His heart on beforehand"; TCNT has "chose"; Rotherham, "fore-approved." "Foreordained" literally means to mark off beforehand. Rotherham has "fore-appointed." "Called," in Paul's use of the word, means more than "invited." It has in it the idea of being brought in.[48]

It has often been remarked that verses 29 and 30 contain an unbroken chain reaching from eternity to eternity. All those foreknown of God are, without exception, eventually glorified.[49]

4. A life of assurance and security (8:31-39)

In verses 28 and 29 Paul made five profound assertions; he now raises five unanswerable questions (vv. 31-35). These five questions grow out of the previous affirmations concerning the unchanging, invincible purpose of God. They are all designed to give to believers a deep sense of spiritual security. This security is based upon God's gracious disposition toward us (vv. 31-33), the redemptive work of Christ (His death for us and His intercession in our behalf, v. 34), and the immutability and strength of the divine love (vv. 35-39).

Paul's discussion of the believer's life in the Spirit — indeed, his discussion of the whole redemptive work of God in our behalf (begun at 3:21 — is concluded with an exultant and triumphant affirmation (vv. 36-39). He enumerates all sorts of powers and beings, present and

---

[47]"All things" refers primarily to the sufferings mentioned earlier (vv.17,18), but of course is not limited to those things.

[48]It should be observed that in this passage *all who are called* are also justified and glorified.

[49]The aorist (past) tense of the verb heightens the thought of certainty of fulfillment.

future, human and superhuman, and exclaims that none of these nor any other creature is able to break the chain of love which binds the heart of God to His people. "Thus does this wonderful chapter . . . leave us who are 'justified by faith' in the arms of everlasting Love, whence no hostile power or conceivable event can ever tear us" (D. Brown, p. 95).

For Further Study

1. Read Romans 6:1-8:39 in a modern translation and look for recurring words and phrases.

2. Use a concordance to study the New Testament teachings about the Holy Spirit. Where are most of the references to the Spirit clustered?

3. Write down in your own words what is taught about the Holy Spirit in Romans 1:1-7:25.

4. Write out in your own words what is taught about the Spirit in Romans 8.

5. Study every occurrence of the word Life in Romans 5-8. (Use a concordance if you wish.) Write out in your own words the essential teaching of each passage.

6. Read in a Bible dictionary articles on Life, Sanctification, Holiness, Salvation, Law, Spirit, Adoption, Prayer, Election, Calling, and Glorification.

Chapter 6

The Faithfulness of God:[1]
The Doctrine of Election

(Romans 9:1-11:36)

It is a great step from the end of chapter 8 to the beginning of chapter 9. From a crescendo of triumph in the love of Christ, Paul's tone declines to lament and anguish. We can imagine, as Moule observes, that after the last words of 8:39 were penned "there was silence awhile in that Corinthian chamber" (p. 244). The most fitting sequel to such a profound revelation of grace and glory is the "silence of the soul." Immediately, a glaring contradiction enters the picture: the dark riddle of Israel's unbelief. Nothing can separate us, Paul exults, but how is it that Israel, the chosen people, stands separated from the love of Christ? The backdrop of God's faithfulness to His saints in 8:28-39 constrains Paul all the more to engage afresh this issue, and he takes it up in chapters 9-11.

The passage has been perplexing to some expositors who commonly assert that Paul concludes his main argument at 8:39, adding chapters 9-11 as an appendix, a parenthesis, or digression. The history of interpretation teaches us that this approach effectively hinders any positive appreciation of the passage. It is our feeling that the doctrinal section culminates in chapters 9-11 and that here is the apex of the argument. Far from being an appendix, the passage at hand is crucial for interpreting the entire letter; without it, much of Romans lies undiscovered.

The fate of Israel had serious consequences for Paul because it became the occasion for some to question the gospel he preached. The people entrusted with the divine promises (cf. "oracles of God," 3:2) had rejected the gospel, thereby raising the twofold implication that God had revoked Israel's promises and simultaneously nullified His covenant faithfulness. Jewish unbelief therefore appeared, at least to Paul's detractors, to cast a pall of suspicion over the ways of God. The question, then, that lies at the heart of chapters 9-11 is this: Does the unbelief of

---

[1]Three main concepts, not separate and distinct but bound together, are unfolded in chapters 9-11. These are: (1) God's redemptive purpose; (2) His faithfulness to His promises; and (3) the all-embracing character of the divine salvation; taking in not Jews only, but both Jews and Gentiles.

Israel signify a failure of God's promises, or a breakdown of His purpose (cf. Gifford, p. 38)? Paul answers with a hearty "No!" God has not cast off His people; His word has not failed; and His purpose remains unchanged and unchanging.

Paul's closely reasoned argument can best be appreciated if, before a detailed exposition is given, we offer a summary statement of the passage. The apostle's primary theme (9:6a) is developed by showing that God's activity in Israel has been consistent from the beginning. In the history of the nation, a plan of selection has been at work (9:11); the spiritual heirs of promise (9:8) have never included all the physical descendants of Abraham (9:6). The principle elucidated here, "the purpose of God according to election" (9:11), is the fulcrum upon which the entire reasoning turns. After this viewpoint of divine choice is established, it is defended in the form of three successive rebuttals to objections, each making a sequential part of the argument.

First, the objection that God has acted unjustly: "Is there unrighteousness with God?" (9:14). The objector complains that God's election is arbitrary and capricious; the accusation is not allowed to stand. Paul's refutation insists upon (1) the freedom and sovereignty of God and (2) the revealed goal of His electing purpose (9:14-29). The question "What shall we say then?" (9:30) introduces the second objection: Why has Israel failed to attain the righteousness of God? Paul answers that Israel has stumbled at Christ; the viewpoint is that of human responsibility. The unbelief of Israel magnifies the faithfulness of God in that God has invited, but Israel will not come (10:1-21). The third objection, which reverts to the divine perspective, is introduced by the question, "Did God cast off his people?" (11:1). The answer is clear; the election of God has not displaced Israel. Its rejection is partial (11:1-10) and temporary (11:11-27). A brief summary paragraph rehearses the entire argument: the divine purpose will run its full course; God has not wavered from His first intention (11:28-32).

Divine faithfulness as the keynote of chapters 9-11 is reflected in the references to God's "mercy" (cf. 9:15,16,18; 11:30,31,32). This is a word that includes love and grace but blends in the quality of steadfastness, in order to capture the unerring faithfulness of God to justify all who believe. Paul's usage stems from the Old Testament, where the corresponding term stands for God's "steadfast love" (RSV) toward Israel. The nation might unilaterally break the covenant, but God remains faithful and issues a promise of restoration (cf. Isa. 54:7,8; Hos. 2:19,20; Jer. 3:12).[1] This persistent refusal of God to wash His hands of wayward

---

[2] The Greek word *eleos* ("mercy") is the translation of the Hebrew word *chesed* ("steadfast love") in the Greek Old Testament. In the prophets *chesed* is a covenant term that denotes the saving faithfulness of God to disobedient Israel.

Israel is the prophetic insight that makes the promise of chapters 9-11 a live possibility — it all depends on the merciful God (cf. 9:16).

The passage can be divided into five parts: (1) a lament for Israel (9:1-5), (2) the saving purpose of God in election (9:6-29), (3) a righteousness of God for all who believe in Christ (9:30-10:21); (4) the mystery of Israel's future restoration (11:1-32), and (5) a hymn of praise to God (11:33-36).

A. Lament for Israel (9:1-5)

As Paul takes up the tragedy of fallen Israel, he bursts forth in an unexpected lamentation; there is no immediate cue for this weeping. Godet remarks that Paul does not prepare us because "it costs him too much to pronounce the fatal word; every reader will divine it from his very silence" (p. 338). This introductory lament reveals the intercessory grief of Paul (vv. 1-3) and the spiritual tragedy of Israel (vv. 4,5).

1. *The intercessory grief of Paul (9:1-3)*

These are the words of a burdened intercessor, not an enthusiastic patriot. They reflect Paul's continuing concern and prayers for the salvation of Israel (cf. 10:1; 11:1-5). Perhaps as "apostle of the Gentiles" (11:13), he had been accused of being a renegade, a traitor to his own people and indifferent to their fate (cf. Acts 21:33; 22:22; 25:24; 2 Cor. 11:31; Gal. 1:20). However, his grief is real and the vehemence of his assertion allays any suspicion that he is "animated by hostility or even indifference to the Jews" (Denney, p. 656).

The *sincerity* of Paul's grief is certified by his union with Christ and the witness of the Holy Spirit (v. 1). The phrase "in Christ" ("as one in union with Christ," TCNT) describes a union with Christ that makes any form of lying impossible (cf. 8:1,10). Even a truthful man may exaggerate the truth, but in the holy presence of Christ no such exaggeration is possible: He is the searcher of hearts (Eph. 4:15; Col. 3:9). A second appeal is made to the approval of conscience, the moral guardian capable of standing over against man either to accuse (cf. 2:15; 1 Tim. 1:19) or to acquit (cf. 1 Pet. 3:16,21). The verdict of conscience is weighty because it is "enlightened by the Holy Spirit" (TCNT, NEB); that is, the witness of conscience is doubly sure for the Christian. Paul speaks the truth in Christ, and his conscience bears witness in the Holy Spirit.

The *burden* of his grief is described in the parallelism of verse 2. The word "heaviness" refers to grief as a state of mind, while its counterpart "sorrow" never loses its physical associations and implies heartbrokenness (cf. Sanday and Headlam, p. 227). Note the heightening of the anguish: (1) it is great ("a great weight of sorrow," TCNT); (2) it is continual ("my heart is never free from pain," TCNT). The "truth" (v. 1) that Paul asserts is affirmed by the depth of his grief; he cannot find words strong enough to convey his feeling.

The *proof* of his grief is expressed in a prayer-wish (v. 3). Although verse 3 can be taken as a prayer, it must not be interpreted as a literal request, as though Paul actually prays to atone for the sin of Israel. The verb "could wish" — the imperfect tense has potential force here — assumes a condition of unreality and must govern the request (cf. Gal. 4:20; Acts 25:22). "Accursed from Christ" (KJV) is literally "anathema from Christ" (ASV), and it means "devoted to destruction" (cf. Deut. 7:26; Gal. 1:8,9; 1 Cor. 16:22). The wish, if fulfilled, would amount to banishment from Christ into perdition, the possibility of which Paul emphatically denies (cf. 8:31-39). Paul's prayer-wish is more reflective than Moses' genuine vow of substitution in Exodus 32:32. It is better to call it, with Dorner, "a spark from the fire of Christ's substitutionary love" (quoted by Denney, p. 657). The reference to "my kinsmen according to the flesh" reveals that Paul cannot evaluate the Jews in purely human terms; as we shall see in verses 4,5, fleshly ties are not the source of his grief.

2. *The spiritual tragedy of Israel (9:4,5)*

The lament grows out of the magnitude of that which Israel had experienced under the Old Testament covenant. The incomparable gifts of God to Israel are bittersweet reminders of the extent of Israel's spiritual tragedy. One can almost hear the tremor in Paul's voice as he breathes the word "Israelites" (v. 4). They are more than Jewish "kinsmen"; the name itself implies the privileges of the chosen people and designates God's special relationship to them in election (cf. Sanday and Headlam, p. 229). In verses 4,5 Paul recounts the legacy of election and covenant in Israel's history. These are the marks of divine favor which "separately and all combined constitute the crowning reason for the apostle's grief" (Griffith Thomas, II, 125).

The are two parts in the catalogue of privileges before us. First, six covenant blessings (v. 4) are arranged in parallelism and may be studied as explanatory couplets.[2] We can summarize the couplets by noting three aspects of God revealed in them: (1) His grace calling out a people, (2) His holiness pervading their worship, (3) His promise setting forth hope.

---

[3] These couplets are: (1) "adoption" ("made God's sons," NEB), conferred at the Exodus (cf. Exod. 4:22; Hos. 11:1), parallels "giving of the law" at Sinai (cf. Exod. 20:1ff.); (2) "glory" is the "splendor of the divine presence" (NEB; cf. TCNT, Goodspeed) in the Old Testament theophanies (called *shekhinah* in Judaism; cf. Exod. 33:18; 40:34) and parallels "service of God," which refers to worship in the tabernacle and temple; and (3) "covenants," where the plural hints at successive renewals of the covenant through Abraham, Moses, and David, parallels "promises," the longed-for messianic hope (cf. Bruce, p. 185).

Second, a royal lineage is traced that connects Israel to the patri-archs and the Messiah (v. 5). The "fathers," Abraham, Isaac, and Jacob, are the noble ancestry from whom the people came; and "Christ," the Messiah, is the flower of that root. The phrase "of whom concerning the flesh" ("from them in respect of His human lineage," Weymouth; cf. 1:3,4) hints at the tragedy: although *from* Israel, Christ does not *belong to* Israel. The offense heightens when verse 5b is read as a doxology ascribed to Christ: "Christ, who is God over all, blessed for ever" (RSV mg.; cf. NASB, NIV, Knox, Weymouth). Moule argues that the context "pointedly suggests some explicit allusion to the super-human Nature of Christ, by the words, 'according to the flesh.' But if there is such an allusion, then it must lie in the words '*over all, God* ' " (*Expositor's Bible* p. 262).[4] Indeed, the sadness in these verses laments Israel's refusal of the highest gift, the divine Son who came to His own.

B. The Saving Purpose of God in Election (9:6-29)

The inference that follows from verses 1-5, namely, that Israel's unbelief means a failure of God's promise, is rejected by Paul. The phrase "hath come to nought" (v. 6a) is a verb that literally means "fallen from its place," and denotes the "non-realization of the promise, its being brought to nothing by the facts" (Godet, p. 346). Paul is certain that the "word of God," His declared purpose (cf. Sanday and Headlam, p. 240), will reach its appointed goal; thus, he begins a step-by-step defense of God's faithfulness. Particularly in verses 6-29, there is a sense of theodicy, a vindication of God's sovereign right in dealing with Israel as He has. The proof to be found is that of revelation: the historical outworking of God's purpose. In a word, divine election (or "God's redemptive purpose," as W. T. Conner put it) is the banner to which Paul rallies. We can discern three leading thoughts: (1) the principle of election (vv. 6-13), (2) the freedom of election (vv. 14-21), and (3) the goal of election (vv. 22-29).

1. *The principle of election (9:6-13)*

The present condition of the Jews is nothing new, Paul argues, for the history of the people shows that not all the physical descendants were recipients of the promise (v. 6b). The chosen people were consti-tuted upon the basis of "God's electing purpose" (v. 11b, Weymouth), that is, a plan that worked on the principle of election. The thought then of verse 6b can be translated "not all descendants of Israel are truly Israel" (NEB), for it introduces a spiritual distinction within the ranks of

---

[4] The punctuation of verse 5b has "probably been more discussed than that of any other sentence in literature" (F. C. Burkitt). Suffice it to say here that on grounds of grammar, context, and Pauline usage, the view that Christ is called God commends itself (so Godet, Gifford, Sanday and Headlam, Nygren, Bruce, and Murray).

the historical people. The true Israel cannot be defined in terms of physical descent, or understood simply "according to the flesh" (v. 3); it is created not by blood and soil, but by the promise of God (cf. Barrett). This "Israel," a part of but not coextensive with the physical descendants, came to be as a result of divine election. The ground then of Paul's reasoning is the principle of election named in verse 11; however, he must first illustrate it in the historical calling of the children of promise.

a. *The case of Isaac and Ishmael: election transcends birthright* (*vv. 7-9*). Paul quotes Genesis 21:12, where God tells Abraham not to oppose Sarah's demand for the expulsion of Hagar and Ishmael, because "in Isaac shall thy seed be called" (v. 7b). The quotation adduces proof that not all the "offspring of Abraham" (NEB) are his true children. The word "seed" is capable of both a collective ("posterity") and individual ("descendant") sense (cf. 4:16,19; 2 Cor. 11:22; Gal. 3:16,19). For Paul, the collective "seed of Abraham" is gradually focused in the one promised seed, Christ (Gal. 3:16). So, Barrett rightly thinks that "behind the difficult theological development of verses 6-13 lies a thought that is fundamentally Christological and soteriological" (p. 181). This process of differentiation between Isaac and Ishmael has a sovereign, redemptive design which becomes clearer as we read further in chapter 9.

The thought of verses 8,9 explicates the meaning of Isaac's chosenness: he was born because of God's promise. Ishmael was a true son of Abraham with as much of his father's blood in his veins as Isaac had, but his birthright belonged to the "children of flesh," not promise (v. 8). Isaac's promised birth in the context of failing age, sterility, and Sarah's laughter (cf. 4:19) depended upon God's visitation: "When I come back at this time next year, Sarah will have a son" (v. 9, Goodspeed; cf. Gen. 18:10). The idea that Isaac is "counted" (v. 8 KJV; "regarded," NASB; "reckoned," NEB) parallels the meaning of "called" (v. 7; "reckoned or considered," Sanday and Headlam, p. 241). Just as God creates righteousness and annuls sin by divine reckoning (cf. 4:8,22) so He freely reckons Isaac to be the seed. "If God drew the distinction at the outset, it could not be wrong to draw it subsequently through all the ages. Thus the Apostle distinguishes between the seed as a whole and the promised seed, in order to emphasize Divine election as the fundamental principle" (Griffith Thomas, II, 133).

b. *The case of Jacob and Esau: election supersedes works* (*vv. 10-13*). So far, Paul has based his argument on the story of Abraham and Isaac, and it could be found to have a flaw. Nygren remarks, "It might be thought, in the case of Isaac, that the basis of his election was the advantage he had in being the son of a free woman, whereas Ishmael was the son of a bondwoman. But when Paul now turns to the choice of Jacob above Esau, there can be no such idea" (p. 363). Jacob and Esau were twins in the same womb, and before either was born, before either had done good or bad (v. 11a), Rebecca was told "the elder [Esau] shall serve the younger [Jacob]" (v. 12; cf. Gen. 25:23). Here the point is clear: the choice of Jacob does not depend upon human conditions of parentage and deed; in fact, "conspicuous unfavourable characteristics" (Moule, *Expositor's Bible* p. 578) in Jacob makes election based on merit absurd.

Paul now defines the governing principle in this episode: "the purpose of God according to election" (v. 11b; cf. "God's electing purpose," Weymouth; "the divine purpose which has worked on the principle of selection," Sanday and Headlam). Sanday and Headlam call it "the key to chaps. ix-xi" (p. 244); Barrett says "this marks out the theme of chs. ix-xi" (p. 182). The word "purpose" is a technical term in Paul that denotes the divine plan for the salvation of mankind (cf. 8:28; 11:2; Eph. 1:11; 3:11; 2 Tim. 1:9;2:10). It reaches into eternity past and claims the unseen future because it springs from the heart of God. Our understanding of God's purpose must be qualified in three ways. First, the present tense verb "might stand" expresses constancy, an abiding condition which is the opposite of "hath come to nought" (v. 6a). God's purpose remained in effect in Jacob's case, and it is still intact for the Jews of Paul's day. Second, its decisive sign is calling, not works; that is, the external purpose is confirmed to us, anchored in the realities of history, by divine call ("him that calleth") not by our works ("not of works"). Third, the phrase "according to election" is modal, pinpointing the way in which the divine purpose works. The purpose of God expresses itself in the act of election so that it is a selecting, discriminating purpose (cf. Denney, p. 661). In summary, the saving purpose of God is perpetually active, revealed in calling, and discriminating among men. It is the richness of this purpose that Paul will display in the remainder of chapters 9-11.

To confirm the propriety in God's prenatal choice of Jacob, Paul adds a quotation: "Jacob I loved, but Esau I hated" (v. 13; cf. Mal. 1:2,3). Since Malachi speaks of the descendants of the twins, the nations Israel and Edom (cf. Mal. 1:4), Paul is evidently pleading that the subsequent history of the nations corroborates the divine action with regard to their respective founders. This is the concept of "corporate personality" (cf. Bruce, p. 193) in which a solidarity exists between the ancestor and his descendants (cf. 5:12-21). Thus, we are not compelled to choose whether Paul views the destiny of the individuals or the status of the nations; the two are vitally intertwined. It also sheds light on the enigmatic statement that God "hated" Esau ("Esau I repudiated," *Modern Language Bible*) which can be rendered in the idiomatic sense "not preferred" (cf. Luke 14:26; John 12:25). The word signifies both the setting aside of Esau and the perpetual enmity between God and Edom. This is no passive indifference between God and man but, as history witnesses, an active "rupture resulting from moral antipathy" (Godet, p. 350).

Two words of caution are in order: the passage neither says (1) that God chose Jacob because He foreknew his faith (Chrysostom), nor (2) that God predestined Esau to eternal condemnation (Calvin). Primarily, Paul thinks here of the course of nations in redemptive history not the eternal destiny of individuals. It helps to remember that even when election focuses on the eternal basis of salvation it is never remote from living history. God's saving purpose appears in the events of history, and it moves through the contingencies of history.

2. *The freedom of election (9:14-21)*

If, as Paul has argued, God's electing purpose takes no account of human merit, then it could be challenged as being arbitrary and cruelly unjust. It is this objection of a supposed interlocutor that Paul frames ("What shall we say then?") in verse 14 and answers the question in verses 15-21. We have seen this procedure at a major step in the doctrinal argument (cf. 3:1-6); the question, "Is there unrighteousness with God?" is again repelled with horror in the characteristic rejoinder, "God forbid" (v. 14; cf. 3:4,6). [5]

In his answer Paul combats an idea that prevailed in rabbinic Judaism and thrives today in humanistic circles, namely, that God's favor is due those who are worthy. This assumption lies behind the charge of injustice; therefore, the apostle drives home the point that the only just mercy is free, sovereign mercy. "Justice presupposes rightful claims, and mercy can be operative only where no claim of justice exists" (Murray, II, 26). We are bidden then to heed His sovereign power not to frighten us into silence but to prepare our hearts for mercy. In the words of Luther, "This is hard to take for the proud who claim to know everything, but it is sweet and welcome to the meek and humble, for they despair of themselves and this is why the Lord accepts them" (p. 268). For Paul, God is still God; therefore, his understanding of God's sovereign being in terms of will (vv. 15-18) and power (vv. 19-21) is the basis of the entire reasoning.

---

[5] There are two misleading approaches to Paul's position. Some, for example, think the apostle does not defend the justice of God and rejects any question of theodicy (Nygren). Others, on the other hand, contend that Paul tries to present an answer to the charge of injustice and fails miserably (Denney, Dodd). Both approaches miss the point. To be sure, the biblical citations (vv. 15,17) and the parable of the clay (v. 20) appear to circumvent the issue by silencing the propriety of questioning God, but there is more here than meets the eye.

a. *God's sovereign will for Moses and Pharaoh (vv. 15-18).* The two quotations in verses 15 and 17 are a double rejection of the charge of injustice; they show us contrasting figures (Moses and Pharaoh), both of whom illustrate the freedom of God's activity. First, in Exodus 33:19 (v. 15), when Moses requests to see the divine glory after his intercession for the people, God "gives him to understand that nothing in him, notwithstanding all he has been able to do up till now in God's service, merited such a favor" (Godet, p. 352). If a man so deserving as Moses can lay no hold on the divine favor, how shall anyone else be entitled to it? The emphasis rests upon "whom" ("whomsoever," Sanday and Head- lam, p. 254), an indefinite pronoun which reserves the choice of those who receive mercy to God Himself.

The conclusion stated in verse 16 is dependent upon the idea of mercy in the previous verse. If God's dealings with man are to be governed by mercy, then they cannot be determined by man's will ("not of him that willeth") or by man's effort ("nor of him that runneth"). Elsewhere, Paul uses running as a metaphor for Christian striving (cf. 1 Cor. 9:24,26; Phil. 2:16; 3:12), but here it means man's achievement that merits salvation. The phrase "of God that [showeth] mercy" (v. 16c) should be translated "the merciful God" (cf. Barrett, p. 183) so that the source of mercy is properly emphasized. Mercy is never grounded in human aspirations; it all depends upon the merciful God.

Second, the quotation of Exodus 9:16 (v. 17) adds a new dimension of thought: God's sovereign will encompasses not only recipients of mercy but also objects of wrath. God who is free to bestow mercy is also free to kindle wrath, as the instance of Pharaoh reveals. Unwittingly, Pharaoh falls into the purpose of God; he has been "raised up" as an actor in the drama of history (cf. Hab. 1:6; Zech. 11:16) to carry out God's ends. Historically, the defiance of Pharaoh to God's will was the occasion of the Exodus, an act of deliverance in which God demonstrated His power and caused His name to be proclaimed throughout the world (cf. Exod. 15:13-16; Josh. 2:9-18; Ps. 105:26-38). In underscoring this twofold purpose in the hardening of Pharaoh, Paul intends us to see a sinister adversary in redemptive history whose obstinance serves God's merciful purpose. Thus, we are prepared for the startling turn of events announced in chapter 11. In the present time, Israel exists (like Pharaoh) for a twofold purpose: (1) to provide the occasion for a divine act of deliverance — righteousness by faith, and (2) to provide the occasion for publishing salvation to the entire world — precisely by rejecting the gospel (cf. 11:11,15,19,25; Barrett, p. 187).

The apparently harsh expression "whom he will he hardeneth" (v. 18) need not be softened. Paul well knew the Exodus account which says that "Pharaoh hardened his heart" (Exod. 8:15,32), but he does not labor here to prove human responsibility (as he does in 9:30-10:21), rather divine sovereignty. Much like the phrase "God gave them up" (cf. 1:24,26,28), hardening implies a refusal of grace so that "the exhibition of God's power upon Pharaoh appears only as the secondary purpose, consequent on his refusal to yield to God's direct will, 'Let my people go'" (Gifford, p. 171). However, Paul passes over this process to the end of the matter; by one and the same operation of His will, God has mercy upon one man and hardens another. "It was through God, in the last resort, that Moses and Pharaoh were what they were, signal instances of the Divine mercy and the Divine wrath" (Denney, p. 663). Paul never says the ways of eternal life and death are arbitrary with God; rather he pleads that in carrying out His saving purpose, God retains liberty of choice in its design.[6]

b. *God's creative power over mankind (vv. 19-21).* That we have followed Paul's thought is confirmed by the twofold objection in verse 19. We could expect, if everything depends upon God's sovereign will, the question to arise, What happens then to man's responsibility? Is it possible to say that man is to blame for anything when God's will stands concealed behind everything? (Nygren, p. 367). The verb "with-standeth" (v. 19) is an intensive perfect which emphasizes the present results of a settled condition; it has been rendered "can resist" (NEB), "can oppose" (Moffatt); but more likely, it means simply: "What man is there who is resisting God's will?" (Sanday and Headlam, p. 259; cf. "there is no resisting his will," Knox). The word "will" (cf. Acts 27:43; 1 Peter 4:3) is used of the deliberate purpose of God. Paul has shown the divine will to be irresistible; therefore, the objector spots a fault in the moral government of the universe. And he pleads, if God governs men under these conditions, how can they be held accountable?

Paul's answer turns to the Old Testament imagery of a potter, a favorite model for God as Creator, which is progressively expanded in the form of three rhetorical questions put to the objector (vv. 20,21). The rebuke sounded in the vocative "O man" (v. 20a, "a mere man," Weymouth) also contains a logical refutation. It reminds us that the relation of every man to God is that of created to Creator; man can never be anything other than God's creature, and his wisest course is not to

---

[6] Calvin is often assailed for proposing the doctrine of reprobation in this passage; i.e., the reprobate are predestined to perdition (p. 362). Not to be missed is his subsequent explanation: "Their perdition depends upon the predestination of God in such a way that the cause and occasion of it are found in themselves" (*Institutes*, III, 23,8). We may chide him for downplaying human responsibility, but it is unfair to caricature him because we overstate his case.

pass judgment upon his Creator. "The eloquence of the contrast between 'O man' and 'God' must be observed" (Murray, II,31). The mistake in this rejoinder is the old one that flourished in Eden (Gen. 3:5) — man's attempt to shed his creatureliness.

The potter image secures the point: God's sovereignty over His creatures derives from His inherent "power" (v. 21a, KJV; "light," ASV) as Creator (vv. 20b,21). The analogy is taken from prophetic descriptions of God's handling of Israel. The allusions are to Isaiah 29:16; 45:9; and Jeremiah 18:6, where God creates the destiny of Israel and the nations in accordance with His own will. Just as the prophets insist upon a sovereign design in history, even to the anointing of a Pharaoh-like servant, Cyrus (Isa. 45:1), so Paul urges that God has creative authority over mankind, in particular, disobedient Israel. If the "molded" can rail against the "molder" (v. 20b; cf. NASB), then God must relinquish His right as Creator, which would be as absurd as saying the potter must answer to the clay (v. 21).

The phrase "same lump" may imply man's common predicament in sin ("mass of perdition," Augustine, Calvin, and Luther), but more clearly shows the creator "making out of a mass of shapeless material one to which he gives a character and form adapted for different uses, some honourable, some dishonourable" (Sanday and Headlam, p. 260). Vessels of "honour" and "dishonour" ("noble . . . menial," Moffatt) reflect the different roles played by individuals (Moses and Pharaoh, vv. 15-17) and nations (Jews and Gentiles, vv. 22-24) in God's plan (cf. 2 Tim. 2:20). We should be wary of running ahead of Paul; he does not say the ignoble vessel is created for perdition; rather it remains useful, like Pharaoh and unbelieving Israel (cf. Bruce, p. 195). To this point, the apostle contends only for the Creator's right to shape "vessels" to His own ends; we have yet to see what those ends are.

Many interpreters have argued that Paul never answers the objection in verse 19 but crushes it. For example, Dodd protests that Paul "is embarassed by the position he has taken up," pushing "unethical determinism to its logical extreme." "Man is not a pot . . . ; he will not be bludgeoned into silence. It is the weakest point in the whole epistle" (pp. 158,159). It would indeed be surprising if such a flimsy conclusion should be the last word of Paul's logic (cf. Godet, p. 357)! All the outcry has obscured these vital points: (1) the main comparison is between the potter as designer and God as Creator, not between the pot and man; (2) the text brings a man to "salutary despair" (Luther) for he learns that nothing can raise him from the shapeless mass of humanity save the Creator's hand; (3) the connection to verses 22-24 shows that the potter's hand is not capricious; the creative power of God is being used for a beneficent purpose which calls mankind to accountability.

3. *The goal of election (9:22-29)*

The desired goal of God's ways with men, which Paul has suspended from view, is now unveiled. It is not morally perverse and arbitrary, but full of mercy — in Denney's words, "an exercise of will of such character that man can have nothing to urge against it" (p. 664). If the absolute right of the Creator has been exercised in abundant mercy to Jew and Gentile, how can anyone challenge the faithfulness of God? The argument here builds closely on what has gone before in redemptive history and brings us to the situation in Paul's day. The passage has two main ideas: the goal of the divine purpose is realized in God's longsuffering (vv. 22-24) and is confirmed in the prophetic promises (vv. 25-29).

a. *Realized in the longsuffering of God (vv. 22-24).* In verses 22-24, Paul finally silences the objection to divine sovereignty raised in verse 19 by use of a long rhetorical question (cf. KJV, ASV, RSV). [7]

The key word is "longsuffering," a word that refers to God's forbearance in granting repentance to men under wrath (cf. 2:4). Instead of destroying the "vessels of wrath," God has "endured with much longsuffering" (v. 22b; "tolerated very patiently," NEB) for a twofold purpose: (1) to demonstrate His wrath and power (v. 22a) and (2) to pour out the riches of His glory (v. 23).

This understanding of the text translates the participle "willing" (v. 22a) in the causal sense of "desiring" (RSV, NEB) or "choosing" (NIV), meaning that God forbears "because He wishes" to show wrath and power (cf. Gifford, Barrett). The alternative rendering is a concessive one [8] ("although God wishes" [cf. Weymouth, Moffatt, Sanday and Headlam]), which argues that longsuffering restrains wrath, giving opportunity for repentance. On this view a paraphrase of the verses would read: "Although God wishes to show wrath, he has delayed it through longsuffering in order to show mercy." This reading is attractive, but two considerations weigh against it: (1) God's longsuffering with Pharaoh is an exact parallel; its motive is the demonstration of God's wrath and power; (2) wrath and power are now present in the world (1:18; 3:25,26); therefore, to those who despise His goodness, God's longsuffering results in hardness, an exhibition of wrath (cf. 2:4,5). In keeping with the overall argument, Paul ties together wrath and mercy

---

[7] The sentence is an "if" clause with the conclusion missing, a construction that is fairly common. The line of thought is as follows: "If God's ultimate purpose is to show mercy (vv. 22-24), how can you question any longer (unexpressed)?"

[8] The Greek participle is capable of either a causal or concessive sense; the primary clue comes from context.

in a remarkable way. Hardened Israel, under deserved wrath for disobedience, is the instrument of God's mercy to the Gentiles (11:12-15, 28-32). That goal is already marked in God's purpose: His longsuffering visits wrath upon unbelieving Israel (cf. 1 Thess. 2:16) even in order to bestow riches of mercy upon the Gentiles.

Answering to this reciprocal function of wrath and mercy are two groups of people, "vessels of wrath" (v. 22b; "objects of retribution," (NEB) and "vessels of mercy" (v. 23; "objects of mercy," NEB), respectively. The word "vessel" was probably prompted by verse 21, but these particular vessels are worlds apart in nature and destiny. First, Paul carefully avoids saying how the vessels of wrath come to be what they are, but he does not hesitate to make God responsible for the destiny of the vessels of mercy. The word "fitted" (v. 22b) literally means "perfected, made ripe" (cf. Luke 6:40; 1 Cor. 1:10) and describes the fitness of the lost for eternal destruction without defining the cause. However, the saved are "prepared beforehand for glory" (v. 23b, TCNT; cf. 8:29) by God Himself. This distinction is consistent with the biblical principle that man is saved by grace and condemned by sin. "Men fit themselves for hell; but it is God that fits men for heaven" (Griffith Thomas, II, 148).

Second, the preparation of the vessels of mercy, eternally grounded in the divine purpose, is manifested in the calling of Jews and Gentiles. The words "even us" (v. 24) stand in apposition to "vessels of mercy" (v. 23), making the situation in Paul's day (i.e., a believing remnant of Jews and saved Gentiles) the historical proof of God's faithfulness. Divine longsuffering over unbelieving Israel has made it possible for both Jews and Gentiles to be called to Christ in gospel preaching.

b. *Confirmed in the promises of the prophets (vv. 25-29).* There can be no sentiment against the calling of the Gentiles and the rejection of the majority of Israel because the matter is confirmed by Scripture. The redemptive goal, seen in the dual operation of wrath and mercy in Israel, contemplated two results, as shown in the Old Testament prophets: (1) divine mercy has been extended to the Gentiles, a people "not beloved" (vv. 25,26; cf. Hos. 2:23; 1:10) and (2) because divine mercy preserved a "seed" (v. 29; cf. 9:8), a remnant of Israel has been saved (vv. 27-29; cf. Isa. 10:22,23; 1:9).

Paul cites Hosea to prove that God promised to call the Gentiles; however, the passage originally applies to the restoration of Israel. He probably understood the promise of Israel's restoration, "either by parity of reason or as a typical prophecy" (Gifford, p. 175), to include the calling of the Gentiles. In reversing His sentence upon Israel, God would embrace in mercy all who were not His people. The phrase "in the place where" is to be taken in a geographical not a logical sense; it has been interpreted as (1) Palestine, where the Gentiles will gather (Munck), and (2) the Dispersion, where God acclaims those in exile who bear the reproach of not being God's people (Sanday and Headlam). The latter view well accords with the idea that wherever they come to faith, there Gentiles, who in time past were not God's people, will be called sons of the living God (cf. 1 Peter 1:1; 2:10).

The proof from Isaiah shows that only a "remnant" (v. 27) of the Jews continues to inherit God's promise and carries out the divine purpose. The remnant doctrine (cf. "seed," v. 29; 9:8) forms a link between what God did among the patriarchs (9:6-13) and what happened to Israel in Paul's time. Additionally, it shows a progressive narrowing in the scope of election from the nation, to a remnant, and finally to Christ, the Elect One (9:30-33). Furthermore, the remnant is an evidence of God's mercy at work and a pledge that Israel as a whole has not been rejected (cf. 11:1,5). The remnant is the climax and conclusion of the exposition thus far. We see that the divine purpose finally focuses on the chosen Seed; election leads to Christ. Because of divine faithfulness, there is righteousness in Him for all who believe.

C. A Righteousness of God for All Who Believe in Christ (9:30-10:21)

The midpoint of Paul's argument, 9:30-10:21, has its background in the crucifixion of Jesus by the Jews and their subsequent rejection of the gospel. To this point, Paul has said that God saved a remnant of Israel and called the Gentiles through His electing purpose; now this circumstance is explained in terms of human responsibility. The way of righteousness by faith in Christ has been preached; the results are that Israel has refused, and Gentiles have accepted. This new standing in Christ, accessible to all — Jew and Gentile alike — makes the plight of the Jews inexcusable. In Paul's mind, divine sovereignty and human responsibility dwell together, each complementing the other.

In his book, *Evangelism and the Sovereignty of God*, J. I. Packer writes: "God's sovereignty and man's responsibility are taught us side by side in the same Bible; sometimes, indeed in the same text [e.g., Luke 22:22]. Both are thus guaranteed to us by the same divine authority; both, therefore, are true. It follows that they must be held together, and not played off against each other. Man is a responsible moral agent, though he is also divinely controlled; man is divinely controlled, though he is also a responsible moral agent" (pp. 22,23). Such an antinomy is before us here: from the divine viewpoint, Israel's defection falls within the will of God (9:6-29); from the human viewpoint, Israel's failure is the result of disobedience (9:30-10:21).

Human responsibility unfolds when we consider the relationship of man to Christ, which is exactly the procedure Paul follows. The theme of chapter 10 is, therefore, Christological, or in concrete terms, how God has been faithful in Christ to provide righteousness to all who believe, without distinction (cf. 10:13; 1:16).[9] Paul undoubtedly says that the Jews are guilty, as noted in the descriptions of their disobedience (cf. 10:3,16,21); however, this serves to show that in becoming guilty toward God, Israel magnifies divine faithfulness in Christ.

This middle point in the argument is the solution to chapters 9-11: chapter 10 looks back to chapter 9, explaining that man's election is realized in the hearing of the gospel, and looks forward to chapter 11, preparing the dramatic end of redemptive history through preaching to the nations. The proclamation of Christ to all is the center of God's near and far purpose for mankind. To put it another way, the corollary of election and eschatology is missionary preaching. Tracing the emphasis to Christ, the text can be divided as follows: (1) the trying cross of Christ (9:30-33), (2) the believer's righteousness in Christ (10:1-13), and (3) the worldwide proclamation of Christ (10:14-21).

1. *The trying cross of Christ (9:30-33)*

Verses 30-33 summarize the argument of 9:6-29 and contain the theme of 10:1-21. In characteristic fashion, Paul concludes the foregoing discussion, "To what conclusion does this bring us?" (v. 30a, Weymouth), with a question and offers an immediate answer. First, Gentiles who never concerned themselves with being righteous before God, have laid hold of righteousness based on faith (v. 30b). (We are to understand "righteousness which is of faith" as righteousness that is "conditioned on faith" [Williams] in contrast to righteousness based on works [cf. v. 32].) Second, Israel, to the contrary, actively pursued the principle of righteousness but failed to attain a rule of life that would yield righteousness (v. 31). This is the sum of the matter as it stands.

Now, Paul confronts the objection, "Wherefore?" (v. 32a); that is, why did Israel fail to reach the aim of righteousness? The venture failed because Israel sought righteousness by an impossible means: "as if it were based on works" (v. 32b, RSV). The subjective phrasing is intentional. Paul will not admit the possibility of securing righteousness by works, so he says the starting point itself is unreal. Denney remarks, "It is an idea of your own, not a truth on which life can be carried out . . .; such an idea, however, rooted in the mind, may effectually pervert and wreck the soul, by making the Divine way of attaining righteousness and life offensive to it; and this is what happened to the Jews" (p. 668).

----

[9] The majority of commentators view the passage as a proof of the guilt of the Jews, but this is too one-sided. To insist upon a primary theme of guilt minimizes the emphasis upon righteousness by faith and obscures the primary link between election and Christ.

The phrase "stumbled at the stone of stumbling" (v. 32b) marks the insurmountable hurdle in Israel's blind run after works. "The stone at which the Jewish nation has stumbled, which has been to them a cause of offence, is the Christ, who has come in a way which, owing to their want of faith, has prevented them from recognizing or accepting Him" (Sanday and Headlam, p. 280). Paul here thinks of the scandal of the cross, "a stumblingblock" (cf. 1 Cor. 1:23), which summoned the Jews from the pretension of self-righteousness to the merit of Christ's shed blood. The cross is God's tribunal, trying the souls of men, providing refuge and redemption for the believer, but becoming a holocaust, plying fierce judgment upon the guilty who will not kneel before it. It is this twofold effect of Christ's coming that Paul intends to portray in the stone of stumbling.

To show that Christ is the "rock of faith" for believers and the "stone of stumbling" for Israel, Paul ties together Isaiah 28:16 (v. 33a,c), which tells how the Lord placed in Zion a precious cornerstone as the ground of faith and assurance, and Isaiah 8:14 (v. 33b), which speaks of a stone that would cause Israel to stumble. As in the earliest testimonies of Christian preaching (cf. Matt. 21:42; Mark 12:10; Luke 20:17; Acts 4:11; 1 Peter 2:6,8), where the stone passages are applied to Christ, these two sayings become for Paul "a testimony as to the double result of Christ's coming into the world, the fall of some and the rising of others (cf. Luke 2:34). They are at the same time a testimony against righteousness by the law and for the righteousness of faith" (Nygren, pp. 377,378).

This paradoxical effect signified in stumbling on the one hand and believing on the other is decisively important to Paul's argument. Christ is the elect stone, "a chief corner stone, elect, precious" (1 Peter 2:6), placed in Israel (cf. "I lay in Zion," v. 33a) by the will of God; consequently, man's election is grounded in the election of Christ (Eph. 1:4). The cross and its power to acquit and condemn is eternally grounded in the electing purpose of God: "this Jesus, delivered up according to the definite plan and foreknowledge of God, you crucified and killed by the hands of lawless men" (Acts 2:23, RSV). Although we might give a psychological account of Israel's blunder, as Barrett believes, "this would only describe the mechanism used by God, who provided the stone for Israel to trip over. . . . election and rejection are both in him, and it is impossible for men to glimpse God's eternal purposes apart from him" (p. 194). Election happens in the preaching of the cross (cf. 1 Thess. 1:4-10), which explains how the classical defense of divine sovereignty (9:6-29) can be followed by the greatest missionary passage in the letters of Paul (10:1-21). The highest mandate to preach the gospel is the knowledge that, in doing so, God is faithfully carrying out His electing purpose in Christ. The development in 10:1-21 traces the twofold effect of the elect stone: (1) deliverance — Jew and Gentile without distinction have righteousness by faith in Christ (10:1-13); (2) downfall — the Jews have stumbled at Christ in unbelief (10:14-21).

2. *The believer's righteousness in Christ (10:1-13)*

This section, which is mainly an exposition of the "righteousness of God" (v. 3), describes the never-to-be-embarrassed faith (9:33b; 10:11) that one can put in Christ. It takes up the "rock of faith" theme from the stone-conflation (9:33) and expands it in three crucial statements about the believer's righteousness in Christ: (1) it is sufficient to fulfill the law's demand (vv. 1-4); (2) it is immediate through the proclaimed word (vv. 5-10); and (3) it is accessible to everyone who calls (vv. 11-13).

a. *It is sufficient to fulfill the law's demand (vv. 1-4).* Verse 1 expresses Paul's prayer for Israel to be saved, renewing the intercession begun in 9:1-3. Nothing that Paul has said about sovereign election alters his active concern for the future conversion of Israel. The intense emotion with which he prays ("my heart's desire" [v. 1], the "good pleasure" which perfectly satisfies Paul's heart [cf. Eph. 1:5,9]) is hardly the mood of a pessimistic fatalist. In praying for the conversion of Israel to Christ (cf. 11:25,26), Paul recalls the misguided strivings of his countrymen that make their lostness so much more pitiable. The empathy of Paul's plea is heightened by four affections in Israel that have turned sour under the heavy hand of the law. These four cardinal errors of the Jews are:

Religious pride (v. 2a). The phrase "zeal for God" ("enthusiasm for God," Weymouth; "zealous for the honour of God," TCNT) refers to a passionate fidelity to God's honor based on performance of religious duty. It was synonymous in Judaism with the pride — and Paul understood from experience the Jewish pride — which resisted the gospel of Christ (cf. Gal. 1:14; Phil. 3:6; Acts 9:1,2; 21:20; 22:3).

Spiritual blindness (v. 2b,3a). The ardent devotion of the Jews is misguided — "an ill-informed zeal" (NEB). It amounts to a blind ignorance of what true righteousness is. Apparently, Paul thinks of the time of Jesus' ministry and the cross (cf. 1 Cor. 2:8) because he uses the word "ignorance" in verse 3a ("they did not recognize," Knox), not "misunderstanding," but later says that the Jews who hear the gospel cannot claim ignorance (v. 19).

Self-righteousness (v. 3b). The words "their own" denote origin, a righteousness that men evolve out of themselves (cf. Phil. 3:9). Denney says, " 'Their own' is the key to the situation. Their idea was that they could be good men without becoming God's debtors, or owing anything at all to Him" (p. 669).

Unyielding stubbornness (v. 4a). The momentum of self-will carries Israel to the point of refusal to acknowledge God as the source of righteousness. The verb ("subject themselves") is reflexive middle, alluding to Israel's stubbornness.

All this striving under law never arrives at its appointed goal of providing righteousness, and that for a reason: It collides with Christ who is the only One who can bring legal religion to an end (v. 4). Christ has introduced a new order of relations between God and man that stands in antithesis to all that Jewish legalism cherished. In what sense, we must now ask, is Christ the end of the law? The word "end" (v. 4) can be taken in the sense of (1) goal, fulfillment ("completion of the Law," *Modern Language Bible*; "consummation of Law," Weymouth) or (2) termination, abrogation ("termination of law," Goodspeed; cf. TCNT, NEB). The church fathers and reformers held the former view, making Christ the perfect fulfillment of the law (cf. Calvin, p. 221); but modern commentators have made an emphatic break between faith and law. The aeon of law has been eclipsed by the advent of righteousness in Christ; therefore, Christ is the cessation of law. Gifford remarks, "Christ is the end of the law as death is the end of life" (p. 183); Denney follows, "Paul is insisting, not on the connection, but on the incompatibility, of law and faith" (p. 669; cf. Godet, Sanday and Headlam, Nygren, and Murray).

The appended phrase "to every one that believeth" (v. 4b) indicates that these two views of "end of the law" are not mutually exclusive. The Old Testament law itself is not abolished, but the principle of law as a way of righteousness has come to an end, superseded by the way of faith. This termination was with a view to righteousness ("unto"); thus, for the believer, Christ is the perfect fulfillment of all that the law requires. On the one hand, Christ is the goal at which the law aimed in that He is the perfect embodiment of righteousness, and that demand is thus fulfilled for the believer. On the other hand, Christ is the cessation of law in that He replaces the old order of legal religion with the new order of the indwelling Spirit (cf. Bruce, Barrett). Paul's point is the sufficiency of faith to appropriate the righteousness of God because Christ fulfills the law's demand and thereby abrogates its claim.

b. *It is immediate through the proclaimed word (vv. 5-10).* Since it is based on performance, "law-righteousness" (v. 5a, Moffatt) requires extensive knowledge and intensive preparation. It is religion of the letter (cf. 7:6) and, being so complicated, is not easy to come by. In fact, the real dilemma, as Paul sees it, is that no one can succeed in law-righteousness because it is conditioned upon obedience: "The man who perfectly obeys the Law shall find life in it" (v. 5b, Phillips; cf. Gal. 3:12; Lev. 18:5). In contrast, "faith-righteousness" (v. 6a, Moffatt) is an immediate possibility because it is a divine possibility. Human inability, which is the shortcoming of law-righteousness, is overcome by divine ability in faith-righteousness.

The *provision* of faith-righteousness is the redemptive work of Christ (vv. 6-8). Paul finds this divine activity prefigured in the words of Deuteronomy 30:11-14, which enjoins obedience to the divine commandment that is neither hidden, nor far off, neither in heaven, nor in the sea, but near — in the mouth and heart. The immediacy of the divine commandment to the people suggests a faith analogy to Paul who puts "his own thoughts — his inspired conviction and experience of the Gospel — into a free reproduction of these ancient inspired words" (Denney, p. 670). Just as God made faith possible by drawing near to Israel in the days of Moses, so He draws near today in the work of Christ, making faith-righteousness possible.

Paul provides a brief, running commentary on Deuteronomy 30:11-14, defining each point with an explanatory "that is" (lit., "interpreted this means") and applying each to the gospel of Christ (v. 6c,7b,8c). First, Christ has come near in His incarnation; He is Immanuel, "God with us" (Matt. 1:23). No one need scale heaven "to bring Christ down from above" (v. 6c), that is, precipitate the Incarnation; it has already happened. Second, Christ has come near in His resurrection; He is risen from the dead (v. 7b). The word "deep" is the "abyss" (NASB, NEB, RSV), used elsewhere in the New Testament for the abode of demons (Luke 8:31) and as a term for a place of torment (Rev. 9:1). It suitably portrays the underworld that Christ has vanquished (cf. 1 Peter 3:19; Eph. 4:9). Third, Christ has come near in His exaltation; He is the ascended Lord who is proclaimed in the gospel message (cf. Phil. 2:10,11). The "word of faith" (v. 8c) is the "message about faith that we preach" (Goodspeed), meaning the gospel preached by Paul (cf. Eph. 6:17; Heb. 6:5; 1 Peter 1:25).

The *appropriation* of faith-righteousness is in believing and confessing the gospel (vv. 9,10). Verse 9 gives the two articles comprising the "word of faith," namely, confession of Jesus as Lord and belief in His resurrection. The order of confessing before believing corresponds simply to the order of mouth and heart in verse 8b; it follows that we should attach no priority to confession because the order is reversed in verse 10. Barrett says, "No distinction is to be drawn between the confession and the faith; the confession is believed and the faith confessed" (p. 200). Obviously, confession with the lips that leads to salvation must be preceded by faith that appropriates righteousness (v. 10); thus, confession with the lips confirms and verifies the faith of the heart (cf. Murray, II, 57).

Although the confession "Jesus is Lord" could have been made before questioning magistrates (cf. Luke 21:12-15; 1 Peter 3:13-16) or in a baptismal setting (cf. Acts 8:16; 1 Peter 3:21), the context here relates it to the apostolic gospel, involving obedience to its claims. Such an acclamation of Jesus' lordship, which belongs to Him in virtue of His exaltation (cf. Eph. 1:20-23; Phil. 2:9-11), can only be made with the help of the Holy Spirit (1 Cor. 12:3). Furthermore, confession, like faith, represents a personal relationship to Christ rather than an external act or assent to a defined truth (cf. Nygren, pp. 382,383). Because the name of Jesus is exalted above every name, a man who calls upon His name invokes Him as Lord. To call upon the name is to confess the faith; therefore, we may look to praying in the name of Christ for the meaning that Paul attaches to confession (cf. v. 13).

c. *It is available to everyone who calls (vv. 11-13)*. The addition of "whosoever" (v. 11) to previously quoted Isaiah 28:16 marks an important advance in the exposition (cf. 9:33). Faith-righteousness is not only "near" (v. 8b), it is available to "all" (v. 12) so as to make it universal in scope. The keynote is universality, marked by the fourfold repetition of the word translated "whosoever" in verses 11, 13 and "all" in verse 12 (cf. "everyone," NEB). This links the heart of chapters 9-11 with the thematic promise of the whole epistle: the gospel is for the Jew first and also the Greek (cf. 1:16). Looking back over the argument, we can see that Paul moves in a calculated sequence. The universal character of the gospel is a blessing that obtains from the faith-way of righteousness, which is, in turn, predicated upon a longstanding purpose in election; in short, the universality of salvation demonstrates the faithfulness of God.

The universality of salvation means that there is one gospel made available for all people regardless of religious or national background. This representative idea is qualified by Paul in three points. First, there is *one well-founded faith* for everyone (v. 11). The phrase "shall not be put to shame" means "will not be disappointed" (NASB); those who put their trust in Christ need not fear that their faith in Him will prove to be ill-founded.

Second, there is *one ever-bountiful Lord* for everyone (v. 12). In 3:29,30, the one God of both Jews and Gentiles is the source of justification; here Paul assigns that role to the lordship of Christ, "the same Lord is Lord of all" (NEB, RSV). There is no distinction between Jew and Gentile in sin (cf. 3:22), hence no distinction in salvation; there is an equal welcome for both. The idea of God's wealth in Christ is a favorite one of Paul's (cf. 1 Cor. 1:5; Eph. 3:8; Phil. 4:19; Col. 1:27; 3:16). Here the present participle "abounding in riches" reflects the faithfulness and readiness of Christ to pour out the blessings that have been prepared in the divine purpose (cf. 9:23; 11:12,33).

Third, there is *one never-failing prayer* for everyone (v. 13; cf. Joel 2:32). "To call upon the name of the Lord" is a technical phrase in the Old Testament for worship and confession (cf. Sanday and Headlam, p. 291); the New Testament formula is calling upon the name of the Lord Jesus (cf. Acts 9:14; 22:16; 1 Cor. 1:2; 2 Tim. 2:22). In verse 14, calling upon Christ is the expression of faith; when compared to verses 9,10, it stands in the place of confession. To confess Jesus as Lord is to call upon His exalted name for salvation.

3. *The worldwide proclamation of Christ (10:14-21)*

The paragraph division at verse 14 is based on the inferential "how then," the appearance of a string of Old Testament quotations, and the renewed discussion of Israel's stumbling. The marked change in tone and style (rhetorical questions with scriptural answers) presents a somewhat obscure structure that is difficult to outline; however, the direction of thought is clear. Having demonstrated that righteousness is available to anyone who calls on the name of Christ, Paul proceeds to show that the universal character of salvation necessitates the publishing of the gospel on a similar scale. In order to call upon the name of Christ, it is necessary to hear the gospel message. If this privilege of hearing has not occurred, then the premise of a gospel for everyone falls apart, and with it, divine faithfulness.[10] In developing the text along these lines we can distinguish (1) the necessity of preaching (vv. 14,15), (2) the persuasion of hearing (vv. 16,17), and (3) the witness of disobedience (vv. 18-21).

a. *The necessity of preaching (vv. 14,15).* Preaching is necessary, not to make the Jew guilty, but to carry out God's electing purpose. Verses 14,15 make up a logical chain[11] of five links (calling, believing, hearing, preaching, and sending) that leads up to the last, the divine commission of preaching. The word "sent" (v. 15a) is a cognate verb of the noun "apostle." As Bruce notes, the "preacher is an 'apostle' in the primary sense of the word; he is a herald or ambassador conveying a message from someone who has authorized him to deliver it" (p. 205).

---

[10] Most interpreters view the passage as an indictment of the Jews. Sanday and Headlam, for example, believe "the object of the section must be to show the reason (although Gentiles have been accepted) the Jews have been rejected" (p. 301). Similarly, Godet: "the ignorance of Israel the cause of their rejection" (p. 385); Barrett: "Israel's unbelief inexcusable" (p. 203). However, three points can be brought against this interpretation: (1) Although they are embraced in the indefinite subjects of verses 14-18, the Jews are not explicitly mentioned until verse 19 (cf. Denney, pp. 672,673). (2) The central idea is the gospel message — its proclamation, hearing, and dissemination (v. 17). (3) The Jews stand guilty because of a worldwide proclamation; therefore, their disobedience mirrors the unwearied faithfulness of God.

[11] Such chain syllogisms or sorites, where the logical predicate of one link becomes the logical subject of the next, indicate a self-evident conclusion (cf. 5:3b-5; 8:29).

Preaching, therefore, is a divinely commissioned task, and it happens because God sends out heralds. "St. Paul argues back from cause to effect, through the series of Prayer, Faith, Hearing, Preaching, Sending; thus the last link in his argument must be the first in the realisation from which the rest follow" (Gifford, p. 187). By quoting Isaiah 52:7, Paul most likely alludes to the welcome "coming of those who bring good news" (v. 15b, Goodspeed), having been sent by the Lord to preach (cf. Barrett, Sanday and Headlam).

We must not overlook Paul's point: "For as the cause of faith among them is the preaching of the gospel, so the cause of preaching is the mission of God, by which it had pleased him in this manner to provide for their salvation" (Calvin, p. 397). Preaching is the pledge and proof of God's saving purpose. In the words of Packer, "the belief that God is sovereign in grace does not affect the *necessity* of evangelism. Whatever we may believe about election, the fact remains that evangelism is necessary, because no man can be saved without the gospel" (p. 97).

b. *The persuasion of hearing (vv. 16,17).* The links of hearing, preaching, and sending hold firm; Paul has proved their strength. But the break comes in the link of faith: Israel (and perhaps others are intended) has heard but not heeded. The quotation of Isaiah 53:1, "Lord, who hath believed our report?" (v. 16b), is marshaled to show that the problem of unbelief is an old one. Verse 17 appears to be parenthetical (Phillips marks it by parentheses), but it is connected to verse 16 by an inferential particle "so" (v. 17a). It takes up another chain of logic that we can paraphrase as follows: "Unbelief (v. 16) implies not hearing, which in turn means no word from God (v. 17), but that is certainly not the case (vv. 18-21)." Israel's unbelief is inexplicable because hearing the word should have aroused faith.

On the positive side, Paul here teaches the potency of the "word of Christ" (v. 17)[12] or the "message about Christ" (cf. NEB, Goodspeed, Sanday and Headlam). Faith arises from the report that comes to the ears of the listener, and this message consists of the word of Christ. There is a close connection here between the proclaimed word and the presence of Christ. Verse 14b is properly translated in the NASB: "And how shall they believe in Him whom [not 'in whom,' RSV] they have not heard?" It strictly means that, when the gospel is proclaimed, Christ Himself is heard through the message (cf. Eph. 2:17; 4:21). This interpretation is altogether suitable in verse 17: the "word" in the gospel is the voice of the ascended Lord, persuading the hearer, arousing faith.

---

[12] The reading "word of God" (KJV) is not in the best Greek manuscripts, and the preferred "word of Christ" is adopted in all modern translations.

c. *The witness of disobedience (vv. 18-21).* This section provides three witnesses against Israel which verify that the "word of Christ" has been heard. The first witness is the voice of the heavens (cf. Ps. 19:4) telling the glory of God "into all the earth . . . unto the ends of the world" (v. 18). How the witness of God in creation demonstrates that Israel has heard the gospel is a question of longstanding debate. The use of Psalm 19:4 has been understood as (1) a description of the universal character of the gospel (Sanday and Headlam, p. 299), (2) an appeal to natural revelation (Murray, II,61), (3) a symbol for the spread of the gospel in the civilized world (Gifford, p. 189), and (4) a literal reference to worldwide preaching (Godet, p. 388). To add another opinion, it may be the testimony of the heavenly assembly and the inhabitants of the earth who have heard the word of the ascended Lord (cf. Isa. 1:2; Ps. 50:4; Col. 1:23; Acts 2:5; Eph. 3:10).

The second witness is the saving faith of Gentiles (vv. 19,20), who confirm that Israel not only heard but also understood the word. Because the Gentiles were a "foolish nation" (Deut. 32:21), one that never sought God (Isa. 65:1), their reception of the gospel message, where the conditions seem so much against it, argues that surely Israel understood (cf. Gifford, Denney). Those who are "no people" (v. 19b) become the instrument of God's purpose to stir Israel to jealousy; this introduces the decisive missionary strategy elaborated under the concept of gospel jealousy in 11:11-14.

The final witness is the faithfulness of God (v. 21), "a picture of the 'everlasting arms' spread open in unwearied love" (Gifford, p. 190) to Israel, "an unruly and recalcitrant people" (NEB; cf. Isa. 65:2). The paradox of Gentile obedience, God being found by those who did not seek Him, is matched by the paradox of Jewish disobedience, God's untiring love being rejected by those whom He constantly sought. The confession of the Gentile stands in contrast to the gainsaying of the Jew, but both are aspects of God's eternal purpose (cf. 11:30,31). The protest that Israel has been mistreated (9:30,31) is silenced by the pleading of divine mercy through the gospel invitation. The guilt of Israel is sealed by its defiance of God's love.

D. The Mystery of Israel's Future Restoration (11:1-32)

The gravity of Israel's stumbling at Christ might hasten the presumption that the nation was forever excluded from the sphere of divine mercy. To be sure, the persistent refusal of divine love signified that a judicial hardening had come upon Israel (10:21), but the gospel call was itself proof that God had not abandoned the effort to save Israel. In asserting that God has not rejected Israel, Paul does not withdraw the premises of election and gospel we have seen in chapters 9 and 10. On the contrary, the theme of chapter 11, the unfolding of mercy in re-demptive history, brings the two ideas together; the future of the Jews with God is grounded in a continuing election and is certified in the preaching of the gospel.

The election theme is brought into play in Paul's reference to the remnant of Jews (cf. 9:27-29) who have believed in Christ (11:5). The gospel theme is found in the Gentile reception of salvation which becomes the means of recovery for hardened Israel (11:14). Even the hope for the salvation of "all Israel" (11:26) is conditioned upon saving faith in Christ (cf. 11:23). The vision before us does not mean that warm-hearted patriotism or universal optimism has the last word on the fate of Israel. Much more, the final word belongs to "mercy"; it is the faithfulness of God to His purpose in Christ that assures a way of salvation for the Jews. Paul presents three concepts that govern his expectation of mercy for Israel: (1) the pledge of mercy in the remnant (vv. 1-10), (2) the possibility of mercy through the gospel (vv. 11-24), and (3) the prophecy of mercy upon all (vv. 25-32).

1. The pledge of mercy in the remnant (vv. 1-10)

The words "I say then" (v. 1a) give the result of the questioning in 10:14-21 and introduce the main thought of this section. The language of the question, "Has God rejected his people?" (NEB), which expects a negative answer, recalls the promise made to Israel in the farewell speech by Samuel. "For the LORD will not cast away his people, for his great name's sake, because it has pleased the LORD to make you a people for himself" (1 Sam. 12:22, RSV). The supposition of God forsaking Israel is imponderable because such an act would negate God's ancient choice. The direct denial in verse 2 adds the clause "which he foreknew" ("whom he chose from the first," TCNT), which means "Israel stood before God's eyes from eternity as His people, and in the immutable-ness of the sovereign love with which He made it His lies the impossibil-ity of its rejection" (Denney, p. 676; cf. 8:29).

a. *The solitary of example of Paul (v. 1b).* The emphatic flourish with which Paul recited his Jewish pedigree can be interpreted in two ways. It might be calculated to disarm criticism for raising the blas-phemous notion that God would cast away His people. If so, the depre-cation "God forbid" finds its motive in Paul's heritage: "No true Israelite could bear the thought that God had cast away His people" (Gifford, p. 191; cf. Denney, Sanday and Headlam).

However, it is likely that Paul regarded himself as an example of the Jewish Christian remnant; therefore, since he was both an Israelite and a believer, his salvation was personal proof that God had not cast away the entire nation (cf. Barrett, Munck). In this view, the Jewish ancestry functions to qualify Paul as a representative of the chosen people.

b. *The elect remnant of Jewish Christians (vv. 2-6)*. The proof now expands from the example of Paul to include a remnant within Israel that obeyed the gospel. This situation parallels the Old Testament account of Elijah: (1) Like Paul, he was a solitary figure pleading against apostate Israel (1 Kings 19:10,14). (2) In Elijah's day, there was a faithful minority of seven thousand who refused to worship Baal (1 Kings 19:18); so in Paul's day, only a faithful remnant adhered to Christ. Bruce notes, "As in Old Testament times, so in apostolic times God's purpose in choosing His people was safeguarded by His reservation of a faithful remnant" (p. 211).

The counterpart of the seven thousand is the "remnant — a selection by grace" (v. 5b, Weymouth); it is chosen by an act of grace, not dependent upon works. The parenthetical explanation introduced in verse 6 connects the present remnant with the electing purpose (cf. 9:11) which guided God's dealings with Israel from the beginning. The principle "of works" (v. 6, "basis of works," NASB) nullifies the meaning of "grace" because it establishes a human claim upon God. It reminds us that if the remnant was saved by grace, then the remainder of Israel must also see its election come to pass under grace. The principle of election by grace will not allow the Jew to bind God to himself by human performance or human ancestry. Grace rules over the future of Israel in chapter 11 as surely as it does over the past history of Israel in chapter 9.

The remnant recalls 9:27-29 where the emphasis is *only* a remnant, but the concept is put forward here as *already* a remnant. The remnant is a testimony that God's grace toward Israel has not ceased. Because the remnant has a redemptive role, it is the divine pledge of coming salvation. These Jewish Christians will come to "fullness" (cf. 11:12); therefore, the remnant is a provisional and productive number, not an unchangeable minority.

c. *The hardened majority of Israel (vv. 7-10)* The shift of emphasis implied by "what then?" (v. 7a) leads us to the consequences of verses 2-6 in respect to the unsaved portion of Israel. Paul reiterates that the saved "election" (v. 7b, "this chosen remnant," Knox), a synonym for remnant, has obtained the righteousness of God which the most of Israel still seeks apart from Christ. These verses measure the condition of unsaved Israel from the viewpoint of unbelief rather than exclusion from the divine election. In rejecting Christ, the majority of Israel, designated by "the rest" (v. 7c), has not been cast away, but has been hardened in disobedience.

The passive verb "were hardened" (v. 7c; "have become callous," Weymouth) admits human responsibility into the process. Barrett states that "it is impossible here to distinguish between 'hardened because disobedient' and 'disobedient because hardened' " (p. 210); however, a clearer distinction is likely. Hardening is the natural and necessary effect of mercy that is rejected, the same effect we saw in the similar word for hardening in 9:18. There is a contingency in hardening based upon the callous disregard of man; therefore, hardening must be interpreted as judicial, a justly imposed sentence upon unbelief (cf. Gifford, Sanday and Headlam). The processes of judicial hardening and human disobedience are concurrent because they happen simultaneously when the gospel is refused.

Paul uses hardening in the metaphorical sense of a covering that grows over the heart, rendering Israel morally insensitive to the word of God (cf. John 12:40; Mark 6:52; 2 Cor. 3:14). This is highlighted in the sequence of Old Testament quotations (Isa. 29:10; Deut. 29:4; and Ps. 69:22, 23) which gives a scriptural basis for the hardening (vv. 8-10). The stress upon hardening as a divine act ("God gave them," v. 8a) is balanced by the description of obstinate Israel falling into its own trap, "snare," "trap," "pitfall," and "retribution" (v. 9, RSV). The phrase "always" (v. 10b) does not mean "forever," as it is rendered in the versions (RSV, NEB, NASB), but refers to the kind of hardening. As long as the condition lasts it will be sustained, not spasmodic. Its provisional character rests in the fact that it will come to an end (cf. 11:25); for now, the Jews bend their backs "continually" (cf. Munck, p. 115).

2. *The possibility of mercy through the gospel (11:11-24)*

Paul now asks the question from 11:1 in a different form, probing whether the stumbling of hardened Israel represents the final purpose of God. The antecedent of "they" (v. 11a) is the "rest," the hardened majority of Israel (v. 7c). Therefore, the question asks, "The hardened portion did not stumble at Christ with the result that they fell into ruin, did they?" (cf. Sanday and Headlam). The contrast between the two verbs "stumbled" and "fall" suggests that the latter means a final, irrevocable fall. It is rendered by Weymouth: "irretrievably"; Williams: "fall in utter ruin"; NEB: "complete downfall." The answer Paul gives is the decisive turning point in the discussion, which for the first time directly expresses the hope and the way of salvation for Israel. In the providence of God, the stumbling of Israel has been the means of salvation for the Gentiles, whose turning to the gospel has the further purpose of provoking Israel to faith.

Although the instrumentality denoted in "by their transgression" (v. 11b, NASB) basically refers to the Jewish rejection which began the

Gentile mission (cf. Acts 13:46; 18:6; 28:28), there is probably an allusion to the Jewish rejection which brought Jesus to the cross, effecting saving riches for the world. The exposition now concentrates on the likelihood of Israel's salvation; accordingly, the verses are dominated by conditional thought (cf. "if," vv. 12a,14a,15a,16a,17a,18b,21a,22c,23a,24a), which underscores the real probability of mercy. Paul's expectation for the recovery of Israel embraces two principles: (1) the phenomenon of gospel jealousy (vv. 11-15), and (2) the continuity of Israel in the people of God (vv. 16-24).

a. *A jealousy arousing faith (vv. 11-15).* This concept, which has received less than generous treatment by some commentators, is much more subtle than first appears. It aims at provoking the Jews to jealousy by the gospel, "stir Israel to emulation" (v. 11c, NEB). Paul equates making Israel jealous with bringing some of the Jews to salvation (v. 14); therefore, the provocation is not a psychological rivalry but a change in the misdirected loyalty of the Jew. In the Old Testament, divine jealousy (Num. 5:14; Exod. 20:5; Deut. 4:24; Ezek. 36:5,6) is aroused to wrath when Israel breaks the covenant; similarly, the jealousy of Israel for God can be aroused by the Gentile entrance into the covenant (cf. 10:19; Deut. 32:21). Upon seeing the covenant blessing received by the Gentiles, the Jew, like an unfaithful marriage partner, will come to repentance and seek "reconciliation" (v. 15).

The *strategy adopted* (vv. 13,14) by Paul is to "magnify" his office of preaching. The fervor with which Paul pursues the jealousy of Israel does not conflict with his role as "apostle of the Gentiles." Whenever Paul speaks of his apostleship and being sent to the Gentiles (cf. 15:15-21; 1 Cor. 9:15,16; Gal. 2:7-9; Col. 1:24-29; Eph. 3:2-11), he suggests the importance of that office. We can credit Johannes Munck with teaching us afresh that (1) Paul's Gentile mission is bound up in God's plan for the end of the age, and (2) the Roman letter is written as a missionary manifesto. Paul will not slight his Gentile readers (v. 13a), and he carefully explains that the Gentiles had a future promise bound up in the restoration of Israel. Just as Israel's "no" leads to salvation, so will its "yes" be a decisive turning point (cf. Munck, p. 119). Paul reasons that the conversion of Israel will inaugurate a blessing for the world even greater than that brought by its downfall.

The *prospect foreseen* (vv. 12,15) is indeed a glorious one. The exact nature of the event is not spelled out, but there are important clues given in "fulness" (v. 12c) and "life from the dead" (v. 15b). First, the word "fulness" means "coming to full strength of numbers" ("full inclusion," RSV; "full quota," Williams) and stands in contrast to "diminishing" (or "loss," v. 12b). Clearly, the contrasts between "remnant" (v. 5b) and "rest" (v. 7c), between "diminishing" (v. 12b) and "fulness" (v. 12c), and between "casting away" (v. 15a) and "receiving" (v. 15b) indicate a future conversion of Israel in a proportion not happening in Paul's ministry. This "fulness" speaks of a revolutionary turnabout, not a trickle of Jews to Christ but a blossoming stream, the wonder of which could be called a "mystery" (11:25). This primary sense of "full number" suitably applies to other passages in Paul (cf. 11:25; Gal. 4:4; Eph. 1:23; Col. 1:19).

Second, the vagueness of the phrase "life from the dead" (v. 15b) has divided the interpreters. The figurative expression can be taken in (1) a historical sense — "an increase of spiritual fervour and blessing in the whole Church of Christ on earth, so great and wonderful as to be comparable to a resurrection from the dead" or (2) an eschatological sense — "the new life of the world to come, the final development and glorious consummation of the kingdom of Christ" (Gifford, p. 195). The historical view emphasizes the fact that Paul does not say "the resurrection of the dead" but hints at a spiritual resurrection of faith in Israel that will vivify the world (cf. Luke 15:24-32; Ezek. 37:3-14). Godet says, "The light which converted Jews bring to the church, and the power of life which they have sometimes awakened in it, are the pledge of that spiritual renovation which will be produced in Gentile Christendom by their entrance *en masse*" (p. 404; cf. Calvin, Gifford, Moule, Murray).

The strength of the eschatological view is that it provides an appropriate advance upon the phrase "reconciling of the world" (v. 15a). The reasoning goes, anything less in magnitude than the resurrection or return of Christ would be anticlimactic in comparison to the reconciliation preached in the gospel. Sanday and Headlam make it the general resurrection, ushering in the messianic kingdom (pp. 325,326). Munck places it among the events surrounding the Second Coming (p. 127). Barrett says it will be the signal for the resurrection (p. 215). The problem is whether "life from the dead" looks to an event within history or to the transition of the ages that ushers in the world to come. On the balance of evidence, the phrase may be an undefined hyperbole, "simply a very strong expression for the greatest conceivable blessing," but in light of verses 25-32, the eschatological setting is most likely (cf. Dodd, p. 177; Denney, p. 679).

b. *A continuity belonging to the chosen people (vv. 16-24).* The discussion of salvation for Israel still moves in the realm of possibility, but Paul's confidence grows in this passage. We can briefly summarize the expanding argument. If, as in the case of the "firstfruit" and the "lump" (cf. Num. 15:18-21) and in the case of the "root" and the "branches" (cf. Jer. 11:16,17), the consecration of the part extends to the whole, then the consecration of a part of Israel reaches the whole (v. 16). The consecrated part of Israel, its firstfruit and root, is the present election, the remnant that stands in line with its ancient predecessor, the patriarchs (Bruce, p. 217).[13] The point is the continuity of divine grace in the people of God. The existence of the chosen people of God, incorporating saved Jews and Gentiles, depends upon God's electing purpose, revealed first in the patriarchs and manifested now in the elect remnant. It is this divine continuity, not the merits of the fathers, that makes the salvation of Israel possible. "Here there is no thought of human pretensions, but of God's free grace based on the choice of His sovereign will" (Nygren, p. 398).

Paul expands the thought further by the allegory of the olive tree (vv. 17-24), which depicts an invigorating continuity between the root (patriarchs) and the engrafted wild-olive branches (Gentile Christians). The strange horticultural method,[14] which Paul recognizes as "contrary to nature" (v. 24), is the strength of his argument. The success of unnatural grafting, whereby Gentiles enter by faith (v. 20b) and receive the rich blessings of the covenant promises (v. 17c), increases the probability that the natural branches, hardened Jews which were broken off (vv. 20a, 21a), can be restored by a similar process. This is not a case of deducing theology from natural processes but an appeal to the restorative power of divine grace (Barrett, p. 217). In terms of first-century probabilities, the salvation of disobedient Israel would be more likely to occur than what had already happened, the grafting of the Gentiles into the people of God.

We have before us in this allegory the two pillars upon which the people of God are founded in all ages: man's faith and God's power (cf. 2 Tim. 2:19). First, the condition of participation is faith (vv. 20, 21). Faith leaves no room for boasting; it demands perseverance from the saved Gentile and repentance from the unsaved Jew. It is misleading to suggest that the continuance of election depends on faith; on the contrary, the true sign of election is persevering faith. "Throughout the New Testament continuance is the test of reality. The perseverance of the saints is a doctrine firmly grounded in the New Testament (and not least in Pauline) teaching; but the corollary to it is that it is saints who persevere" (Bruce, p. 219). Second, the ground of assurance is God (vv. 23, 24). That "God is able" (v. 23b) does not cancel the requirement of faith, but it means that only divine grace will ever bring Israel to faith.

---

[13] The metaphors have been applied to Christ, to the remnant, and to the patriarchs (Gifford, pp. 195, 195). With the majority of commentators, it is best to apply both metaphors to the elected line which began with the patriarchs. This is consistent with the use of "root" in the allegory of the olive tree.

[14] W. M. Ramsay (*Pauline and Other Studies*, pp. 219-250) shows how such a grafting procedure may have been practiced in the first century.

3. The prophecy of mercy upon all (11:25-32)

This concluding section brings the exposition to its goal in the revelation of a mystery, made known to rebuke Gentile conceit (v. 25) and to proclaim divine mercy (v. 32). The term "mystery" does not refer to esoteric knowledge but to a divine secret, once hidden in eternity but now revealed in history. Paul generally used the word in reference to the eternal purpose of God to redeem humanity that is revealed in Christ and the gospel (cf. 1 Cor. 2:1; 15:51; Eph. 1:9; 6:19; Col. 1:26,27). In this passage, the mystery lies concealed in the relationship of hardened Israel to the saved Gentiles. We have already seen the crucial factors, the hardening of Israel (vv. 7-10) and the call of the Gentiles (vv. 11-15), but the new disclosure is that the hardening will subside after the fullness of the Gentiles. The prophecy, then, reveals the unusual way in which Israel will be saved. The following analysis offers the three points that will be developed below: (1) the judgment of God upon disobedient Israel is a limited hardening, touching only a part of the people; (2) when the full complement of the Gentile world has received the gospel, then the hardening of Israel will disappear; (3) as a consequence, the whole of Israel will be saved by believing in Jesus the Messiah.

a. *The fullness of the Gentiles (v. 25).* The hardening of Israel has distinct limitations. First, the prepositional phrase "in part" is adjectival, more naturally modifying "hardening" ("blindness," KJV) and indicating a quantitative limit, only a "part of Israel" (RSV). Second, a temporal limit is imposed by "until," which in its context must be translated "until the time when" (cf. 1 Cor. 15:25). The condition will remain until a crucial event in redemptive history has transpired, "until the full number of the Gentiles come in" (RSV).

Finally, the nature of this event can be fixed by two considerations: (1) the verb "come in" has a technical sense, "entering the kingdom of God" (cf. Matt. 7:13; 23:13; Mark 9:43-47; Luke 13:24) and therefore refers to the Gentile reception of salvation; (2) the phrase "fulness of the Gentiles" means the full complement of converts from the Gentile world, a corporate idea parallel to the "fulness" of Israel in verse 12. Therefore, this fullness signifies an eschatological condition, the completion of the gospel mission among the nations of the world, whose fulfillment would coincide with the lifting of hardness from Israel (cf. Godet, Gifford, Sanday and Headlam, Barrett).

b. *The salvation of all Israel (vv. 26,27).* To resolve the thorny issues arising from these verses, we need to consider two important questions. First, what condition is stated in the connective "and so" (v. 26a)? There are three possible views of "and so" that fit the requirements of grammar and context: *modal*, "and in that manner"; *temporal*, "when that has happened"; and *correlative*, "in the following manner."[15]

The *modal view* stresses the logical sense of "so" and connects it to the preceding clause in verse 25: "The hardening will subside when the Gentiles are all saved, and in that manner, all Israel will be saved." It emphasizes that "by the whole Gentile world coming into the kingdom and thus rousing the Jews to jealousy" (Sanday and Headlam, p. 335), the conversion of all Israel will happen (cf. Williams, Gifford, Godet).

The *temporal view* of "so" makes the expected fullness of the Gentiles a chronological and necessary prerequisite to Israel's salvation: "This partial blindness has come upon Israel only until the Gentiles have been admitted to full strength; when that has happened, the whole of Israel will be saved" (NEB). The temporal sense of "then" is a well-attested idiom, used in the New Testament to summarize a preceding sequence of events (Acts 17:33; 20:11; cf. Bruce, p. 222).

The *correlative view* notes the common use of "so" to introduce a following statement; in this case, it corresponds to "as it is written" (v. 26b). The correlation "so . . . as" would ground the salvation of Israel in the event described in the scriptural quotation (vv. 26b, 27): "In the following manner, all Israel will be saved, just as it is written, the Redeemer will come from Zion." There is little to choose among the three, as described above, except emphasis; perhaps the temporal view best secures the meaning of the other two.

The other question is, What is the meaning of the phrase "all Israel"? The designation is an Old Testament formula indicating the totality of the people (cf. 2 Chron. 12:1; 1 Sam. 7:5; 1 Kings 8:65) and must be understood in a collective sense, "Israel as a whole" (cf. Knox, NEB). It means "a future conversion of the Jews, so universal that the separation into an 'elect remnant' and 'the rest who were hardened' shall disappear" (Gifford, p. 199)

It may be helpful to state what it does not mean. First, it does not mean "every Israelite"; it no more means the salvation of every Jew than "fulness of the Gentiles" means the salvation of every Gentile. Paul thinks here in terms of collectives not individuals. Second, "all Israel" does not mean the "sum total of elect Jews who believe Christ during the gospel era." What would be worthy of a "mystery" in the evident fact (tautology) that the present election will be saved? To project the results of Christian preaching over the centuries into this prophecy crushes the drama of the whole chapter. Third, it does not mean the "Israel of God" (Gal. 6:16) which is the church of Jews and Gentiles. The sustained contrast between Israel and the Gentiles in chapters 9-11 forbids this

---

[15] The crucial word is "so," Greek *houtos*, an adverbial particle with a wide range of usage in the New Testament.

identification. When all Israel is saved, there may yet be unbelieving Jews, but the historical entity called Judaism will become subject to the gospel so that the church will incorporate the synagogue and Jews everywhere will be recognized as true Christians.

The deliverance that Israel will experience is described by the quotation of Isaiah 59:20,21 plus Isaiah 27:9 (vv. 26b,27); it is a spiritual restoration in the new covenant, granting forgiveness of sins. The phrase "out of Zion" ("from Zion," RSV) is probably a reference to the heavenly Jerusalem (Gal. 4:26) and alludes to the redeeming work of Christ which will be consummated at the second advent. "St. Paul uses the words to imply that the Redeemer, who is represented by the Prophets as coming from Zion, and is therefore conceived by him as realized in Christ, will in the end redeem the whole of Israel" (Sanday and Headlam, p. 336). The hope of Israel resides in the covenant mercy revealed in Jesus the Messiah, the "Deliverer" (1 Thess. 1:10), whose saving work extends from the Incarnation to the Second Coming. There is nothing here about a special way for the Jews in a restored theocracy in Palestine; Paul views the salvation of Israel as a possibility of grace through faith, connecting it with the here and now of the gospel. Israel will come by the way of the cross.

c. *Mercy upon the disobedient (vv. 28-32)*. This paragraph rehearses the entire argument and ties up the loose ends of chapters 9-11. We now see God's ultimate purpose for the world; it is mercy for Jew and Gentile alike. In a remarkable intertwining of the themes we have followed, election and gospel, Paul replays in summary fashion the roles of Jew and Gentile in God's purpose by means of two carefully structured sentences. *Jewish disobedience* (vv. 28,29) has two aspects: from the viewpoint of the gospel, the Jews are God's enemies for the sake of the Gentiles who have been blessed with salvation by their rejection (v. 28a); from the viewpoint of election, the Jews are God's beloved because of the purpose He began with the patriarchs (v. 28b). Both aspects of Jewish disobedience fit into God's purpose which never changes "for the gifts and the call of God are irrevocable" (v. 29, RSV).

Then, *Gentile obedience* (vv. 30,31) also has two aspects: from the viewpoint of the gospel, the Gentiles, who were once disobedient, are now receiving mercy in the time of Jewish disobedience (v. 30); from the viewpoint of election, the Jews are now disobeying, when the Gentiles are receiving mercy, in order that they may now[16] also receive mercy (v. 31). Again, both aspects flow in God's present purpose, shutting out both Jew and Gentile in sin that they both could come in mercy (v. 32).

---

[16] This "now" is not to be overlooked (cf. NASB); the best Greek texts have it. It means that Paul held an imminent hope for the conversion of Israel (cf. 13:11-14).

The "all" here has nothing to do with universalism but speaks of the universality of salvation because of the universality of sin. The door of mercy is as wide as the pit of sin; as surely as sin attaches to every man, so surely, mercy beckons to every man. "God's purpose in shutting Jews and Gentiles together in a place where their disobedience to His law must be acknowledged and brought to light was that He might bestow His unmerited mercy on Jews and Gentiles alike" (Bruce, p. 223; cf. 3:23; Gal. 3:22).

E. A Hymn of Praise to God (11:33-36)

Because God has shined light on the dark problem of Jew and Gentile, Paul breaks out in hymnic praise of His glory. The height of the argument has ended in the wondrous depth of God; the truth declared in verse 32 leads Paul to adoring wonder, which is a fitting climax not only to chapters 9-11 but for the entire doctrinal portion, chapters 1-11. Gifford says, "The wrath 'revealed from heaven against all unrighteousness' (i. 18), has given place to the mercy which embraces all the nations of the earth" (p. 201). Munck believes that "Paul turns with his readers to that praise of God which to him is the goal of his mental endeavor to trace God's working in the world" (p. 142). This doxology praises an unfathomable triad of virtues in God (v. 33a), if we follow the versions that render, "O depth of wealth, wisdom, and knowledge in God" (NEB, cf. RSV, Goodspeed). Then, each is extolled in turn but in reverse order (vv. 33b-36). We can briefly note the refrains.

1. *Praise of God's knowledge (11:33b)*

Knowledge applies chiefly to the apprehension of truth; here, it probably means the divine intuition which foreknows the outcome of all the factors in history before they come to pass. It is the theoretical, intellectual power to make inscrutable judgments and choose unsearchable ways (cf. Weymouth, Knox). "Who would have thought of the means just described by which his mercy is brought to bear on all men" (Barrett, p. 228).

2. *Praise of God's wisdom (11:34)*

Wisdom is God's designing of all the elements of His knowledge into a revealed purpose for mankind (cf. Col. 1:9, 28; 1 Cor. 1:30; 2:6,7). It denotes the admirable skill by which God includes the free actions of man in His plan and transforms them into the means for the accomplishment of His purpose. The quotation of Isaiah 40:13 reminds us that God's wisdom is all His own; He needs neither consultants nor research assistants.

3. *Praise of God's riches (11:35,36)*

God's wealth is the inexhaustible store of spiritual blessings available in Christ (cf. 2:4; 9:23; 10:12; Col. 1:27). This quotation of Job 41: 11 (v. 35) affirms that it is impossible to build up a store of merits and outgive God. As Gifford says, "no gift of His is a requital of benefits first conferred on Him, but all are of His own free grace and overflowing bounty" (p. 203). No one can make God a debtor because He is the "Source, Guide, and Goal of all that is" (v. 36, NEB). The last line is the proper place where our observance of divine faithfulness should lead us for it is the chief end of man to give God the glory.

For Further Study

1. Use a Bible dictionary to study the terms Election, Calling, and Faith, paying attention to the relationship of each with preaching the gospel.

2. How is it that we can believe in election and still be concerned about evangelism?

3. Trace the theme of chapters 9-11 back into the previous chapters of Romans. How does 9-11 fit into the overall outline of the letter?

4. List the references to Israel and define Paul's uses of the term.

5. Answer these questions about the prophecy of Israel's salvation. Has the prophecy been fulfilled? Should it be considered a central part of Paul's thinking?

6. How does Paul use the word mercy?

Chapter 7

The Service of God:
The Doctrine of Obedience
(Romans 12:1-15:13)

We have now reached the division of the epistle which generally is called the practical section in contrast to the preceding doctrinal portion (chs. 1-11). We have seen the saving relationship of God to the world in the four biblical concepts of wrath (1:18-3:20), righteousness (3:21-5:21), life (6:1-8:39), and mercy (9:1-11:36). Now the response of the saved man to God is presented in terms of a surrendered life of service. Griffith Thomas suggests: "We must observe the three pivots of the Epistle suggested by the word 'Therefore.' In ch. v. 1 we have the 'Therefore' of Justification; in ch. viii. 1, the 'Therefore' of Sanctification; in ch. xii. 1, the 'Therefore' of Consecration. This is the order: Salvation, Sanctification, Service" (III,1).

Paul has no doctrine which does not imply a corresponding practice; it is therefore characteristic of his thinking to follow a doctrinal exposition by an ethical exhortation (often marked by the transitional particle, "therefore" [e.g., Eph. 4:1; Col. 3:5]).[1] "Doctrine is never taught in the Bible simply that it may be known; it is taught in order that it may be translated into practice" (Bruce, p. 225; cf. John 13:17). For Paul, in particular, the superstructure of Christian ethics is raised on the foundation of Christian revelation.

It is to be noted that what Paul affirms in chapters 6-8, the believer's union with Christ in the fellowship of the Spirit, he here enjoins: live now in union with Him! The earlier section (chs. 6-8), laying down the general principle of the believer's "newness of life," describes that life in general, sometimes mystical, terms (cf. 6:4,11,18,19). The present passage (12:1-15:13) gets down to particulars. Godet aptly says: "The believer is dead unto sin, no doubt; he has broken with that perfidious

---

[1]This pattern of doctrine followed by exhortation is common to the epistolary form; cf. Ephesians 1-3/4-6; Galatians 1-4/5-6; Colossians 1,2/3,4; 1 Thessalonians 1-3/4,5; 1 Peter 1:1-2:10/2:11-5:14; Hebrews 1:1-10:18/10:19-13:25. In more practical letters like 1 and 2 Corinthians, the two emphases are mingled.

fiend; but sin is not dead in him, and it strives continually to restore the broken relation. By calling the believer to the conflict against it, as well as to the positive practice of Christian duty, the apostle is not relapsing into Jewish legalism. He assumes the inward consecration of the believer as an already consummated fact; and it is from this fact, implicitly contained in his faith, that he proceeds to call him to realize his Christian obligations" (p. 424). Because obedience has its wellspring in saving faith, it can be exhorted; it is not obedience in principle but in thought and attitude, word and deed, wrought out in the concrete situations of life" (cf. Cranfield, *Scottish Journal*).

Sanday and Headlam think that the primary idea running throughout these chapters is "that of peace and unity for the Church" in all the aspects of life, internal and external (p. 351). The passage begins with a general appeal for consecration to God and the living of a transformed life (12:1,2). This is followed by a discussion of the Christian's duty to God and his fellow believers (12:3-21), duties to the state and one's fellow citizens (13:1-14), and duties touching the relations between weak and strong Christians (14:1-15:13). The first appeal (12:1,2) is the foundation upon which the rest is built. The remaining sections relate broadly to the religious, civic, and moral spheres of life. The entire section is pervaded by the thought of the Christian life as a life of service to God.

A. The General Appeal for Self-consecration (12:1,2)

It is agreed by commentators that the first two verses of chapter 12 introduce the practical division of the epistle (12:1-15:13) and spell out its theme. Nygren calls the passage, "the basic rule of Paul's ethics" (p. 416); Barrett, "the ground of Christian ethics" (p. 230); Godet, "the basis of Christian conduct" (p. 424). D. Brown sees it as a statement of "the general character of all Christian service" (p. 121). Gifford speaks of it as an appeal for "personal consecration to God's service," explaining that this personal consecration is "the inmost centre of the spiritual life" from which flows all else that is discussed in this portion of the letter.

The appeal is voiced in the verb "beseech" ("appeal," RSV; "entreat," TCNT), which may be used in the sense of "exhort" (cf. Eph. 4:1; 1 Cor. 4:16; 1 Thess. 4:1; 1 Tim. 2:1; 1 Peter 2:11) or of "encourage" (cf. 2 Cor. 7:6,13; Col. 2:2; 4:8). Here it clearly means "exhort" and conveys the idea of "tender entreaty" (Gifford, p. 204). Yet the word also has a connotation of authority, suggesting a summons to obedience issued in the name of the gospel. Cranfield remarks, "The apostle is not by any means pleading for a favour; he is claiming in Christ's name an obedience which his readers are under obligation to render" (*Scottish Journal*, p. 6).

1. *The ground of the appeal is the mercies of God (12:1a)*

The "therefore," supported by the reference to "the mercies of God," looks back to all that Paul has written in the preceding chapters (1:18-11:36). The word "mercies" ("compassions," Norlie)[2] is a fitting summary of the entire action of God in behalf of men through Jesus Christ as set out in the whole of chapters 1-11. Its use in 12:1, however, is especially appropriate, in view of the climactic declaration in 11:32 of God's all-embracing mercy. Calvin goes to the point: Paul's entreaty teaches us "that until men really apprehend how much they owe to the mercy of God, they will never with a right feeling worship him, nor be effectually stimulated to fear and obey him" (p. 450). The apostle attracts us, therefore, by the sweetness of grace to the obedience of faith.

2. *The substance of the appeal is the surrender of self (12:1b,2b)*

We now come to the heart of the matter: What am I as a Christian to do in obeying God? Paul's answer has two closely related aspects; the upward look is dedication, "present your bodies," and the inward look is transformation, "be ye transformed." These two things, relating to the body and the mind, epitomize the dynamics of Christian obedience.

a. *Dedication is the sacrifice of self to God (vv. 1b,c).*

The verb "present" is that which is used in chapter 6 of presenting one's self and the members of his body to God and righteousness or to sin and iniquity (6:13,16,19). The word basically denotes the presenting of a ritual sacrifice, but it is used of the presentation of Christ in the temple (Luke 2:22), of Paul presenting his converts to God (Col. 1:28), and of Christ presenting His church to Himself (Eph. 5:27). The term has an obvious sacrificial connotation in the present passage.

That which we are to present to God is our "bodies." The context may call attention to the body "as the instrument by which all human service is rendered to God" (Denney, p. 687). Gifford thinks "The body is claimed first for God's service, because there was great need to warn new converts from heathenism against sins of the flesh" (p. 204). However, the term may be used in the sense of "self," denoting, as Calvin says, "not only our bones and skin, but the whole mass [totality] of which we are composed" (p. 452). The NEB therefore translates it: "offer your very selves to him." D. Brown uses the expression, "your whole embodied selves" (p. 121).

---

[2] The Greek word for "mercies" is used here for the first time in Romans. A similar, but somewhat weaker, term is used eight times (counting both its noun and verb forms) in chapters 9-11. The word in the present passage speaks of tender compassion, and the plural calls attention to its manifold expressions.

The self-sacrifice of the Christian is qualified by three terms: "living," "holy," "acceptable to God." "Living" contrasts it with the sacrifices of Jewish and pagan rituals, which were offered up in death. There is perhaps an allusion in the word to 6:13, where believers are urged to present themselves to God "as alive from the dead." "Holy," which means consecrated, dedicated, shows that the Christian's self-sacrifice is marked by a continuing process of sanctification (cf. 1 Peter 1:16). "Acceptable" suggests that the sacrifice is true and proper, one that God desires and will accept (cf. "well pleasing," 2 Cor. 5:9).

The act of offering up self to God is defined by Paul as the Christian's "spiritual service" ("reasonable service," KJV). The noun ("service"), which was used of the temple service discharged by worshiping Israelites (cf. 9:4; Heb. 9:1,6), denotes the service of worship. The adjective ("spiritual" or "reasonable"), which occurs elsewhere in the New Testament only in 1 Peter 2:2, literally means "pertaining to reason." Sanday and Headlam understand the two words together to mean "a service to God such as befits the reason; i.e., a spiritual sacrifice and not the offering of an irrational animal" (p. 352; cf. 1 Peter 2:5). Knox translates, "worship due from you as rational creatures"; Phillips, "act of intelligent worship"; NASB, "spiritual service of worship"; and NEB, "worship offered by mind and heart."

b. *Transformation is the conformity of self to the new age (vv. 2a,b).*

"This world" (or "age," cf. Luke 16:8; 1 Cor. 1:20; 2:6,8) is evil (Gal. 1:4) and is ruled by Satan, the "god of this world" who blinds the minds of unbelievers (2 Cor. 4:4). "This age" stands opposed to the "age to come" (cf. Eph. 1:21), which has already dawned for believers (1 Cor. 10:11; 2 Cor. 5:17). Since the cross, " 'this age' can no longer be the regulative principle of life for those who have died and been raised with Jesus" (Barrett p. 232; cf. 6:3-6). The Christian's life must be shaped by the new age for he is destined to be conformed to the image of Christ (Rom. 8:29). It seems unlikely that we should make an external-internal distinction between the verbs "conform" and "transform"; as synonyms, they treat the same matter from negative and positive aspects (cf. Denney, Cranfield). Phillips, however, translates it: "Don't let the world squeeze you into its mold, but let God remold your minds from within" (v. 2a,b). The latter idea (transformation by the renewal of the mind) is "the one true preservative against 'conformity to the world'" (D. Brown, p. 122).

The force of the tense[3] in the two verbs is noteworthy; it can be brought out by translating: "stop being conformed . . . continue being transformed" (cf. Williams). The conforming, which is happening, is to

---

[3]The present imperative in a prohibition indicates that a current action is to cease; in an exhortation, it indicates that a current action is to continue.

stop; the transforming, which is also happening, is to go on indefinitely (Cranfield, *Scottish Journal*, p. 17). This ongoing process of transformation flows from the inner being, the renewed mind (v. 2b), which in contrast to the mind enslaved by the flesh (cf. 1:28; Col. 2:18) has been purified by the gift of the Spirit (cf. 2 Cor. 3:18; 4:16; Titus 3:5). In a decisive surrender ("present," v. 1, aorist tense), the believer offers himself and then is progressively transfigured by the Spirit who has reshaped the mind, "in which the surrender in purpose becomes a long series of deepening surrenders in habit and action, and a larger discovery of self" (Moule, *Expositor's Bible*, p. 329). The renewal of the "mind" refers to the new attitudes and ideals that characterize the Christian. The model of this transformation is Jesus Himself, whose inner glory as the Son of God transfigured His outer appearance (cf. Matt. 17:2; Mark 9:2).[4] "The mind and memory, reason and emotion, indeed, everything in the Christian's life, the inmost and the outward, from the highest to the lowest, all must be included in this metamorphosis into harmony with the new aeon" (Nygren, p. 419).

3. *The outcome of the appeal is the proving of the will of God (12:2c).*

The verb "prove" means to put to the test, to prove by testing; it then comes to mean "to approve as genuine" (cf. 2:18; 1 Cor. 16:3; 2 Cor. 8:2; Phil. 1:10).[5] Like a precious metal that passes through the assayer's hands, the will of God may be tested and proved genuine by the believer. That is to say, the life being transformed by the renewal of the mind results in a new perception which recognizes and embraces the will of God. "An unrenewed mind cannot do this; it is destitute of moral discernment — has no proper moral faculty" (Denney, p. 688; cf. "reprobate mind," 1:28). The will of God is what He wills, what He desires of His people. Sanday and Headlam understand it to include "all that is implied in moral principle, in the religious aim, and the ideal perfection which is the goal of life" (p. 354). The Christian should contemplate it with eagerness and commit himself to carry it out in life.

It is best to read the three adjectives, "good," "acceptable," and "perfect" as substantives, defining the will of God: "what God's will is — all that is good, acceptable, and perfect" (TCNT; cf. RSV, NEB, NASB).

---

[4]The Greek word rendered "transformed" is used elsewhere in the New Testament only in Matthew 17:2 and Mark 9:2 (where it is used of Jesus' being "transfigured" before His disciples) and in 2 Corinthians 3:18. The English word "metamorphosis" is derived from the Greek word.

[5]The Greek word is used more than twenty times in the New Testament, and is rendered in KJV by various terms: prove, try, approve, discern, etc. A close parallel to the present passage is Ephesians 5:10.

B. Duties to God and Fellow Believers[6] (12:3-21)

In 12:3ff. Paul shows how the believer's consecration to God (12:1,2) is carried out in the performance of specific duties. He presents first those duties that relate more directly to God and one's fellow believers, the stress being on a ministry of edification in the life of the church. Conscious of a special commission from God, Paul reminds his readers that it is in that capacity he addresses them: "For I say, through the grace that was given me, etc." Moffatt renders it, "In virtue of my office, I tell every one of your number." The passage which follows teaches "body language," that is, how a Christian is to think of himself in terms of other members of the body of Christ and how he is to perform his ministry according to individual needs and separate gifts. The passage is replete with imperative constructions and can be outlined around the hortatory ideas of sober thinking (vv. 3-5), diligent ministry (vv. 6-8), and unfeigned love (vv. 9-21).

1. Think soberly — a sane self-estimate (12:3-5).

There is a fourfold play on the verb "to think" in verse 3: "exaggerated thinking . . . proper thinking . . . purposeful thinking . . . sober thinking." The RSV translates this unique series, "not to think of himself more highly than he ought to think, but to think with sober judgment" (cf. NASB). D. Brown, observing that it is not possible to convey in good English the play on words which the Greek text exhibits, offers a literal rendering: "not to be high-minded above what he ought to be minded, but so to be minded as to be sober-minded" (p. 123). The verb translated "think soberly" ("make a sober estimate," Weymouth, NEB; "have a sane estimate," Phillips) means to keep one's senses, to be orderly and restrained, sound-minded. The Bible elsewhere represents it as the opposite of madness (2 Cor. 5:13); it is used also of the sobriety to which Jesus returned the demoniac of Gadara, when he was put "in his right mind" (Mark 5:15). In *Salvation and Behavior,* Graham Scroggie comments: "Self estimate must be on one or other of three levels: super, above; sub, under; or sane, right. On the super level are the superiority complex people; and on the sub level are the inferiority complex people, they are both off the right level" (p. 81).

a. *The measure of a sane self-estimate is the divine gift of faith (v. 3c).* When Christians measure themselves by the standard God has given them in their faith, then they will achieve a proper opinion of themselves. Faith stands "for all those gifts which are given to man with

---

[6]This section, though relating mainly to one's duties to God and his fellow Christians, is not to be interpreted exclusively in this manner, for in verses 14-21 non-believers are perhaps mainly in view.

or as the result of his faith" (Sanday and Headlam, p. 355). D. Brown calls it "the inlet to or seed-bed of all the other graces" (p. 123). It may be used here in the special sense of power for the carrying out of one's duties.

The emphasis is upon diversity ("to each," NASB) and sovereignty ("God has allotted," NASB), a twofold pattern which recurs in similar passages (cf. 1 Cor. 12:9; Eph. 4:7). There is no room for high-mindedness in the man who owes everything he has to God (1 Cor. 4:7). Indeed, the close connection of verse 3 — observe the first word, "for" — with what is enunciated in verses 1 and 2 suggests that "humility is the immediate effect of self-surrender to God" (Gifford, p. 206).

b. *The motive for a sane self-estimate is the unity of the body (vv. 4,5).* Both the diversity and the unity of the Christian community are recognized by Paul. The diversity ("many members") has an analogy in the human body (v. 4), a favorite figure used by Paul for the corporate life of Christians (cf. 1 Cor. 12:12; Eph. 4:16; Col. 1:18). The thought is that Christians have diverse functions within the body of Christ and that all are necessary to the proper working of that body. Therefore, no one member is to think of himself as being alone important.

The idea of unity is brought out in the phrase "one body in Christ" (v. 5a). The teaching is that there is a common relation to Christ that unites the church, and this unity makes it imperative that each person perform his duty for the good of the whole. The words "individually members one of another" (v. 5b, NASB, RSV) imply that this unity preserves individuality; the focus is diversity unified through interdependence. "The individuals retain their value, only not as independent wholes, but as members one of another. Each and all exist only in each other" (Denney, p. 689).

2. *Minister diligently — the exercise of spiritual gifts (12:6-8)*

The discussion now turns to the ministry of individuals within the body of Christ. The list of seven spiritual gifts, amplified in 1 Corinthians 12:8-10, 28 and Ephesians 4:4-16, includes the officers of the church but is not restricted to them. The word "gifts" actually refers to any gift of God's grace (Greek, *charisma*, 1:11; 5:15; 6:23; 11:29), but here it means endowments that God bestows on the members of the church to be used in His service. Barrett remarks: "In this sense the whole life of the Church, not its ministry only, is 'charismatic'; but the total effect of the passage (cf. 1 Cor. xii-xiv) shows that this supernatural conception of the Church's life does not exclude the notions of discipline and authority" (p. 237).

The construction of verses 6-8 is somewhat obscure, there being no finite verb expressed in the Greek. So, most translations begin a new sentence with "And having then gifts" (v. 6a), and they then supply a hortatory verb for the exercise of each gift (v. 6b, 7a, 8b; cf. KJV, ASV, Weymouth, TCNT, Phillips). The RSV inserts the hortatory verb at the beginning: "Having gifts . . . , *let us use them:* if prophecy, in proportion to our faith, etc." (author's italics). The NEB is somewhat similar: "The gifts we possess differ . . . , and *must be exercised accordingly:* the gift of inspired utterance, etc." (author's italics). In looking at the gifts, we can easily forget Paul's point that seems suspended for the moment. The appointed tasks arise out of the received gifts; so the Christian must tend to his own sphere of ministry, neither begrudging others nor inflating his own position. There is no hint of anything official in this passage; the church as a whole ministers, and each member has a function of ministry to one extent or another, as the nature of the gifts will show.

a. *The gifts of inspired utterance include prophecy, teaching, and exhortation (vv. 6b, 7b, 8a).* Prophecy (v. 6b) was second only to apostleship in Paul's evaluation (cf. 1 Cor. 12:28; Eph. 4:11); its preeminence therefore makes it preferable to glossolalia (tongue-speaking; cf. 1 Cor. 14:1, 39). Prophecy is *sometimes* prediction but *always* the immediate proclamation of God's word through human lips. Because of the danger of false prophecy, the prophet must speak within the limits of faith, "as far as the measure of his faith will let him" (Knox).

Teaching (v. 7b), which imparts the truth of God, suggests the work of the pastor (Eph. 4:11); exhortation (v. 8a), which applies the truth by encouragement (cf. Acts 13:15), suggests the work of the preacher, but the two functions must have overlapped. "Each means a communication, effected in different ways, of the truth of the Gospel to the hearer; in the one it is explained, in the other applied. Yet it could never be explained without application or applied without explanation" (Barrett, p. 238).

b. *The gifts of sympathetic service (vv. 7a, 8b, c, d) are ministry, giving, ruling, and showing mercy.* The word "ministry" (from the root of which our word "deacon" comes) is the general term for charismatic service (1 Cor. 12:5) and was applied to the apostolic ministry (11:13; 2 Cor. 4:1; 6:3), the social ministry for the needy (15:25, 31; 2 Cor. 8:4), and to the deaconship (Rom 15:1, RSV; 1 Tim. 3:8). The one who gives ("He who contributes," v. 8b, RSV) must do so with "simplicity" (KJV). The Greek word, used eight times in the New Testament, is rendered in five different ways in KJV: simplicity, singleness, liberality, bountifulness, and liberal. Here it may denote singleness of purpose, meaning that the giver has no ulterior motive in his act of giving (cf. Montgomery). Or, the idea may be that of wholehearted generosity (cf. ASV, TCNT). The NEB sees in the term the thought of heartiness. It is worthy of note that the gift (*charisma*) of giving goes beyond the possession of wealth to the "person's spiritual capacity, his God-given inclination to give" (Cranfield, *Scottish Journal* p. 34).

The "one who presides" (v. 8c, Weymouth) can be a person who takes the lead in the church (1 Thess. 5:12; 1 Tim. 5:17) or in the household (1 Tim. 3:5,12), though perhaps the former is the interpretation to be preferred. However, there is certainly no episcopal office in view here. Following the suggestion of several interpreters, we may take the term as a reference to the church leader who cares for the weak and needy (cf. Cranfield). Zeal and energy are required for the fulfillment of his task. The one "helping others in distress" (v. 8d, NEB), on behalf of the congregation, probably tends the sick, relieves the poor, or cares for the elderly and disabled. Nothing affords more consolation to the distressed than the sight of helpers full of "cheerfulness" (cf. Calvin, p. 463). It is to be observed that these last four gifts look to the everyday needs of people, revealing a large portion of New Testament church ministry to be social in character.

3. *Love sincerely – the display of unfeigned affection (12:9-21)*

After considering the importance of humility and spiritual gifts, Paul is ready to show us "a more excellent way" (1 Cor. 12:31). "The sequence of ideas is exactly similar to that in 1 Cor. xii, xiii, and obviously suggested by it" (Sanday and Headlam, p. 360). In the section that follows, love is the ruling thought, but Paul does not entangle it in the sloppy sentimentalism that haunts the word in modern religious talk (cf. Dodd, p. 198). It is first of all, love "without hypocrisy" (v. 9a), that is, "sincere" (TCNT), "genuine" (RSV). In the ministry of the church, the Christian's love must be the real thing, not counterfeit (cf. Moffatt). Nygren (pp. 425,426) effectively paraphrases verses 9-21, with love as the subject throughout, on the pattern of 1 Corinthians 13. We can best define the all-embracing character of unfeigned love by briefly commenting on its active features.

a. *Love to the brother within (vv. 9-13).* Up to this point, Paul has spoken of love of man toward God only once (8:28), but there has been a profuse outpouring of references to the divine love toward mankind (cf. 5:5,8; 8:35,39; 9:13,25; 11:28). We now hear of the love which the Christian owes his fellow man (cf. 13:8-10), and particularly in verses 9-13, the exercise of love toward the Christian brother. Love of the brethren fulfills the new commandment that Christ gave (John 13:34,35) and signifies that we are members of the family of God (cf. 1 Thess. 4:9; Heb. 13:1; 1 Peter 1:22; 1 John 5:1,2).

Holy earnestness (v. 9b) gives love a robust character. Love regards evil with horror and weds itself to that which is good. "Love is not a principle of mutual indulgence; in the Gospel it is a moral principle, and like Christ who is the only perfect example of love, it has always something inexorable about it" (Denney, p. 691).

Love embraces the Christian brother and eagerly shows him honor (v. 10). "Tenderly affectioned" is the translation of a word which denotes natural affection between blood relatives. "Love of the brethren" (lit., "brother-love"; Greek, *philadephia*) conveys much the same thought. Knox expresses it: "Be affectionate towards each other, as the love of brothers demands." Whether "preferring one another" (v. 10b) means to take the lead in showing honor ("outdo one another," RSV; cf. Goodspeed), or to give a higher place ("give pride of place to one another," NEB; cf. TCNT) is difficult to say. Both ideas make good sense and marshal strong evidence.

The boundless energy of love is pointed up in verse 11a; it never wearies. The Greek suggests unflagging zeal. Williams has "never slack in earnestness." Moreover, love is aglow with the Spirit (cf. RSV, Denney, Bruce, Barrett), serving the Lord (v. 11b).

Joyful perseverance (v. 12) reflects the buoyancy of love in the light of the future inheritance (cf. 5:2-5; 1 Peter 1:3-9). Love rejoices because of hope (cf. 1 Cor. 13:7), stands firm in time of trouble, and persists in prayer (cf. NEB). Barrett writes: "Christian rejoicing, which endures through affliction, is rooted in the hope of what God will do, and at all times the Christian looks beyond his immediate environment to God in prayer" (p. 240).

Enthusiastic sharing (v. 13) is love going out of the way to relieve the needs of the saints and to open a haven to the weary. The Christian is to share his goods with fellow Christians and pursue hospitality, an important duty in the New Testament church (cf. Heb. 13:2; 1 Tim. 3:2; Titus 1:8; 1 Peter 4:9). Phillips paraphrases "hospitality," "never grudging a meal or a bed to those who need them."

b. *Love to the enemy without (vv. 14-21).* With the change of construction in verse 14, we also enter a new atmosphere for the display of love. John Brown remarks: "Having thus stated how the Roman Christians ought to behave to their fellow-sufferers, the Apostle proceeds to show how they should conduct themselves to the authors of their sufferings" (p. 467). These guidelines, which focus on those outside the kingdom of God, are particularly reminiscent of the Sermon on the Mount.

Gracious forbearance (v. 14) is the response of love to its enemies (cf. Matt. 5:44; Luke 6:28; James 3:9-12). Love calls down blessings upon the persecutor, not curses. In connection with the preceding injunction of verse 13, Griffith Thomas says "we are to 'pursue' hospitality, and we are also to bless those who 'pursue' us" (III,39).

Sympathetic understanding (v. 15) reveals the capacity of love to identify with the highs and lows of others. Love is joyful with the happy and sorrowful with the mourner. The Christian can stand beside his fellow man to have time and room for him in real human joy and real human sorrow without compromising with his evil or pretending to share his presuppositions (cf. Cranfield, *Scottish Journal*).

Likable humility (v. 16) draws a circle of love around the unlovely and, having excluded snobbery, invites them to full privileges of fellowship. Love seeks harmony among Christians (cf. 2 Cor. 13:11; Phil. 2:2; 4:2), decries haughtiness, and takes "a real interest in ordinary people" (Phillips, cf. NEB). The real danger of conceit is that it closes the door of Christian friendship (cf. Prov. 3:7).

Honorable aims (vv. 17,18) make love a noble virtue, never stooping to the base standard of the world. Love does not repay evil for evil (cf. Matt. 5:43,44; 1 Thess. 5:15; 1 Peter 3:9; 1 Cor. 13:5,6); it gives no cause for slander from anyone (cf. Prov. 3:4; 2 Cor. 4:2; 8:21); and within its power to do so, love lives peaceably with all men (cf. Matt. 5:9). The Christian has no control over others; if the peace is broken, they must be at fault.

Spacious temperament (v. 19) is that restraint in love that leaves room for "the law of divine retribution to operate whether now or on 'the day of wrath' (ii. 5)" (Bruce, p. 230). Love never avenges itself because vengeance is the proper work of God (Deut. 32:35). We must "leave room for God's anger" (Goodspeed; cf. NASB, NEB) for, as the Scripture shows, judgment is His prerogative.

Overcoming kindness (vv. 20,21) is the mellowing power of love to turn an enemy into a friend. Love overcomes evil with good, just as God has proceeded against the enmity of mankind (cf. 5:8). The phrase "heap coals of fire on his head" (v. 20b), quoted from Proverbs 25:21,22, refers to the burning shame (Moffatt) an enemy feels when kindness is returned for evil, which may also lead to his repentance. "Heap benefits on thine enemy; for thereby thou shalt cause him the salutary pain of shame and regret for all the evil he has done thee; and thou shalt light up in his heart the fire of gratitude instead of that of hatred" (Godet, p. 439).

C. Duties to the State and Fellow Citizens (13:1-14)

Christian duty does not end in the ministry of the church, but it reaches in an ever-widening sphere to the entire civic domain. Having pleaded for love to the outsider (12:17-21), Paul abruptly moves from the inner corporate life of Christians to their outer walk in the community at large, which ties together the loosely framed themes of chapter 13. The majority of interpreters treat the injunctions concerning the state (vv. 1-7), the neighbor (vv. 8-10), and the approaching day (vv. 11-14) as three disconnected topics (cf. Sanday and Headlam, Bruce, Barrett). But throughout the passage there is emphasis on the world at large as an arena in which the Christian renders service to God. This he does by obeying rulers (vv. 1-7), loving his neighbors (vv. 8-10), and watching for "the day" (vv. 11-14).

1. Submit to the governing authorities (13:1-7)

There is nothing surprising in Paul's raising the question of the Christian's obligation to governing authorities. Since the Christian cannot indulge in vengeance (12:17-19), he must look to the state to suppress evildoers (v. 4). Likewise, since the state serves the good of men (v. 4), to actively support it can be regarded as part of the debt to love one's neighbor (cf. Cranfield, *Scottish Journal*, p. 62). This emphasis on submission to governing authorities may also owe something to the turbulent situation in Rome. It is likely that the introduction of Christianity into the Jewish community of Rome had caused rioting, provoking the emperor Claudius (ca. A.D. 49) to drive many Jews out of the city.[7]

This likelihood is strengthened by the appearance of two Jewish Christians, Aquila and Priscilla, in the Acts record of Paul's first visit to Corinth. They had just come from Italy "because Claudius had commanded all the Jews to leave Rome" (Acts 18:2, RSV). Although Christians were not responsible for such disturbances, the suspicion of anarchy was a common grievance voiced against them (cf. Acts 17:6,7). "It was all the more necessary, therefore, that Christians should be especially careful of their public behaviour, and give their traducers no handle against them, but rather pay all due honour and obedience to the authorities" (Bruce, p. 233). Three affirmations sum up the reasons given by Paul for such obedience.

a. *The state is a divinely ordained institution (vv. 1,2).* The key idea in this passage is expressed in the words, "let every soul be subject unto the higher powers" (v. 1, KJV). They are not, however, to be understood as a demand for a blind servitude to the state but as an appeal

---

[7]Suetonius tells us that Claudius "expelled the Jews from Rome because they were constantly rioting at the instigation of Chrestus" (*Life of Claudius*, 25,2). Many scholars believe the reference to "Chrestus" is a variant spelling of "Christ," hence the commotion was connected with the gospel movement in Rome (cf. Sanday and Headlam, Bruce).

for a submission to the authority ordained of God that preserves and orders society. The verb "to be subject, obey" is used in the New Testament of the loyal submission of the Christian to God (James 4:7), to the leaders of the church (1 Cor. 16:16), to civil authorities (Titus 3:1; 1 Peter 2:13); of wives to their husbands (Eph. 5:22; Col. 3:18); of slaves to their masters (1 Peter 2:18); of the young men to elders (1 Peter 5:5); of the church to Christ (Eph. 5:24). The phrase "higher powers" (v. 1, KJV) or "governing authorities" (NASB, RSV) clearly refers to civil authority; it likely includes "both the person and office of such as are set in authority" (Gifford, p. 211). Paul elsewhere uses the same word with the meaning of "angelic authorities" (cf. 8:38; Col. 1:16; 2:10,15; Eph. 1:21; 3:10; 6:12),[8] but these powers are neither commissioned in the service of God nor are they to be obeyed by Christians.

Paul views the institution of government as having a special claim to man's allegiance because it is divinely ordained (v. 1b). God is the source of all authority and power, and therefore "no human authority can exist except as the gift of God and springing from Him" (Sanday and Headlam, p. 366). The truth that God is the ruler of all nations and master of history was well known in the Old Testament (cf. 2 Sam. 12:8; Jer. 27:5,6; Dan. 2:21). In His providence, God protects man from the ravages of unbridled sin by raising up civil authority, just as He provides men with sun and rain (cf. Barrett, p. 245).

Resistance to the state therefore amounts to rebellion against "a divine institution" (NEB), which act will incur punishment (v. 2). Bruce notes the misuse of verse 2 and cautions that "The state can rightly command obedience only within the limits of the purposes for which it was divinely instituted — in particular, the state not only may but must be resisted when it demands the allegiance due to God alone" (p. 237).

b. *The state is the minister of true justice (vv. 3,4).* The state carries out the task that is expressly forbidden to the Christian, executing wrath upon those who do wrong (v. 4b; cf. 12:17,19). Paul consistently sees the ruler in the twofold role of praising the good (v. 3c) and punishing the evil (v. 4b); therefore, the obedient Christian has no cause to fear authority. It might seem that Paul is oblivious to the possibility of injustice in government, but he had personally experienced mistreatment from authorities (Acts 16:22,37; 2 Cor. 11:23-25). Nygren believes "his judgment did not rest on accidental experiences and impressions; it is part of his total theological outlook" (p. 429). The grounds for his

---

[8]Oscar Cullmann (*Christ and Time*, pp. 191-205) has argued for a double reference in "powers" — to civil authorities and also to invisible angelic powers acting through them; "the State is indeed the executive agent of invisible powers" (p. 195). His case has not been widely accepted by interpreters of Romans.

optimistic view of rulers is found in verse 4: "they are God's servants appointed for your good" (TCNT). The magistrate can be called a "minister of God" (Greek, *diakonos*), both in preserving good and executing wrath, as surely as a Christian can (12:7) or even Christ Himself (15:8). The purposes to which the ruler ultimately gives effect are, in spite of all contrary appearances, not his own, but God's (Cranfield, *Scottish Journal*, p. 74). We can be sure the state exists to a good end because it is the instrument of God's purpose (cf. 8:28).

In the darker side of God's purpose, civil authority is God's "avenger who brings wrath" (v. 4c, NASB); that is, civil authority is the present manifestation of God's wrath that restrains evil. Although it does not vindicate the moral right of capital punishment, the "power of the sword" (v. 4b, NEB) alludes to the powers of life and death vested in the state.

c. *The state is the franchise of public conscience (vv. 5-7).* Paul now explains that Christians should submit to the state not only out of expedience, avoiding wrath, but also out of propriety, "for conscience' sake" (v. 5). The Christian lives "by a higher principle and he obeys the Government, not because he fears retribution which follows on disobedience, but because his conscience bids him do so" (Dodd, p. 205). This reference to conscience suggests the spirit and limit of obedience to the state, for "when it comes to order something contrary to God's law, there is nothing else to be done than to make it feel the contradiction between its commission and its conduct" (Godet, p. 444). The Christian motivation to citizenship, which transcends fear of reprisal, recognizes the positive good for society as a whole that God has made the responsibility of the state.

Paul adds: "That is also why you pay taxes. The authorities are in God's service and to these duties they devote their energies" (v. 6, NEB). It is because conscience recognizes the divine appointment of government that we subsidize its activity through taxes. The antecedent of "this very thing" (v. 6b) can be the general work of the state (Gifford, Barrett) or the specific task of tax gathering (Cranfield). In the latter case, Paul is saying that even as tax-collectors, these authorities are working energetically as the "officials" of God and that justifies their function. We must remember that the levy of taxes was a volatile issue in the Roman world; it was, indeed, the trumped-up charge of tax evasion that helped nail Jesus to the cross (cf. Luke 23:2). There may be an echo of Jesus' true teaching in verse 7: "Render to Caesar the things that are Caesar's" (Mark 12:17, RSV). Paul enlarges upon the idea of paying taxes, which Christians knew from Jesus' words, and adds "respect" (literally "fear") and "honor" to that due public officials (v. 7c). Respect and honor are paid to earthly rulers, not in view of their prestige and influence, but because Christian conscience sanctions their place of service in God's plan.

2. *Be a debtor to love* (13:8-10)

Having sketched the Christian's duty as a citizen of the state, which is "no small portion of love" (Calvin, p. 485), Paul proceeds to show that our sense of debt is really the principle of love for others. We should note the occurrence of the plural noun "dues" (v. 7a) which in Greek reappears in the cognate verb "owe" (v. 8a), thus forming a smooth transition from the previous section (cf. Denney, NEB). The Christian should leave no debt outstanding against him, except the obligation to mutual love, a debt that can never be cancelled. In the third century, Origen wrote: "The debt of love is permanent, and we are never finished with it; for we must pay it daily and yet always owe it" (*Ad Rom.*, col. 1231, Dodd's translation). However, the genuineness of love has a legitimate test in whether or not a Christian repays his other debts.

In verse 8, Paul does not use the Greek word for "neighbor" (as the versions would suggest) but the phrase "the other." It is possible, therefore, to translate this sentence "he who loves has fulfilled the other law" — the "other law" being the second great commandment, "Thou shalt love thy neighbour as thyself" (Matt. 22:39; Mark 12:31). But, the translation "neighbor" is preferred by all the versions. The significance of "the other," the Greek of which means another of a different kind, has been pointed out by Barrett: "Love for the neighbor can too easily be misinterpreted as 'love for the likeminded man who is congenial to me'; love is not Christian if it cannot include love for the man who differs from me in every way" (p. 250).

We may ask in what fashion does the love of neighbor fulfill the law of God. Paul's premise, a precept widely used in the New Testament (cf. Luke 10:27; Gal. 5:14; James 2:8), is that the Ten Commandments (Exod. 20:13-17) are summed up in one rule (cf. NEB; Lev. 19:18), namely, to love one's neighbor as oneself (v. 9). Therefore, if the Christian discharges the debt of love, he has performed the full requirement of the law. However, as we have already seen, the debt to love is never fully discharged; therefore, when rightly understood, the whole law is perpetuated and is being fulfilled in the Christian law of love.

3. *Prepare for the approaching day* (13:11-14)

Verses 11-14 set the seal of urgency on fulfilling the debt to love by describing the critical nature of the times. The passage is the counterpart to 12:1,2 where the reader is urged to live in conformity with the new age, but what there appeared as a faraway frontier now becomes a nearby horizon. The introductory words, "And that" (v. 11a), look back to all of Paul's exhortations in chapters 12 and 13 and heighten the force of what has been said (cf. 1 Cor. 6:6; Eph. 2:8; Heb. 11:12). Weymouth translates: "Live thus, realizing the situation"; TCNT: "This I say, because you know the crisis we have reached"; Phillips: "Why all this stress on behavior? Because, as I think you have realized, the present time is of the highest importance." The obedience of the faithful grows with the expectancy of Christ's return; therein lies Paul's definition of New Testament watchfulness (cf. Matt. 25:31-46; 1 Thess. 5:1-11; Heb. 10:24,25; James 5:7-11; 1 Peter 4:7-11). We can outline the nature of this eschatological vigil around the notes of nearness (v. 11), earnestness (vv. 12,13), and readiness (v. 14).

a. *Nearness that signals the approaching day (v. 11).* Paul has already told us that the life of the age to come has spilled over into this present world (cf. 5:5; 8:23; 12:2) and that the Christian lives between the times; that is, the interim between Christ's ascension and second advent. Our attention is drawn to the end of this era in the word "time" (v. 11a), which, in this context, refers to the overlapping of the ages, the last epoch of history preceding Christ's return (cf. 3:26; Gal. 4:4; 1 Cor. 4:5; 7:29; 10:11; Eph. 1:10; Heb. 9:26). That a Christian understands the impending close of this era is reason enough to "awake out of sleep" (v. 11b). The kind of time it is means that it is already time to rouse up from spiritual drowsiness (cf. TCNT; 1 Thess. 5:6-8; Eph. 5:14).

The imminent event in Paul's thinking is the nearness of salvation (v. 11c), the future aspect of our deliverance in Christ, namely, the consummation of salvation realized at the coming of Christ (cf. 5:9; 8:23; Phil. 2:12; 1 Thess. 5:8,9; 1 Peter 1:5; Heb. 9:28). It is closer now than when Paul and his readers first came to know the Lord (v. 11c, NEB). How close is it? That question, a widely debated one, has no definitive answer. Although we can plead for an imminent expectation in Paul's hope (cf. 11:31; 1 Cor. 15:51; 1 Thess. 4:15), it is another thing to say he was convinced that Christ would necessarily come in his lifetime.

b. *Earnestness that befits the approaching day (vv. 12,13).* With the trumpet of the Lord's advent ringing in his ears, Paul sounds the reveille for God's soldiers in this world. The picture is that of a soldier stripping off his attire and donning the armor of battle. The exhortations "let us therefore cast off" (cf. 1 Peter 2:1; James 1:21; Col. 3:8; Eph. 4:22,25; Heb. 12:1) and "let us put on" (cf. Col. 3:10,12; Eph. 4:24; 1 Thess. 5:8; Gal. 3:27) are common figures of admonition to Christians (v. 12). The struggle to be engaged is between night-life activities and day-life service (cf. 2 Cor. 6:14; Eph. 5:8; Col. 1:12,13; 1 Thess. 5:4-8).

God musters the Christian for fighting, not sleeping; our lives are to be equipped with the armor that God provides, "the armour of light" (cf. Eph. 6:13-18).

Parallel to "casting off" and "putting on" is the appeal to "walk becomingly" (v. 13). Six sins, named in three pairs, are especially to be avoided. Griffith Thomas groups these six sins under the headings of (1) intemperance, (2) impurity, and (3) discord (III, 64). "Revelling" ("carousing," NASB) is the lack of moral restraint (cf. 1 Peter 4:3) that would naturally lead to "drunkenness." "Chambering" is unlawful sexual intercourse; and its companion, "wantonness" ("licentiousness," RSV; cf. 2 Peter 2:2), is a shameless, open exhibition that shocks public decency. The last pair, "strife and jealousy," represents the passions that abuse true love; both evils grow from a malignant ambition (cf. Gal. 5:20; 2 Cor. 12:20).

c. *The readiness that welcomes the approaching day (v. 14).* Instead of indulging in these sensual vices, the Christian clothes himself in the Lord Jesus Christ. Putting on Christ interprets the meaning of putting on the armor of light (v. 12b): "Let Jesus Christ himself be the armour that you wear" (NEB; cf. Weymouth, Cranfield). Therefore, in this context, putting on Christ refers to clothing the soul in the moral disposition and habits of Christ (cf. Gifford). This exhortation is similar to the plea in Colossians 3:10-12 and Ephesians 4:24 to put off the old man and put on the new.

In contrast to Galatians 3:27, which states the indicative fact that believers have "put on Christ" by virtue of their union with Him through faith (cf. Rom. 6:3-6), this verse has imperative force, calling the believer to continual renewal of the relationship once begun.

It has its negative counterpart in "put a stop to gratifying the evil desires that lurk in your lower nature" (Williams). A man who allows his fleshly appetites to go on unchecked is not wrapped up in Christ. It was this insight that brought Augustine from the despair of a tarnished past to the light of full salvation. Under the intuition of providence, Augustine read verses 13,14 in silence, and he tells us: "No further would I read, nor had I any need; instantly at the end of this sentence, a clear light flooded my heart and all the darkness of doubt vanished away" (*Confessions*, 8,29).

D. Duties Touching the Relations Between Weak and Strong Christians (14:1-15:13)

Paul now passes to a subject of urgent importance for his readers — the dispute of the "strong" and the "weak" in the Roman church. Here is the scene: "This Christian [the weak in faith], not untrustful, at least in theory, of the Lord alone for pardon and acceptance, is, however, quite full of scruples which, to the man fully 'armed with Christ,' may seem, and do seem, lamentably morbid, really serious mistakes and hindrances" (Moule, *Expositor's Bible*, p. 376). Paul takes up the task of reconciling these two brothers. Our discussion will highlight the following points:

1. *The problem of the strong and the weak (14:1-12)*

The two groups that emerge, the "strong" (those who have a "robust conscience" [cf. 15:1], NEB) and the "weak" (those who are "overscrupulous in their faith" [cf. 14:1], Goodspeed), are both Christian. The weak were not so completely emancipated from ritual abstinence as were the strong; their weakness consisted of an immature faith that had not grasped the full meaning of Christian liberty. We may suppose their views to have tended toward legalism, especially in its ceremonial aspects, because Paul mentions three ascetic tendencies in chapter 14: (1) the eating of vegetables instead of meat (v. 2), (2) the hallowing of certain feast or fast days (v. 5), and (3) the prohibition to drink wine (vv. 17,21). Similar ascetic practices, widespread in the Graeco-Roman world, troubled the Galatian (Gal. 4:10,11) and the Colossian (Col. 2:16,17) Christians. However, in those churches, Paul denounces them as heretical, in fact, a dangerous subversion of justification by faith. His conciliatory spirit in Romans indicates that the scruples in question are, from the viewpoint of the gospel, matters of indifference.

For all the attempts to identify these specific groups in Rome, no satisfactory answer is forthcoming.[9] It is a fair inference that the weak are Jewish Christians who are offended by the conduct of the Gentile majority in the church. In view of the sketchy information, we must base this probability on 15:7-13, where the discussion passes over into an exhortation for unity between the Jew and Gentile (cf. Gifford, Denney, Barrett). Although Paul had not been there (15:22,23), it must be granted that he had some knowledge of the Roman church (perhaps through Aquila and Priscilla, cf. Acts 18:2). Throughout the letter, the truth of the gospel is applied to Jew and Gentile without distinction; in this passage, Paul narrows his target to an old problem that surely existed in Rome: the unity of Jewish and Gentile believers. In sum, the origin and exact divergence of the views of the strong and weak are obscure, but the effects of the rift are clear enough.

---

[9]Many able commentators believe that Paul, writing on the basis of past experience, addresses this problem to prepare the church in case it did arise. This view argues that (1) the sting of real controversy is absent, (2) the admonitions are preventive measures along the lines of 1 Corinthians 8-10, and (3) the lack of precise information indicates that the problem is not yet a specific difficulty in the Roman church.

a. *The serious magnitude of the problem threatens the fellowship of the church (v. 1).* The verb "receive" often is used of God's gracious reception of man (v. 3), but here it means for a man (the strong) to welcome another (the weak) into Christian fellowship. The description of the "weak in faith" (a present participle) implies a temporary condition that could change (Godet, p. 454). It would be natural for the strong to welcome the weak, thinking to win them over from their inferior views, but Paul will not agree to that. There is to be no purpose of reforming the weak — "accept him without attempting to settle doubtful points" (v. 1b, NEB). Or the meaning can be, "not for the purpose of passing judgment on their scruples" (TCNT, cf. RSV). No genuine fellowship exists where the invited feel they must pass a test to gain full acceptance. "Fellowship among Christians is not to be based on questioning and disputing, toward the result that the one adopts the other's view and accepts it as the norm of action. Such sameness is not a Christian ideal. Acceptance ought not to rest on such secondary considerations" (Nygren, p. 443).

b. *The harsh feelings in the problem arise from matters of indifference (vv. 2-5).* How often piddling opinions and trivial issues keep Christians apart! We might have expected Paul to take sides with the strong since he undoubtedly agreed with them (cf. 14:14), but Paul was so completely free from spiritual bondage "that he was not even in bondage to his emancipation" (Bruce, p. 243). In areas of life that were open to question, Paul took the course of pleasing all, in order to preserve the unity of the church (cf. 1 Cor. 10:23-33). The apostle argues that the opinions which divide the strong and weak are not all that important. Why debate unessential matters and thereby rupture the community of faith?

The strong ate any kind of food in good conscience, whereas the weak were strict vegetarians (v. 2), perhaps in order to avoid eating meat consecrated to a pagan deity or in pursuit of Jewish dietary law (1 Cor. 8:7; 10:28). Again, the strong made no distinctions between days, but the weak venerated certain days as more sacred than others (v. 5), a reference to ceremonial days on the religious calendar rather than the sabbath (cf. Col. 2:16; Gal. 4:10). Paul's reasoning is clear: "The fundamental principle is that such things are in themselves indifferent, but that each person must be fully assured in his own conscience that he is doing right" (Sanday and Headlam, p. 386).

In other words, this is a classic case of straining at the gnat and swallowing the camel (cf. Matt. 23:24); the principles involved give no cause for such a disturbance. Paul's concern is the contempt in which the two parties hold each other; the strong despised the weak, and the weak censured the strong (v. 3). The burden of rebuke rests upon the weak who inclined to criticize the strong for taking too many liberties. Often the pampered use their solicitude as an effective weapon, but Paul represses the "tyranny of the weak" in its very beginning (v. 3b, cf. Denney). Judgment upon the strong is forbidden; "God, after all, has made room for him" (Knox). Just as the servant in a human household is upheld by the master of the house, so the strong has a sure footing in *his* Master (Christ) and does not stand upon the carping standards of the weak (v. 4). Each man should be "fully convinced in his own mind" (v. 5b, TCNT), and, forbearing the contentions of others, be big enough to look over such small concerns.

c. *The neglected factor in the problem is each man's responsibility to God (vv. 6-12).* The truth is that both sides are trying to do the will of God. Whatever each does, eating or not eating, hallowing or not hallowing the day, he does it "for the Lord's sake" (v. 6, Weymouth),[10] dedicating his activity to the honor and glory of God. Therefore, if both aim at serving God, then both should know that they will answer to God for their hostile attitudes. Calvin says: "Let a reason for what he does be clear to every one; as an account must be given before the celestial tribunal; for whether one eats meat or abstains, he ought in both instances to have regard to God" (p. 498). The factor to be remembered in the squabble is that, in living and dying, the Christian belongs to God. What Paul means in verse 7 (as shown by v. 8) is that the Christian lives out his life under the lordship of Christ and even death will not remove him from that responsibility. The popular meaning given verse 7 (when quoted out of context) follows *as a corollary*: "each Christian's life affects his fellow-Christians and his fellow-men, and therefore he should consider his responsibility to them" (Bruce, p. 245).

The certainty that we shall answer to God rests in the death and resurrection of Christ (vv. 8,9). The threefold "we live . . . we die . . . we are" in verse 8 shows that the all-embracing criterion for Christian conduct is one's relation to the Lord. Life demands it; death cannot end it. This "eternal claim of the Lord" has been made good in Jesus' death and resurrection (cf. Moule). The very "purpose of Christ's dying and coming to life" (v. 9a, Weymouth) was that He might be Lord over us in life and death (cf. Phil. 2:9,11; Rev. 2:18).

Here is the clinching reason for dropping this incessant criticism of one another — Christ is Lord, the right to judge belongs to Him (vv. 10-12). Both the weak and strong will stand, not at each other's, but at

---

[10]The clause "and he that regardeth not the day, to the Lord he doth not regard it" (v. 6b, KJV) is not found in the best Greek text and is, therefore, omitted in the modern versions.

the "judgment — seat of God"[11] (v. 10c); therefore, let premature judgment cease. The believer's confession of Christ in His exaltation (Isa. 45:23; cf. Phil. 2:10,11) certifies that he shall also stand before Him in judgment (v. 11). Paul concludes the whole problem in a word: "Each of us then will have to answer for himself to God" (v. 12, Moffatt). "The strong, then, is right; but if he boasts of his superiority he instantly becomes as wrong as the man he despises. The weak is mistaken, yet accepted; and he must not put himself in God's place, and judge the strong" (Barrett, p. 261).

2. *The principle of walking in love (14:13-23)*

As Paul demonstrated the citizen's obligation to the state to be the deeper one of love (13:8-10), so he proceeds to argue the question of Christian fellowship from the deeper point of view. Although the Christian is free to follow his conviction in matters of indifference, remembering that he must answer to God, he ought to consider the impact of his conduct on the lives of other Christians. All that Paul has said to this point is true, but the principle of "living by the standard of love" (v. 15a, Williams) is higher than all, giving place for the feelings and consciences of others. This is the particular duty of the strong, to be considerate of others, because the exercise of freedom (in itself right) could become the occasion of stumbling for the weaker brother. In the case of eating meat, the weak, out of deference to the strong, might yield and eat, all the while feeling in his conscience that it was wrong. The effect upon the weak would be guilt — I have sinned (v. 23) — but the blame for his fall would belong to the strong who prepared his stumbling (v. 21). This principle for the conduct of the strong can be summarized in four affirmations.

a. *It is a principle that measures a man in the light of the cross (vv. 13-15).* Because of the coming judgment of God, neither the strong nor the weak are in a position to judge one another (v. 13a). Paul presses his point by a play on the verb "to judge," which in its second usage in verse 13a has the weakened sense of "resolve" (TCNT) or "decide" (RSV). The only matter left to decide is whether one will "trip up or entangle a brother's conscience" (Knox). The "stumbling-block" (cf. 1 Cor. 8:9) Paul has in mind is "the setting of an example which might lead another into sin" (Bruce, p. 251). Paul, agreeing with the strong (v. 14), knows that no food is "unclean" (cf. Mark 7:14-23; Acts 10:9-16; 1 Cor. 10:25,26). But if eating certain food offends a weaker brother, who

---

[11]The better attested reading is "judgment — seat of God" (RSV, NEB, NASB), but the KJV reading, "judgment seat of Christ," is very early and parallels the wording of 2 Corinthians 5:10. In any case, Paul teaches that God will judge the world through Christ (cf. 2:16; Acts 17:31).

considers it unclean, then the strong Christian must desist in the name of love (v. 15). The eating of "unclean food" in the presence of the weak tampers with his conscience and brings him to spiritual ruin. There is an overriding consideration here: "Christ died to save this man from his sins, and will you for his sake not give up some favourite food" (Sanday and Headlam, p. 391). We must take the divine measure of the worth of a fellow Christian. If we measure men by the cross, "it will do more than anything else to preserve our souls in the same attitude of loving regard, unselfish consideration, and willing self-sacrifice" (Griffith Thomas, III, 89).

b. *It is a principle that acknowledges the nature of the kingdom of God (vv. 16-18).* It is often true that a good thing (in this case, Christian freedom in eating) becomes the occasion for slanderous talk (v. 16, cf. NEB). The phrase "evil spoken of" ("to blaspheme," cf. 1 Cor. 10:30) refers to the fact that Christian liberty "will inevitably get a bad name if it is exercised in an inconsiderate loveless fashion" (Denney, p. 705). A person who insists upon the primacy of "meat and drink" has totally missed the basis of the Christian faith. Life in the "kingdom of God" (cf. 1 Cor. 4:20; 1 Thess. 2:12; Gal. 5:21) attaches no importance to eating and drinking (v. 17a). They are absolutely insignificant in comparison to those present foretastes of the coming kingdom: "rightness of heart, finding our peace and our joy in the Holy Spirit" (v. 17b, Knox). After the model of Jesus' teaching (Matt. 5:6,9,10,12; 6:31-33), Paul places the kingdom virtues first among Christian priorities. He enlarges the prospect in that righteousness, peace, and joy are fruits of the Holy Spirit (Gal. 5:22) who has already brought the blessings of the age to come (cf. 8:23). The man who keeps his eye on the kingdom "pleases God" (v. 18, TCNT), and he will give no occasion for anyone to blaspheme his conduct ("approval of men," cf. v. 16).

c. *It is a principle that pursues the aim of mutual edification (vv. 19-21).* Barrett remarks: "It cannot make for the unity of this one body [in Christ, cf. 12:5] if the several members are more concerned to practise their private convictions than to live in love" (p. 265). Paul now draws our attention to the harmony and upbuilding of the community of faith. The "peace" and "mutual upbuilding" (v. 19, Williams) point to the church and not the individual (cf. Sanday and Headlam). The church is God's building (1 Cor. 3:9), and, instead of ruining "the work of God for the sake of food" (v. 20a, NEB), the Christian ought to be building it up (cf. 1 Cor. 14:26; 1 Thess. 5:11). The practical rule implied here is that before a Christian acts on a private conviction, he "must ask how such action will affect the peace of the Church, and the Christian growth of others" (Denney, p. 706). To fail in this respect brings inevitable harm to "that man who eateth with offence" (v. 20b). This phrase can refer to the strong, meaning "it is wrong for any one to make others fall by what he eats" (RSV; cf. NEB, TCNT); or, to the weak, "it can be harmful to the man who eats it with a guilty conscience" (Phillips). The vagueness of the Greek construction may point to the fact that Paul is thinking of both possibilities (cf. Barrett); however, verse 21 is a maxim for the strong. Abstinence (no meat or wine) and restraint ("nor any thing") are noble indeed if they are done to preserve the conscience of a brother and edify the church (v. 21, cf. 1 Cor. 8:13).

d. *It is a principle that safeguards the character of faith (vv. 22,23).* In concluding his argument for love, Paul addresses the strong in faith with a motive to charitable self-restraint (cf. Gifford). The faith of the strong is a personal conviction, to be kept between the Christian and God (v. 22a), not to be flaunted in a reckless way over the weak in faith. The strong are emancipated not to "disturb the neighbours with shouts of freedom and acts of license" but to serve them in love (Moule, *Expositor's Bible*, p. 391). Their blessing is a reassuring faith: "Happy is the man who can make his decision with a clear conscience" (v. 22b, NEB). *Modern Language Bible* expresses it, "Happy the man who has no qualms of conscience in what he allows himself to do." However, the case of the weak is far different. If he eats meat with a guilty conscience, his very doubts will condemn him — "one who has misgivings stands self-condemned if he eats" (v. 23a, Weymouth). The word "damned" (KJV) or "condemned" (the weaker sense the English word once had) refers to an accusation of the heart that contracts a sense of guilt. Whatever his motive for eating, it does not come from faith ("does not arise from his conviction," v. 23a, NEB) if the weaker Christian feels guilty. Therefore, the weak must safeguard the limits of his faith; if he oversteps his own conviction in complying with the standard of the strong, then he has sinned (v. 23b). Paul calls both the strong and the weak to act with a clear conscience, a reassuring faith, and in doing so, they will not sin.

3. *The pattern of the ministry of the Lord (15:1-13)*

The great example of charitable service is Jesus Christ, whom Paul sets forth in this paragraph as the model of conduct for the strong and weak. We are still dealing with the problem of chapter 14, but now the discussion takes on a new dimension. Paul's "argument widens into a plea for patience and forbearance (enforced by the example of Christ) and for the union of all Christians, Jew and Gentile, in common praise" (Denney, p. 707). The references to the ministry of Christ (vv. 3,8) show that Paul, like Peter and John, believed the Christian must walk in the steps of Jesus (cf. 1 Peter 2:21; 1 John 2:6). In appealing to the example of Jesus in burden-bearing (vv. 1-6) and in uniting Jew and Gentile (vv. 7-13), Paul passes to the broad, underlying purpose of God in redemption with which he began the letter.

a. *The concern of Christ for the burdens of others (vv. 1-6)*. The debt of love for others, which is never fully paid (13:8), places an obligation upon the strong to "bear the weaknesses of those without strength" (v. 1, NASB). The word "bear" is used literally (John 19:17) and figuratively (Luke 14:27) of bearing the cross; the discipleship of the cross involves the command to "bear the burden of one another's failings" (Gal. 6:2, Knox). "It is so easy for a man whose own conscience is quite clear about some course of action to snap his fingers at his critics and say 'I'll please myself.' He has every right to do so, but that is not the way of Christ" (Bruce, p. 254). The words of verse 2 limit and explain what Paul means by "please his neighbour" (cf. 1 Cor. 9:20-23). The rule is that we are to please men (not indulge them, Gal. 1:10; Eph. 6:6) for the purpose of their absolute good, further defined as, their edification (cf. 14:16,19).

The phrase "Christ . . . pleased not himself" (v. 3) sums up the earthly life and work of the Lord. The mind of Christ was fastened upon the needs of others (Phil. 2:4-8), not his own interests. Instead of adducing an incident from Jesus' life, Paul quotes the psalmist to prove his point: "The reproaches of them who reproached thee fell upon me" (v. 3b, Ps. 69:9). The words declare that in His suffering, Christ bore the reproaches or sufferings of others. Therefore, the Scripture, revealing the purpose of God, gives enduring hope for the believer that through Christ the trials of life will be won. Verse 4 is a digression, showing the special use of Scripture to foster hope: "so that, through patient endurance [cf. 5:3], and through the encouragement drawn from the Scriptures, we might hold fast to our hope" (TCNT). The thought seems to be that the scriptural forecast of Christ's suffering in the will of God encourages us to pass through our present difficulties in hope (cf. Barrett).

Because He is the "source of all fortitude and all encouragement" (v. 5a, NEB; cf. 2 Cor. 1:3), Paul asks God to grant the gift of mutual concern to the entire church (vv. 5,6). This petition discloses three cardinal precepts for the proper fellowship of God's people. The first precept is harmony of thought, "be likeminded one toward another" (v. 5b). The RSV translates: "live in such harmony with one another"; NEB: "agree with one another." The second precept is imitation of Christ, "according to Christ Jesus" (v. 5b) which must mean "in accordance with the character or example of Christ" (Sanday and Headlam, p. 396; cf.

Eph. 4:24; Col. 2:8). The final precept is unity of praise, "with one mind and one mouth glorify God" (v. 6) or "that you may unite in a chorus of praise and glory to God" (Moffatt). "When one common aspiration reigns in the church, secondary diversities no longer separate hearts; and from the internal communion there results common adoration like pure harmony from a concert of well-tuned instruments" (Godet, p. 469).

   b. *The welcome of Christ for Jew and Gentile (vv. 7-13).* Paul now summarizes the teaching that began at 14:1 by placing the unity of the strong and the weak in the wider purpose of God's mercy for all humanity. This connection makes it probable that the relation of Jew and Gentile is at the center of the problem between strong and weak. We note the recurrence of a threefold structure in this passage like the preceding one in verses 1-6; a description of Christ's example (vv. 7-9a, cf. v. 3a), a proof from the Old Testament (vv. 9b-12, cf. v. 3b,4), and a prayer of hope (v. 13, cf. vv. 5,6). The exhortation to "welcome one another" (v. 7a, Weymouth) is grounded in the fact that Christ has welcomed Jew and Gentile into the kingdom of God. Paul returns to the opening premise of this long discussion (cf. 14:1,3), basing the believer's fellowship on the welcome extended by Christ. The words "to the glory of God" (v. 7b) can be construed with the believers' welcome of each other (Denney) or with the welcome Christ gives all (Sanday and Headlam). Barrett adds: "But it is probably not wrong to take them with both verbs. Christ's act in welcoming men is directed to the glory of God; but so is the unity of Christian men in love. When the strong receive the weak, and the weak the strong, they are in the most significant way glorifying God" (p. 270).

   In order to welcome Jew and Gentile, Jesus "became a servant of the Jewish people" (v. 8a, NEB); that is, He was sent "unto the lost sheep of the house of Israel" (Matt. 15:24). The grand scope of God's redemption is portrayed by Paul in the twofold purpose of Christ's earthly work: (1) that he might confirm God's faithfulness to the promises given to the patriarchs (v. 8b), and, in doing so, (2) that the Gentiles might also glorify God (v. 9a). Christ came to "show God's truthfulness" (Goodspeed) by fulfilling the covenant promises to the Jews, and "at the same time" (NEB), to include the Gentiles among the people of God, thus glorifying God for His mercy. This reciprocity of God's purpose for Jew and Gentile exactly corresponds to what we have already seen in chapters 9-11 (cf. 11:28-32). As Paul did throughout chapters 9-11, he strings together a chain of Old Testament quotations to establish the calling of the Gentiles in the eternal plan found in Scripture (vv. 9-12, cf. Deut. 32:43; Ps. 18:49; 117:1; Isa. 11:10).

A final prayer rounds out the great didactic portion of this letter (v. 13). The petition is Paul's way of saying, "Let us stand back and look at the picture of God's righteousness and the life of faith it brings." Following Moule's account (*Expositor's Bible*, pp. 404,405) we can note: (1) it is a life lived in direct contact with God, "the giver of hope" (Weymouth); (2) it is a life not starved but full, "fill you" (cf. Eph. 3:19; (3) it is a life bright and beautiful, "all joy and peace" (cf. Phil. 4:5-7); (4) it is a life of faith, "through your continuing faith" (Williams); (5) it is a life of heavenly hope, "overflow with hope" (NEB, cf. 5:2; (6) it is a life indwelled by the Holy Spirit, "in the power of the Holy Spirit" (ASV). These blessings of salvation — hope, joy, peace, power, the Spirit — upon Jew and Gentile heal all wounded spirits and bathe the fellowship of believers in the very life of God.

For Further Study

1. How does Paul explain the surrendered life of obedience to God?

2. List the guidelines in chapter 12 for effective ministry in the church and compare them with the spiritual gifts in 1 Corinthians 12 and Ephesians 4.

3. How far must a Christian citizen carry his obligation to the state? Does Paul's teaching apply to a totalitarian regime?

4. What is the ruling principle of conduct for the believer in the world and among the brethren?

5. In a Bible dictionary, study the nature of the Colossian heresy. How does it differ from the problem of the strong and the weak?

6. What are some modern "matters of indifference" that often divide church fellowships?

Chapter 8

Conclusion

(Romans 15:14-16:27)

The letter hastens to a close. The theme of Romans, "the just shall live by faith" (1:17), has been treated from all sides, doctrinal and practical. The body of the letter (1:18-15:13) describes the gospel of God's righteousness which Paul proclaimed to his generation. It has the character of a manifesto, setting forth the compass points of Paul's preaching. We cannot imagine a better way for Paul to introduce himself to the Roman church than by this theological self-confession.

So, having run the course of his gospel, the apostle turns to personal explanation, completing the circle of discussion that introduced the letter (1:1-17, cf. Godet). Nygren remarks: "like the introduction to the epistle, this conclusion is also unusually rich in inclusiveness" (p. 452). Personal touches noted in the introduction — the gospel revealed in Christ (1:1b-5), greeting to readers (1:6,7), and Paul's sense of debt and desire to visit Rome (1:8-15) — now reappear in basically reverse order. First, Paul explains his spiritual obligation to the church and divulges his plan to visit. Then, he expands his greetings to Roman Christians and concludes with a benediction, summing up the gospel of God. We will briefly discuss these concluding words as follows: (1) a narrative of the apostolic mission (15:14-33), (2) personal greetings to Roman Christians (16:1-23), and (3) a final doxology in praise of God (16:24-27).

A. A Narrative of the Apostolic Mission (15:14-33)

This personal narrative, which at first sight appears out of character, reveals the missionary vision which shaped the writing of Romans. In *A Man in Christ*, James Stewart gives a memorable description of Paul's situation: "Written on the eve of his last journey to Jerusalem, [Romans] looks back on all he had learnt of Christ since he had given Him his heart, and gathers up the ripe fruits of those years of experience and meditation and ever deepened consecration" (p. 25). The writing of Romans marks the beginning of a new epoch in the missionary career of

159

Paul, In his vision of a waiting world, he sees Rome as a vital link in the evangelization of the westernmost region of the Empire. Hammered out in the heat of the gospel mission, Paul's letter and plans are more than personal; they are divinely commissioned, bound up in God's plan for the apostle to the Gentiles. As we shall see, verses 15-33 (corresponding to 1:8-15) give four aspects of the apostolic mission as it relates to the church in Rome.

1. *Reasons for writing the epistle (15:14-16)*

In a tactful, apologetic spirit, Paul disclaims any scorn for the spiritual awareness of the Romans (v. 14). "He has written strong words, and does not wish by tactlessness to ruin his relations with the church in Rome before setting foot in the city" (Barrett, pp. 274,275). A comparison with the Galatian letter, where no such compliment occurs, "shows that St. Paul's words must be taken to have a very real and definite meaning" (Sanday and Headlam, p. 403). Paul's sincere appreciation of the faith of his readers discloses two reasons for the writing of Romans.

a. *To remind the Romans of what they already believe (vv. 14,15a)*.
Paul is personally confident that these believers are genuine Christians "full of goodness" (cf. Eph. 5:9), "furnished with a Christian learning" (TCNT), and "competent to counsel one another" (Williams). Notwithstanding admonition and rebuke, where Paul has "written very boldly" on some points (v. 15a, NASB; cf. 6:12-19; 8:9; 11:17-24; 12:3; 13:3,7,13,14; 14:1,4,15; 15:1), he intends "to suggest to their memory what they must know already but may be overlooking" (Denney, p. 711). Paul writes to undergird the faith of the church (of which he was knowledgeable) and to equip the church for the task ahead (not instruct them for the first time).

b. *To claim the Romans for the priestly service of the gospel (vv. 15b,16)*.
The letter is backed by a divine commission ("because of the charge with which God has entrusted me" [v. 15b, TCNT]) to minister to the Gentiles. The phrase "ministering the gospel of God" (v. 16b) portrays Paul as a "priest of God's good news" (Goodspeed). Like the Levites of old, he stands at the altar of God, acting as a priest of the gospel, and the offering which he makes is the Gentile church (cf. NEB). This "living sacrifice" (12:1) is acceptable to God (1 Peter 2:5) because it has been "made holy by the Holy Spirit" (v. 16c, *Modern Language Bible*). We must note that the priestly service is the preaching of the gospel to the Gentiles. In view of his commission, the faith of the Romans comes within the scope of Paul's ministry in the Gentile world.

He claims the Romans for that offering to the Lord gathered from all nations (Isa. 66:20; cf. Murray).[1]

2. Results of preaching among the Gentiles (15:17-21)

God has crowned the Gentile mission with such success that Paul can write to the Romans with confidence. In the fellowship of Christ, Paul finds reason "for boasting in things pertaining to God" (v. 17, NASB). Paul's "glorying" should be understood in relation to verse 16; he has "ground for pride in the service of God" (v. 17, NEB). Murray observes: "There is nothing of egoism in his glorying; it is glorying in God's grace and when thus conditioned it cannot be too exuberant" (II,211). Paul will not speak of anything "except what Christ has accomplished" (v. 18, NASB) through him. The results of Christ's working through Paul, which "is the vindication of Paul's action in writing to Rome" (Denney, p. 712), are described from two points of view.

a. *The conversion of Gentiles has been certified by signs of divine activity (vv. 18a,19a).* Paul describes the obedience of the Gentiles in terms of the "power of God unto salvation" (1:16), the saving manifestation of Christ through the gospel. Here is a threefold account of the saving authority of the gospel: (1) human instrumentality, "by word and deed" (v. 18b), a reference to Paul's preaching ministry (cf. 2 Cor. 10:11); (2) attendant miracles, "signs and wonders" (v. 19a, cf. 2 Cor. 12:12; Heb. 2:4; Gal. 3:5); and (3) divine enablement, "by the power of the Spirit of God" (v. 19a), the influence of the Spirit who accompanies the preaching of the word (cf. 1 Cor. 2:4). The power of God that saves the Gentiles is announced through preaching, exemplified in signs and wonders, and bestowed by the Spirit (cf. 1 Thess. 1:5,6). It is noteworthy that a trinitarian pattern of thought emerges when Paul portrays divine activity in the gospel ("minister of Jesus Christ . . . gospel of God . . . sanctified by the Spirit," v. 16; "pertain to God . . . things which Christ . . . Spirit of God," vv. 17-19; cf. 2 Cor. 13:14).

b. *The mission in the east has been completed by fully disseminating the gospel (vv. 19b-21).* The phrase "fully preached" (v. 19c) means to "carry out completely," that is, "completed the preaching of the Gospel" (NEB, Goodspeed) in the eastern provinces. First, Paul names the southeastern and northwestern extents of the region in which he preached, "from Jerusalem and round about unto Illyricum" (v. 19b). From its starting point in Jerusalem (Acts 1:4,8; 8:14; 9:29), Paul carried

---

[1]As noted by several interpreters (Gifford, Godet, Denney), it follows from this passage that the church in Rome is primarily Gentile in composition.

the gospel to the frontiers of Illyricum (the Roman province bordering the eastern shore of the Adriatic Sea), perhaps during the eighteen months he spent in Macedonia and Achaia on the third missionary tour (cf. 2 Cor. 2:12,13; Acts 20:1-6). It is evident that Paul had not preached to every individual but had covered in a representative way the provinces within the named limits (cf. Dodd, Bruce, Barrett). Second, he limits the mission in the east by a selective principle: "In all this it has been my ambition to preach the good news only where Christ's name was unknown" (v. 20a, Goodspeed). This missionary method, laying a foundation and letting another build (1 Cor. 3:10), was not to avoid rivalry but to evangelize as many of the unreached as possible (v. 21, cf. Isa. 52:15).

3. *Plans for future missionary ventures (15:22-29)*

This is where the Romans come into Paul's thinking; with no further task in the eastern provinces, he is ready to come to Rome (vv. 22,23). The gospel dissemination that detained Paul in the east had run out of room (v. 23a); now his desire of many years will come to pass. Paul envisions a new field of endeavor, divulging an itinerary with three key stages.

a. *A journey into Spain (vv. 24, 28b) is the goal of Paul's enlarged field of work (cf. 2 Cor. 10:15,16).* Although Spain may have had other appeals, it is the most feasible place for Paul to work, seeing the eastern mission was completed and Rome already had a church (cf. v. 20). There is no certain evidence that Paul reached Spain.[2] The possibility of such a journey rests on the release of Paul from Roman imprisonment (cf. Acts 28:16,30). It would then fall during the period of the Pastoral Epistles (cf. a possible reference to Gaul in 2 Tim. 4:10).

b. *The strategic importance of Rome (vv. 24b, 29) makes the church a vital link in Paul's itinerary.* In traveling to Spain, Paul will pass through Rome (in accord with the principle of v. 20) to fellowship (cf. v. 24c, 1:11,12) and to share the blessings of the faith (v. 29). The words "brought on my way thitherward by you" (v. 24b; "helped on my way there," NASB, Barrett) probably mean the church will take some responsibility, as a co-laborer, in the Spanish mission (Dodd, p. 229; cf. 1 Cor. 16:6; 2 Cor. 1:16; Acts 15:3; 3 John 6; Titus 3:13). Paul's passing visit would secure Rome as a missionary center, having been prepared for the task by this very letter.

---

[2]Clement of Rome (A.D. 95) wrote that Paul traveled to the "bounds of the west" (*Epistle to the Corinthians* 5:7). J. B. Lightfoot concludes that Spain is intended (*Apostolic Fathers*, pt. 1, II, 30); Sanday and Headlam think the identification is doubtful (p. 414).

c. *The Gentile collection for Jerusalem (vv. 25-28a) is the immediate prospect in Paul's plans.* The relief fund for the "poor among God's people at Jerusalem" (v. 26b, NEB) is certainly more than an ecumenical money-raising endeavor. If not, why does Paul take such a large body of Gentile believers as representatives (Acts 20:4) and why does he hazard his life for it (v. 31; cf. Acts 20:22; 21:13)? This collection from "Macedonia and Achaia" (v. 26, cf. 2 Cor. 8,9), Galatia, and Asia Minor (cf. 1 Cor. 16:1-4) is a spontaneous gesture of brotherly love (v. 27). Through the offering, the Gentile Christians fulfill their spiritual indebtedness ("a debt they owed them," v. 27a, Weymouth) to the Jerusalem church. But, in Paul's eyes, the offering must have his personal seal (v. 28a), as Bruce notes: "it was the climax of Paul's Aegean ministry and an act of worship and dedication to God before he set out for the west. It was, indeed, the outward and visible sign of that 'offering up of the Gentiles' which crowned his priestly service as an apostle of Jesus Christ" (p. 264; cf. Munck, pp. 11,12).

4. *Prayers from Rome requested by Paul (15:30-33)*

The Jerusalem trip is a foreboding one; uncertainties and perils lie ahead for Paul. Such risk is reason enough to earnestly implore the Romans to pray for him. The grounds for this entreaty are the lordship of Christ ("by our Lord Jesus Christ," v. 30) and the love of the Spirit (shared by the brethren, Gal. 5:22). The prayers requested involve a common struggle (Godet, p. 486): "strive together with me" (v. 30b). The word "strive" (literally "agonize") is an intense metaphor drawn from athletic games (cf. Phil. 1:27; 4:3; Col. 4:12) and used of our Lord's agony in Gethsemane (Luke 22:44; Matt. 26:42). The Romans will take part in the contest Paul must fight "by praying on his behalf to God, for all prayer is a spiritual wrestling against opposing powers" (Sanday and Headlam, p. 415).

There is a threefold intention in the request, indicated by the repetition of "that" (vv. 31a,b, 32a). The first relates to personal danger: "to be rescued from those in Judaea who reject the Faith" (v. 31a, TCNT). The second concerns the church reception in Jerusalem: "that my errand to Jerusalem may find acceptance with God's people" (v. 32b, NEB). These two conditions anticipate a third one pertaining to Rome: "so that by God's will I may come to you with joy and be refreshed in your company" (v. 32, RSV). Denney says: "Paul looks forward to a time of joy and rest beyond these anxieties and dangers, as the ultimate end to be secured by their prayers" (p. 717). To help in this struggle, the apostle touches his request with a prayer of his own, invoking peace upon his prayer warriors (v. 32).

B. Personal Greetings to Roman Christians (16:1-23)

The major critical problem of Romans involves the unity of chapter 16 with the rest of the letter. "It has been widely held that this final chapter was directed not to Rome but to Ephesus — that it was for Ephesus that Phoebe was bound and that the friends to whom Paul sends greetings lived in Ephesus" (Bruce, p. 266).[3] However, the unity of chapter 16 has been defended by able scholars (e.g., Sanday and Headlam, Dodd, Bruce, Barrett), and we can briefly note their arguments. (1) First-century inscriptions and travel customs indicate that twenty-six acquaintances of Paul could have migrated to Rome (vv. 3-16). (2) No manuscript of Romans exists without chapter 16, and it is difficult to imagine (if it was an independent letter) how it came to be attached to chapters 1-15. (3) The tensions of Jewish legalism in Rome (14:1-15:13) imply the presence of false teachers like those in Colossae and Galatia (vv. 17-20). (4) Such a list of greetings for people in Ephesus (where Paul ministered three years) would be unlikely because others would surely ask: "Why leave me out?" The traditional Roman view of chapter 16, which holds the field among commentators, is to be preferred.

When closing letters it was Paul's custom to include personal words such as commendations (1 Cor. 16:10-17; Col. 4:7-9), individual greetings (1 Cor. 16:19,20; Col. 4:10-15), and warnings (Col. 4:17; 1 Thess. 5:12-22; 1 Tim. 6:20,21). This chapter consists in the main of personal greetings to believers in Rome; as such, it has four distinct parts: (1) a commendation of Phoebe (vv. 1,2), (2) greetings to friends in Rome (vv. 3-16), (3) a warning against false teachers (vv. 17-20), and (4) greetings from Paul's companions (vv. 21-23).

1. A commendation of Phoebe (16:1,2)

When completed, the Roman letter evidently was carried to its destination by Phoebe, a member of the church in Cenchreae (RSV, NEB), some nine miles east of Corinth on the Saronic Gulf (cf. Acts 18:18). Paul commends Phoebe to be received into the fellowship of the Roman church: "receive her in the Lord in a manner worthy of the saints" (v. 2a, NASB). The obligation to practice the law of love falls to the church (cf. 15:7) which should welcome her as a fellow Christian. Such letters of introduction and commendation were commonly used in the early church (Acts 18:27; 2 Cor. 8:18-24; 3 John 9,10), although Paul says he

---

[3]Adherents to the Ephesian theory argue as follows: (1) Paul, being a stranger in Rome, would not know twenty-six people; (2) the false teachers of verses 17-20 do not appear elsewhere in Romans; (3) chapter 16 is a short, covering letter carried to Ephesus, introducing what we know as Romans (actually a circular letter); (4) the doxology (vv. 25-27) occurs at two different places in the Greek manuscripts (14:23; 15:33), indicating that Romans once circulated in a shortened form.

did not need one (2 Cor. 3:1). Dodd remarks: "A church must know that
a stranger arriving and seeking hospitality as a fellow-Christian is a
genuine member of the Christian society, and not a parasite or a spy" (p.
234). Paul enjoins the church to "give her any help she may require" (v.
2b, Moffatt), suggesting a definite task for her in Rome.

Phoebe's commendation rests upon her life in Christ; three creden-
tials of her faith are notable. She is a "sister" (v. 1a), a word denoting
spiritual kinship as a sister in the Lord (cf. 1 Cor. 7:15). Phoebe also is
called a "servant" (Greek, *diakonos*, v. 1b) of the church, which can be
translated literally, "a deaconess" (RSV, Phillips, Williams) or in the
general sense of one "who holds office in the congregation" (NEB). It is
doubtful that the word has an official sense in Romans (cf. 13:4; 15:8);
furthermore, the office-bearing features of the diaconate may be over-
stated for even later passages in the New Testament (cf. 1 Tim. 3:11).
Phoebe might naturally be described as she is here if, like the house of
Stephanas at Corinth (1 Cor. 16:15), she had given herself "to the
ministry of the saints" (Denney, p. 717). Finally, she is a "succourer of
many" (v. 2b, KJV), a word which signifies help and protection. Barrett translates it "protectoress" (cf. Goodspeed); ASV, "helper"; NEB,
"good friend." Since the word is used of a wealthy patron in Jewish
communities, it may suggest "that Phoebe was a person of some wealth
and position who was thus able to act as a patronness of a small and
struggling community" (Sanday and Headlam, p. 418). Phoebe was to
Cenchreae what Lydia was to Philippi (Acts 16:15).

2. *Greetings to friends in Rome (16:3-16)*

Identification of the twenty-six individuals named in verses 3-16
must be left to the probabilities explored in technical studies.[4] For our
purposes, this list of greetings opens a door into the everyday world of
the first-century church. Griffith Thomas calls this a "galaxy of saints,"
affording a "remarkable picture.of the heart of the great Apostle, and of
the real condition of Christianity in his day" (III, 153,154). Greetings
and testimonies to these believers, intended partly at least to encourage
them "to act in a manner corresponding to their past life, and not fail in
their religious course, nor ever grow languid in their pious ardour"
(Calvin, p. 544), tell us much about them.

a. *The richness of their fellowship emerges from the remarkable
diversity of individuals named.* Jewish Christians, e.g., Priscilla and
Aquila (v. 3, cf. Acts 18:2), Andronicus and Junias (v. 7, "my fellow-
countrymen," NEB), mingle with Gentile believers, among whom are

---

[4]See Sanday and Headlam, pp. 418-429. The classic treatment is the excursus on
"Caesar's Household" in J. B. Lightfoot, *St. Paul's Epistle to the Philippians*, pp. 171-178.

Epaenetus, Paul's "first convert to Christ from Asia" (v. 5b, NASB), Urbanus (a common Roman name), and Stachys (a rare name associated with the imperial household, v. 9). Women have an important place among the men: Priscilla, Mary, Tryphaena, Tryphosa, Persis, Julia, along with an unnamed mother and sister. Some are common slave names (Ampliatus, Rufus, Hermes, Philologus, Julia), others belong to prominent freedmen (Narcissus, Asyncritus, Patrobas), and many appear in the imperial household (e.g., Andronicus, Apelles, Nereus). Aristobulus (v. 10b) and Herodion (v. 11a) probably belonged to Jewish nobility; the name Persis (v. 12b) means "Persian woman." Everything hints at a fellowship that transcends all barriers of race, culture, and sex; they are all one in Christ Jesus (Gal. 3:28).

b. *The closeness of their faith is suggested by family and household associations.* Paul salutes the congregation ("church," v. 5a) which meets in the home of Priscilla and Aquila. We must recall that New Testament Christianity was conducted on a family basis, and because there were no church buildings, the church gathered in believers' homes (cf. Acts 12:12; 1 Cor. 16:19; Col. 4:15; Philemon 2).[5] In fact, we hear of entire households becoming Christians together (Acts 10:44-48; 16:15, 30-34; 18:8; 1 Cor. 1:16). This family element in organization was congenial to the idea of the church as "the household of God" (Eph. 2:19) or "the household of faith" (Gal. 6:10), and its members as children of God, brothers and sisters in the Lord (Dodd, p. 237). Besides Priscilla and Aquila, household churches are associated with the two groups of five believers each in verses 14 and 15; likewise, Christian gatherings are named in the households of Aristobulus (v. 10b) and Narcissus (v. 11b). Furthermore, note the family relationships: (1) Priscilla and Aquila are wife and husband, as are probably Julia and Philologus; (2) Tryphaena ("dainty") and Tryphosa ("delicate") may be the names of twin sisters; (3) Rufus is named with his mother, and Nereus with his sister. Such ties to the home and family made early Christianity a unique way of life.

c. *The fruitfulness of their labor shows a deep commitment to Christ.* When we ask what accent occurs most frequently in this list, the answer is clear: "for Christ," "in Christ," "in the Lord," "of Christ." These friends of Paul share in a common dedication; they are fellow workers who have risked their very necks (v. 4a), laboring for the Lord (v. 12) even to the point of strenuous toil (vv. 6, 12). Two are "noted men among the missionaries," having been converted before Paul (v. 7b, Goodspeed). In this fellowship, we find men who are "well proved in

---

[5]No clear evidence for separate church buildings appears within the Roman Empire before the third century A.D. (Lightfoot, Sanday and Headlam).

Christ's service" (v. 10a, NEB), one "eminent in the Lord" (v. 13a, RSV), a woman who "mothered" Paul in the faith (v. 13b), dear Christians who are "beloved" (vv. 5b, 8a, 9b, 12b). The pledge of their friendship, made known to one another by a "holy kiss" (v. 16a, cf. 1 Thess. 5:26; 1 Peter 5:14), calls for the admiration of all the Gentile churches (v. 16b).

3. A warning against false teachers (16:17-20)

The greetings break off with a sudden outburst against agitators who present a threat to the Roman church. The circumstances behind this admonition can only be conjectured, but the tone and style are not altogether foreign to the letter. "Against errors such as these St. Paul has throughout been warning his readers indirectly, he has been building up his hearers against them by laying down broad principles of life and conduct, and now just at the end, just before he finishes, he gives one definite and direct warning against false teachers" (Sanday and Headlam, p. 429). The Romans are to mark and avoid these troublemakers whenever they surface in the church (v. 17). Paul identifies them with three labels: (1) they stir up dissensions and put stumblingblocks in the way (v. 17b, cf. Gal. 5:20); (2) they are slaves not to Christ but "to their own appetites" (v. 18a, TCNT; cf. "whose God is their belly," Phil. 3:19); (3) they deceive the hearts of unsuspecting people with "fair and flattering words" (v. 18b, RSV).

We can conclude that these agitators were well suited to the antinomian practices that are alluded to in Philippians 3:17-21 and Colossians 2:20-3:4. In a speech to the Ephesian elders at Miletus, which occurred a few weeks after the writing of Romans, Paul hints at similar perversions (Acts 20:29,30). Here also, however impending the threat of actual disturbance, Paul wants his readers to beware, being well versed in the good and unspotted by the evil (v. 19b). Discord is the work of Satan, and Paul knows that the "God of peace" (not discord, 1 Cor. 14:33) will give the Romans quick victory if they stand their ground (v. 20a, an allusion to Gen. 3:15). An interim benediction following an emotional passage (v. 20b) should not surprise us in Romans (cf. 1:25; 9:5; 11:36; 15:13,33).

4. Greetings from Paul's companions (16:21-23)

Now, in a postscript, the circle of friends in Corinth add their greetings. Timothy, a youthful colleague in the apostolic mission (Acts 16:1-3), joined Paul in Macedonia (cf. 2 Cor. 1:1) before coming to Corinth. The other three (v. 21b) cannot be identified with certainty, but it has been suggested that Lucius is Lucius of Cyrene (Acts 13:1) or Luke the physician; Jason, Paul's host at Thessalonica (Acts 17:5-9); and Sosipater, Sopater of Beroea (Acts 20:4). At this point, Tertius (v. 22), the amanuensis who wrote the letter, apparently takes up the pen (note the first person address). Paul normally used a secretary (cf. 1 Cor. 16:21; Col. 4:18; 2 Thess. 3:17; Gal. 6:11), but Tertius is the only one we know by name. Gaius is the first name of Titus Justus, who opened his home to Paul on his first visit to Corinth (Acts 18:7; cf. NASB, NEB). Erastus, whose name likely has been found in a first-century Latin inscription from Corinth, is the city treasurer ("chamberlain," v. 23b). Since Quartus is Latin for "fourth," and Tertius for "third," would it be, asks Bruce, "excessively far-fetched to think of him as Tertius' brother, born next after him (p. 281)?"

C. A Final Doxology in Praise of God (16:24-27)[6]

This doxology is unusual, not for its serene loftiness (cf. Eph. 3:21; Phil. 4:20; 1 Tim. 1:17), but for its length and manner of summing up the great thoughts of the epistle. Its ideas have much in common with 8:18-30 and still more with the drift of chapters 9-11. In particular, there is a recognizable echo of the dominant themes in the opening salutation (1:1-7) concerning the Old Testament prophecies and the calling of the Gentiles to faith. It is best then to view the doxology as a mosaic of thought and language issuing from the letter itself (cf. Sanday and Headlam). The best commentary on the individual parts are their corresponding notices in the letter: (1) "power to establish you" (v. 25a, cf. 14:4), (2) "according to my gospel" (v. 25b, cf. 2:16), (3) "preaching of Jesus Christ" (v. 25c, cf. 10:18), (4) "revelation of the mystery" (v. 25d, cf. 1:16; 11:25), (5) "now is made manifest" (v. 26a, cf. 3:21), (6) "scriptures of the prophets" (v. 26b, cf. 1:2), (7) "commandment of the everlasting God" (v. 26c, cf. 10:15,16), (8) "obedience of faith" (v. 26d, cf. 1:5), (9) "God only wise" (v. 27a, cf. 11:33).

Bruce believes that such a rounding off of the letter on the same note that was struck at the beginning suggests that Paul himself penned the last words (p. 282). This suggestion leans on Moule's vivid portrayal of the closing scene, in which Paul ponders in silence after his friends have left him alone. We can imagine that tracing through the letter afresh rekindles its most inspiring words; Paul must give the Romans one more sentence "to express his overrunning heart." Moule remarks: "He takes the papers, and the pen. With dim eyes, and in large, laborious letters, and forgetting at the close, in the intensity of his soul, to make perfect grammatical connection, he inscribes, in the twilight, this most wonderful of Doxologies. Let us watch him to its close, and then in silence leave him before his Lord, and ours" (*Expositor's Bible*, p. 437).

---

[6]Verse 24 (KJV) is not found in the best Greek text; therefore, it has been omitted from the modern versions (e.g., NASB, NEB).

For Further Study

1. What are some reasons for viewing the Roman letter as a missionary manifesto?

2. Using a Bible dictionary and other helps, trace the missionary activities of Paul after he arrived in Rome (Acts 28). Did he carry out the plans of 15:14-33?

3. Name some characteristics of first-century church life that can be gleaned from chapter 16.

4. Study the functions of an Apostle, Deacon, and Amanuensis in a Bible dictionary.

Bibliography

Arndt, W. F. and Gingrich, F. Wilbur. *A Greek-English Lexicon of the New Testament and Other Early Christian Literature* (Chicago: The University of Chicago Press, 1957

Arnold, Albert, N. and Ford, D. B. *Commentary on the Epistle to the Romans* in "The American Commentary on the New Testament," Alvah Hovey, ed. (Philadelphia: The American Baptist Publication Society, 1882)

Barclay, William. *The Letter to the Romans* in "The Daily Study Bible" (Philadelphia: The Westminster Press, 1955)

Barrett, C. K. *A Commentary on the Epistle to the Romans* in "The Harper's New Testament Commentaries" (New York: Harper & Row, 1957)

Bengel, Johann Albrecht, *Gnomon of the New Testament*, 6th ed., vol. 3 (Edinburgh: T. & T. Clark, 1866)

Brown, David. *The Epistle to the Romans* (Edinburgh: T. & T. Clark, 1950)

Brown, John. *Analytical Exposition of the Epistle of Paul the Apostle to the Romans* (New York: Robert Carter and Brothers, 1857)

Bruce, F. F. *The Epistle of Paul to the Romans: An Introduction and Commentary* in "The Tyndale New Testament Commentaries," vol. 6 (Grand Rapids: Wm. B. Eerdmans Publishing Company, 1963)

Calvin, John. *The Epistles of Paul the Apostle to the Romans and to the Thessalonians.* Translated and edited by John Owen. In "Calvin's Commentaries" (Grand Rapids: Wm. B. Eerdmans Publishing Company, 1947)

Cranfield, C. E. B. *A Commentary on Romans 12-13* in "Scottish Journal of Theology Occasional Papers" (London: Oliver and Boyd, 1965)

———— *A Critical and Exegetical Commentary on The Epistle to the Romans* in "The International Critical Commentary," vol. 1 (Edinburgh: T. & T. Clark Limited, 1975)

Dargan, E. C. *An Exposition of the Epistle to the Romans* (Nashville: The Sunday School Board, 1914)

Davidson, F. and Martin, Ralph P. "Romans" in *The New Bible Commentary: Revised* (Grand Rapids: Wm. B. Eerdmans Publishing Co., 1970)

Denney, James. *St. Paul's Epistle to the Romans* in "The Expositor's Greek Testament," vol. 2 (London: Hodder and Stoughton, 1900)

Dodd, C. H. *The Epistle of Paul to the Romans* in "The Moffatt New Testament Commentary" (New York: Harper and Brothers Publishers, 1932)

Franzmann, Martin. "Romans" in *The Concordia Bible with Notes: New Testament* (London: William Collins Sons & Co., 1971)

Gifford, E. H. *The Epistle of Paul to the Romans* in "The Speaker's Commentary" (London: John Murray, 1886)

Godet, Frederic. *Commentary on St. Paul's Epistle to the Romans*, translated by A. Cusin (New York: Funk & Wagnalls, Publishers, 1883)

Guthrie, D. and Motyer, J. A., editors. *The New Bible Commentary: Revised* (Grand Rapids: Wm. B. Eerdmans Publishing Company, 1975)

Haldane, Robert. *An Exposition of the Epistle to the Romans*, reprint edition (Marshallton, Del.: The National Foundation for Christian Education, 1970)

Hodge, Charles. *A Commentary on the Epistle to the Romans*, 19th ed. (Philadelphia: James S. Claxton, 1866)

Jowett, J. H. *Great Pulpit Masters*, vol. 5 (New York: Fleming H. Revell Co., 1950)

Lenski, R. C. H. *The Interpretation of St. Paul's Epistle to the Romans* (Columbus: Wartburg Press, 1945)

Lightfoot, J. B. *Biblical Essays* (London: Macmillan & Co., 1893)

Luther, Martin. *Lectures on Romans* in "The Library of Christian Classics" (Philadelphia: The Westminster Press, 1961)

Meyer, Heinrich August Wilhelm. *Critical and Exegetical Handbook to the Epistle to the Romans*, translated by John C. Moore and Edwin Johnson (New York: Funk & Wagnalls, Publishers, 1884)

Moule, H. C. G. *The Epistle of Paul the Apostle to the Romans* in "The Cambridge Bible for Schools and Colleges" (Cambridge: Cambridge University Press, 1892)

————. *The Epistle of St. Paul to the Romans*, in "The Expositor's Bible" 6th ed. (New York: Hodder and Stoughton, n.d.)

Munck, Johannes. *Christ and Israel: An Interpretation of Romans 9-11*, translated by Ingeborg Nixon (Philadelphia: Fortress Press, 1967)

Murray, John. *The Epistle to the Romans* in "The New International Commentary on the New Testament," 2 vols. (Grand Rapids: Wm. B. Eerdmans Publishing Company, 1965)

Nygren, Anders. *Commentary on Romans*, translated by Carl C. Rasmussen (Philadelphia: Fortress Press, 1949)

Robertson, Archibald Thomas. *Word Pictures in the New Testament*, vol. 4: *The Epistles of Paul* (Nashville: Broadman Press, 1931)

Sanday, William, and Headlam, Arthur C. *A Critical and Exegetical*

Commentary on the Epistle to the Romans in "The International Critical Commentary," 5th ed. (Edinburgh: T. & T. Clark, 1902)

Shedd, W. T. G. *A Critical and Doctrinal Commentary on the Epistle of St. Paul to the Romans,* reprint edition (Grand Rapids: Zondervan Publishing House, 1967)

Stifler, James M. *The Epistle to the Romans* (Chicago: Moody Press, 1960)

Stott, John R. W. *Men Made New* (Downers Grove, Illinois: Inter-Varsity Press, 1966)

Thomas, W. H. G. *St. Paul's Epistle to the Romans: A Devotional Commentary,* 3 vols. (London: The Religious Tract Society, 1911)

Zahn, Theodor. *Introduction to the New Testament,* translated under the direction of M. W. Jacobus, vol. 1 (Grand Rapids: Kregel Publications, 1953)

All Scriptures, unless otherwise identified, are quoted from the American Standard Version. Other translations referred to are as follows:

Conybeare, W. J. *The Epistles of Paul: A Translation and Notes,* reprint edition (Grand Rapids: Baker Book House, 1958)

Goodspeed, Edgar J., *The New Testament: An American Translation* (Chicago: The University of Chicago Press, 1951)

Good News for Modern Man. The New Testament in Today's English Version (New York: American Bible Society, 1966). Referred to in the Study Guide as TEV.

Moffatt, James, *The New Testament: A New Translation* (New York: Harper and Brothers, 1950)

Montgomery, Helen Barrett, *The New Testament in Modern English* (Valley Forge: Judson Press, n.d.)

New American Standard Bible (Nashville: Broadman Press, 1960). Referred to in the Study Guide as NASB.

New International Version: New Testament (Grand Rapids: Zondervan Bible Publishers, 1973). Referred to in the Study Guide as NIV.

Norlie, Olaf M., *The New Testament: A New Translation* (Grand Rapids: Zondervan Publishing House, 1961)

Phillips, J. B., *The New Testament in Modern English* (New York: TheMacmillan Company, 1962)

Rotherham, J. B., *The Emphasized Bible* (Grand Rapids: Kregel Publications, reprint edition 1967)

The Modern Language Bible. The New Berkeley Version (Grand Rapids: Zondervan Publishing House, 1959)

The New English Bible (Oxford and Cambridge: University Press, 1965). Referred to in the Study Guide as NEB.

The Holy Bible: Revised Standard Version (New York: National Council of Churches of Christ, 1952). Referred to in the Study Guide as RSV.

The Twentieth Century New Testament: A Translation into Modern English (Chicago: Moody Press, n.d.). Referred to in the Study Guide as TCNT.

United Bible Society, *The New Testament of Our Lord and Savior Jesus Christ* by John A. Broadus. (American Bible Union Version, n.d.) Referred to in the Study Guide as ABUV.

Weymouth, Richard Francis, *The New Testament in Modern Speech*. Newly revised by James Alexander Robertson (New York: Harper and Brothers, n.d.)

Williams, Charles B., *The New Testament: A Private Translation in the Language of the People* (Chicago: Moody Press, 1949)